The Handbook for SMART School Teams

Anne Conzemius and Jan O'Neill

Solution Tree

Copyright © 2002 by Solution Tree
(formerly National Educational Service)
304 West Kirkwood Avenue
Bloomington, IN 47404
(800) 733-6786 (toll free) / (812) 336-7700
FAX: (812) 336-7790
e-mail: info@solution-tree.com
www.solution-tree.com

Cover design by Grannan Graphic Design, Ltd.

Text design and composition by MacAllister Publishing Services, LLC

Illustrations by Cheryl B. Moloney

Printed in The United States of America

ISBN 1-879639-85-8

Dedications

For Quinn William Van de Grift (*AEC*)

For Betty Ward (*JKO*)

Acknowledgements

There are so many people whose encouragement, patience, confidence, and support have given us the extra energy to persist as we wrote this book. A few deserve special mention here. A warm thanks to Drs. Bob and Betty Bush, dear friends, mentors, and professional colleagues whose dedication to learning has been an inspiration to so many. To Al MacIlroy and Toni Morgan we extend a lifetime of gratitude for giving more than anyone could ever expect (and to Tasha and Tom for lending them to us). To Pat Alea, Ann Zanzig, Michelle Larson, and Sue Reynard, our eternal thanks for your laughter, support, assistance, and guidance—what would we do without you? Our thanks to Rick DuFour and Bob Eaker who so graciously invited us into the Solution Tree family, and to Jeff Jones and the amazing staff at Solution Tree whose support and light spirit continue to be a source of inspiration and joy. To our families—parents, siblings, children (Sara, Jim, and Luke), and of course to our most steadfast and loyal supporters, our husbands, Bill and Hank—thanks for listening, waiting, cheerleading, and chiding at crucial times throughout this exhilarating and exhausting process.

To our friends, teachers, colleagues, Peter Scholtes, Brian Joiner, the late Bill Hunter, and George Box for their unswerving dedication to continuous improvement as a way of life—working with them has been life-changing. And finally, we owe so much of what we know and continue to learn to our friends and colleagues in the field who make learning their life's passion. To our fellow educators: our deepest gratitude for the work you do each and every day.

—Anne Conzemius
Jan O'Neill
Madison, WI
Email: qld@qld-llc.com

Table of Contents

About the Authors

The authors are the founders and managing partners of Quality Leadership by Design, LLC, where they design and implement personalized, needs-based solutions to help educational institutions, government agencies, and private sector businesses continuously improve operations. Both have professional roots in education, and together, they have devoted years of work to developing products and services schools can use to boost academic success.

Anne Conzemius, a former school psychologist, has spent many years working in quality improvement in both the public and private sectors. She has served as the Executive Assistant to the State Superintendent for the Wisconsin Department of Public Instruction, where she headed the department's strategic planning and restructuring initiative. Anne holds Master's degrees in Educational Psychology and in Industrial Relations and Human Resource Management, both from the University of Wisconsin, Madison. She is an adjunct faculty member for Cardinal Stritch University in Milwaukee.

Jan O'Neill began her career teaching elementary and middle school students and has diverse experience in early childhood education, special education, multicultural education, and the Montessori method. As an independent consultant, she pioneered the systemwide application of quality principles in municipal and state governments and in healthcare. Jan has developed and implemented numerous training and improvement efforts for public and private sector clients. She holds a Master's degree in Public Policy and Administration from LaFollette Institute, University of Wisconsin, Madison. Jan is an adjunct faculty member for Cardinal Stritch University in Milwaukee.

You can reach Anne or Jan at QLD, Yarmouth Crossing, #188, 2935 South Fish Hatchery Road, Madison, WI 53711. E-mail: qld@qld-llc.com or visit www.qld-llc.com.

Foreword

by Richard P. DuFour and Robert Eaker,
authors of *Professional Learning Communities at Work:
Best Practices for Enhancing Student Achievement*

Nearly two decades have passed since the National Commission on Excellence in Education argued in "Nation at Risk" that national security was in peril because of substandard education in the nation's public schools. The Commission made frequent references to decline, deficiencies, threats, risks, afflictions, and plight. It made no attempt to be subtle in offering its reason why foreign competitors were overtaking American business and industry: the failure of public education. The foundations of society were being eroded, the American way of life was in peril, and our future as a nation was in question—all because of the bad teaching going on in American schools.

The attempts to reform American education have continued almost unabated ever since. For some reason, the unprecedented economic boom enjoyed by the United States in the mid to late 1990s offered no respite. After all, if economic downturns could be traced to poor performance in schools, as "Nation at Risk" suggested, schools should get much of the credit for rising economic prosperity. Oddly, the correlation between the economy and school performance seemed to disappear when things were going well. In fact, during this period of prosperity, state legislatures around the nation continued to rail against public schools, demanding higher standards and greater accountability.

An unstated, but unmistakable, premise of this collective call for accountability in K-12 education was that schools and teachers needed to be awakened from their lethargy by threats of dire consequences. Educators have been told that they must improve results or their students will be sent to other schools, the state will take over their school, or the school will be closed. The assumption behind this threatening posture seems to be that schools could get better results if educators were simply willing to demonstrate greater commitment or to put forth more effort.

Some educators have responded to these attacks by launching their own counteroffensive. Any attempt to hold schools accountable for students achieving academic standards elicits knee-jerk reactions of opposition. States have no business imposing on local control. Standards rob teachers of their creativity and the ability to individualize instruction. *Drill and kill* has sucked all the joy out of learning. Assessments are invalid or discriminatory. The assumption here seems to be that if educators will be sufficiently oppositional, state standards and testing will disappear.

The Handbook for SMART School Teams is based on a different set of assumptions. Authors Anne Conzemius and Jan O'Neill recognize and honor the commitment and effort being demonstrated by our nation's teachers. They regard teachers with respect and empathy rather than disdain. They understand that improving student achievement is not a function of scaring teachers into caring, but rather that it is a function of helping teachers acquire the knowledge and skills to grow.

But if Conzemius and O'Neill will not be included among those who denigrate educators, neither will they be among those who call for an end to student assessment and school accountability. They embrace rather than reject different forms of achievement data and offer strategies to help teachers work collaboratively to use that data as an engine for continuous improvement.

When we wrote *Professional Learning Communities at Work: Best Practices for Enhancing Student Achievement*, we argued that the most promising strategy for sustained, substantive school improvement was helping educators develop their capacity to function as professional learning communities. We called for schools in which teachers worked together in collaborative teams that engaged in collective inquiry on the big questions of teaching and learning. We envisioned teachers participating in action research and working together in continuous cycles of analyzing examples of student work or student achievement data, identifying areas for improvement, developing strategies to bring about the improvement, supporting each other as they implemented the strategies in their respective classrooms, gathering new information and data resulting from the improvement initiative, analyzing that information and data to see what worked, and then starting the process all over again.

The Handbook for SMART School Teams gives teachers specific tools and strategies to do exactly what we proposed. It is a rich resource for those who continue to believe that the best way to improve schools is to develop the people within them. Conzemius and O'Neill not only call for the focus, reflection, collaboration, and leadership capacity that characterize SMART schools, but they also offer extremely useful tools for getting the job done in the real world of schools. Their work makes a valuable contribution to the literature on school improvement. More importantly, their ideas and suggestions will resonate with grateful teachers and administrators.

Introduction
SMART Thinking for Critical Times

When we think about the complexity of the educational enterprise today and the growing demands on the resources and energy of educators, it's easy to see why people feel tugged and pulled in all directions. Consider the enormity of the task:

- **We must educate the whole child**—Assuring that children can read, write, and compute; know basic scientific facts and processes; are knowledgeable about history, geography, social, civic, and economic issues and events; learn and apply creative expression through art, music, and dance; and are physically, socially, and emotionally healthy.
- **We must attend to children's daily needs**—Feeding and transporting them, providing a safe environment in which to learn, disciplining them, teaching them, and even attending to their most basic physical needs when they are not yet skilled to do so for themselves.
- **We must prepare children for all possible futures**—Preparing them to be good workers, good parents, good citizens, and good selves. They need to learn technology skills, employment skills, problem-solving and critical-thinking skills, organizational skills, communication, teamwork, and conflict-resolution skills.
- **We must meet the needs of *all* children**—Educating and caring for all the children who come to school representing a full spectrum of abilities, ages, attitudes, interests, economic conditions, and experiences, including those who speak different languages and come from diverse cultural backgrounds.
- **We must meet the needs of multiple stakeholders with differing expectations**—Satisfying the needs and desires of parents, grandparents, community members, social service agency employees, politicians, journalists, those in higher education and business, and taxpayers.

- **We must be accountable to our government**—Meeting the continuous onslaught of new initiatives and requirements that come from state and federal mandates (mostly unfunded) whether we believe they are in the best interests of the children or not.

When these demands are viewed collectively, it's no wonder educators feel as though they are under attack. It's also a testament to educational practices that we have been able to accomplish as much as we have considering the enormity of the challenge. But the list also demonstrates why there is growing interest in finding new and better ways to educate our children. The ability to meet these demands—and do them *all* well, at the same time, for a sustainable period—is well beyond the capacity of most current educational systems.

In recent years, however, some schools and districts across the country have discovered new ways to work together that fundamentally increase their capacity to learn and grow. This book is about some of these practical methods and tools that allow districts, schools, and educators at all levels to better serve their students and communities.

The Key: Linking Learning and Improvement

The principles that underlie all of the approaches described in this book are simple:

- Make *learning* something that an entire school does.
- Apply that learning to achieve continuous *improvement*.

To some people, continuous improvement in education means that test scores go up every year. That is one way to look at it, but it is just a small part of the picture.

In its broadest sense, continuous improvement is a state of mind, the belief that no matter what I do well, there's a way to do it better next time. When we think this way, everything we do is fair game. Improvement becomes something that applies to both things our schools are currently doing poorly *and* things we think we are doing well.

Figure 1 PDSA Wheel

The only way to continuously improve is to continuously come up with new and better ideas that can be shown to produce better results. And the only way to come up with those ideas is through learning.

Nothing is more motivating and energizing for a group of educators than learning something new and useful—especially if what's learned has potential impact on their teaching and children's learning. Learning happens when

- Theory and practice interact
- Past experience and new knowledge meet
- Data confirm or negate perceptions
- Separate, isolated events or facts emerge into patterns, trends, or new ideas
- Two or more individuals' creative potentials collide

The link between learning and improvement is illustrated by a model called PDSA that is commonly used to implement a continuous improvement process:

PLAN a change or action.

DO the change or action (on a small scale at first).

STUDY the results to learn what did and did not work.

ACT by refining the idea or by implementing it on a broader scale.

PDSA is most often depicted as a wheel (see Figure 1), to capture the idea that learning is ongoing.

> You don't just learn knowledge; you have to create it. Get in the driver's seat, don't just be a passenger. You have to contribute to it or you don't understand it.
>
> —Dr. W. Edwards Deming

First developed by Dr. Walter Shewhart and later adapted and taught by Dr. W. Edwards Deming, PDSA is a process of learning by trying out approaches on a small scale, reflecting on the results, and then either abandoning the approach if it does not work well or institutionalizing it if it does.

You will find PDSA thinking embedded throughout this book. It influences everything from how to hold effective meetings (p. 64) to making process improvements (p. 191) and developing school improvement plans (p. 219). When an entire school community is thinking PDSA, learning and improvement become second nature. Successes are quickly implemented on a broad scale so that all can benefit from the new methods or approaches; mistakes are seen as learning by "failing forward," another opportunity to do better the next time around. With PDSA, schools can move rapidly up the learning curve to understand how and why progress is (or is not) being made.

A SMART Way of Thinking

Believing that learning and improvement should be explicitly linked is one thing; finding tools and methods that let you act on that belief is entirely different. SMART goals are very effective tools for making this translation. These goals are

Strategic and Specific

Measurable

Attainable

Results-based

Time-bound

Strategic goals are linked to strategic priorities that are part of a larger vision of success for the entire school district (see also Chapter 10). *Strategic and specific* means that these goals will have both broad-based and long-term impact because they are focused on the specific needs of the students for whom the goal is intended.

Measurable means being able to know whether actions made the kind of difference we wanted: being able to measure a change in results because of those actions. Measurement can and should occur in a number of different ways using a variety of different tools and strategies. Seeing results across measurements that yield consistent patterns gives us greater confidence that our actions truly have made a difference.

A goal needs to be *attainable*: within the realm of our influence or control, and doable given current resources. To know whether a goal is attainable, you must know your starting point (baseline), how much time you have to accomplish the goal, and what kinds of resources you have to make the necessary changes. Setting a goal that is attainable then becomes an art of balancing the degree of stretch that will make the goal compelling without making it unattainable.

SMART goals are *results-based:* aimed at specific outcomes that can be measured or observed. Results-based goals define not only *what is expected*, but they also communicate a *desired end point*. Results could come in the form of student achievement in a particular area, a percentage of students who improve in a certain area, or as a demonstration of learning that can be defined and measured. (Refer to page 244 for more information on results versus process goals.)

Finally, SMART goals are *time-bound*. As mentioned before, putting a time element in a goal helps you determine attainability. But even more importantly, agreeing on a time frame for achieving the goal helps to keep it a priority. It makes the goal more compelling by giving it some urgency. Having a time limit as part of a goal makes it imperative that we periodically check how well or swiftly we are progressing toward the goal. This helps to keep the goal a dynamic part of the improvement process.

In short, SMART goals let us monitor which of our efforts are making a difference and by how much. For example, here's a SMART goal from an intermediate school: *Within the next 2 years, increase by 50%*

the number of 6th and 7th grade students scoring at proficient or advanced levels in reading and math. (Currently, only one third of students score at those levels.) This goal is

- **Specific and Strategic.** It deals with students in grades 4 and 5 and with reading and math skills, both of which are strategic priorities in the district.
- **Measurable.** The district knows how many students have scored at the desired levels in the past, and therefore can easily compute whether that figure increases by 50%.
- **Attainable.** It is neither so conservative to be uninspiring nor so high that people will think it is impossible to achieve.
- **Results-based.** It describes the *outcome* (higher reading and math scores), not a process or activity that might contribute to that goal, such as implementing a reading program.
- **Time-bound.** It gives a time frame to achieve the goal: within the next 2 years.

Because SMART goals provide a basis for assessing progress, and a tool for assuring that team efforts are focused on strategically important targets, they become the engine that drives continuous improvement and learning.

SMART Goals Make SMART Schools

Having a single team that uses SMART goals will not increase a school's capacity for improvement, but applying this thinking *throughout* a school can have enormous impact. In SMART Schools

- Everyone knows what the priorities and expectations are and can align their efforts to achieving them (because they have agreed on strategic, specific, and attainable goals).
- Everyone knows how success is defined, how it will be measured, and when.
- As a part of the overall strategy, everyone is involved in finding ways to achieve the priorities (within the context of his or her own work) and collectively learns what is and is not working.
- Decisions are well informed and resources are targeted, giving successful new initiatives a far better chance of being sustained and continuously improved over time.

Now that's SMART!

SMART schools build shared responsibility for continuous learning and improvement. They create an environment where specific actions are aligned with strategic intent and are continuously monitored for effectiveness using multiple measures over time. SMART schools use teams as vehicles for collaborative goal-setting, problem-solving, and decision-making, thus assuring that strategies are mutually agreeable and attainable. SMART Schools have a results orientation; they use good processes to target high-priority needs in a timely way.

Becoming a SMART School

In SMART schools, continuous improvement is not an event—it is a way of thinking and being. Individuals, teams, schools, and entire school districts engage in the ongoing process of learning. You may have heard this referred to in the contemporary literature as a *learning organization* or as a *professional learning community*. It doesn't really matter what you call it, as long as it results in everyone sharing responsibility for the improvement of student learning.

How do schools become communities of continuous learners? Across the country, you will find hundreds of models used to represent the basic elements of continuous improvement. This book is built on a simple framework for becoming SMART (Figure 2), incorporating the best of continuous improvement within a culture of shared responsibility.

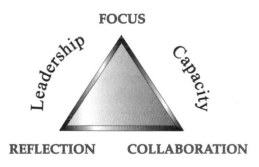

Figure 2 Framework for Becoming SMART

Note. Copyright © 2001 by QLD, LLC. Reprinted with permission.

Focus, Reflection, Collaboration, and Leadership Capacity

"A strong professional learning community consists of

(a) the staff sharing clear goals for student learning [*focus*],

(b) collaboration and collective responsibility among staff to achieve the goals [*collaboration*],

(c) professional inquiry by the staff to address the challenges they face [*reflection*], and

(d) opportunities for staff to influence the school's activities and policies [*leadership capacity*]."

The words in brackets show the link between this statement and the Framework for Becoming SMART.

Source: "Capacity: Lessons from urban elementary schools." Presented to the annual meeting of the American Educational Research Association, New Orleans, April 28, 1999.

An Example of Pareto Thinking

A team of elementary teachers became concerned about what they thought were too many fights on the playground. They believed that a lack of supervision was leading to fights that caused an increasing number of injuries that kept students out of class. They asked their principal to try to secure funds to hire another playground supervisor. Wisely, the principal suggested that they gather some data to determine

- When and where injuries were occurring.
- What types of injuries were children were suffering.
- What was causing the injuries (fights, playground equipment, bad weather, etc.).
- How much instructional time was lost as a result of students missing class due to injuries.

The data showed that while fights were up slightly over the previous year, the majority of class time lost was due to falls and cuts caused by aging equipment and poor overall playground conditions. Once the teachers were able to narrow their investigation to the few causes for the majority of lost class time, their recommendation to the principal changed—fix the playground equipment and repave the surface to eliminate surface cracks.

(continued on page 9 sidebar)

Here is a brief overview of this framework; each element is discussed in more detail in the following sections:

- **Focus** means being clear about *where* you want to go.
- **Reflection** means using data and information to understand where you are now and what impact your actions have.
- **Collaboration** means working *together* to create learning and improvement.
- **Leadership capacity** grows as the other three elements work together. People develop the skills and knowledge to take effective action, and have the authority to act on ideas that are consistent with the organization's vision and plans.

Schools that use a framework like this achieve the results that are most important to them. They know their priorities, know how they are progressing toward achieving their goals, and continuously monitor and adjust what they are doing for the sake of improved results.

Focus

Focus helps us to think clearly about what we are doing and why. Focus helps schools and school districts decide not only what is most important to do, but also what *not* to do or what to *stop* doing. Working toward focus helps to separate the daily urgent issues from the important priorities that need to be nurtured on a longer-term basis. Focus helps schools and individuals stay centered on the purpose of what they're doing, no matter what it is.

Focus is absolutely essential in a learning community. In many ways, focus is what defines the community—what it is, who it serves, its values, and its reason to exist. Without focus, a community attempts to be all things to all people and ends up doing very little with any depth.

Creating Focus

Creating focus is SMART because it helps schools know their true priorities. Many schools create focus by developing statements that capture the essence of a school's mission, vision, values, and goals (see Chapter 9). All of these work together to create focus. As a community matures, its vision and goals will change because continuous learning will shape and inform new ideas. What remains intact, however, are the values and the purpose (mission) that define the uniqueness of that particular community.

The essence of focus, however, is captured in a concept known as the **Pareto principle**.

Vilfredo Pareto, a turn-of-the-century economist who was studying the distribution of wealth, first defined the Pareto principle. He discovered that 80% of the wealth was held by 20% of the people. From this basic principle, financial and business decisions were made based on targeting a small percentage of the population while influencing a large percentage of the wealth. Renowned management expert Joseph Juran applied the principle to management practices and came up with these simple tenets:

- **80/20 Rule:** 80% of the trouble comes from 20% of the problems.
- **Focus on the vital few:** Only a few (20%) of the causes account for the majority (80%) of the problems (losses, failures, time spent, or errors). Focus on improving the few that will achieve the greatest gain. Though often low in visibility, the 20% are high in leverage.
- **Avoid the trivial many:** Because the 80% are so much larger in number (volume, frequency, occurrences, or incidence), they often seem overwhelming and critically important. But though large in number, these trivial many are low in impact. More often than not, they are symptomatic of the fewer underlying causes (the 20%). Addressing the vital few can solve, eliminate, or reduce the trivial many.

In short, Juran showed us that we should focus on improving the few that will achieve the greatest gain.

(continued from page 8 sidebar)

Chapter 9 of this book provides more details on how your school can identify its vital few priorities. These priorities are derived by comparing where your school is now in relation to your vision. Additional guidance appears in Chapter 6, where you will find different data tools (including a Pareto chart) that can help you determine the areas in need of greatest attention or work.

The majority of class time lost was due to falls and cuts caused by aging equipment and poor overall conditions.

Reflection

Reflection encompasses everything that schools and individuals do to understand where they are now, and what they can learn from previous or current practices. To reflect well requires the blending of objective data and feedback with more subjective (but equally valid) knowledge, experience, and observations. In that way, reflection helps us go beyond our best guesses or informed hunches about what is or is not working.

Like focus, reflection generates both enthusiasm and clarity. By taking time to reflect on what we are learning about our practice, we can actually accelerate the improvement process. Reflection at the school and classroom levels gets to the heart of the teaching and learning process. When we reflect on data and monitor progress over time, we can determine whether the strategies we are using or the changes we are making are having a positive impact on students.

Data play an essential role in a school's ability to be reflective. Unfortunately, too often when people hear the word "data" they automatically associate the use of data with inspecting what is happening in a classroom or school. It is important not to confuse *reflection* with *inspection*:

- Reflection exists within a culture whose core value is learning and improvement; inspection exists within cultures that seek to assign blame.
- Reflection is a growth-driven process; inspection is a defects-driven process.

Within the SMART school context, data are used solely to learn and to improve the system, not to punish people or distort results (see the sidebar "Choice in the Use of Data" and Figure 3).

Collaboration

Collaboration is a core value and a critical component of learning communities. The work of continuous improvement cannot be done in isolation. Collaboration is most effective when everyone contributes skills, knowledge, and experience in pursuit of improved results.

Choice in the Use of Data

We have a choice about how we use data in schools: We can use data as the basis for learning and inquiry to discover better methods for doing our work, or we can use data as an *extrinsic motivator* to reward or punish people.

When asked to show that our results are improving, we can do one of three things:

- **Distort the data.** (Change test scores.)
- **Distort the system.** (Stop teaching things that are not on the test.)
- **Improve the system.** (Use data to inform decisions and measure the impact of improvements on learning.)

Obviously, only the last option leads to deep learning and lasting improvement. But it takes hard work to create an environment that truly supports the open use of data, no matter what that data tell you.

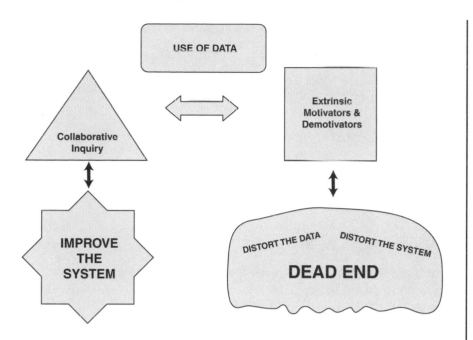

Figure 3 Use of Data
Note. Copyright © 2001 by QLD, LLC. Reprinted with permission.

The greatest value of collaboration is the diversity of thought and perspectives that it brings to the creative process. Without a collaborative approach, focus and reflection can easily lead us to conclusions that support what we think we already know.

Collaboration for its own sake is not enough. **Collaboration is a process we use to achieve *shared* goals.** Having people share their knowledge, expertise, and experience gives us a better understanding of the challenges we face. The end result of collaboration is both a better solution, program, or idea, *and* a greater commitment and capacity to implementing that solution, program, or idea. Collaboration builds community, fuels motivation, renews the spirit, and enhances innovation. When people come together around a common purpose, each contributing his or her unique perspective and skills, and ultimately achieve a mutually defined goal, there is an infusion of energy into the school that is unmatched by any single initiative or program.

This book focuses on one particular vehicle for collaboration: teams. The first lesson to learn about teams is that they need to be used in an environment of focus and reflection to reach their fullest potential.

Synergy for Improvement

Each of the elements of the framework for becoming SMART can be thought of as separate pieces that work at any level of the organization, but they are most useful in combination. Teams, individuals, schools, and whole school districts can apply these ideas in all of their improvement efforts. Skillful collaboration develops interdependent relationships, where all are focused on a common purpose and set of goals, where people need each other to achieve those goals, and where data are used to reflect progress toward the goals. Skillful collaboration results in synergy: The effectiveness of a group exceeds what the individuals can accomplish on their own.

Unfocused collaboration—teamwork void of data and purpose—is counterproductive. Teams in these situations produce superficial content, have vague notions about things that perhaps should be changed, and are often engulfed in unresolved conflict and shotgun approaches to problem solving.

Teams are more than just groups of people coming together to accomplish something. They serve a unique purpose and when they are performing at high levels, they are generative—they create new knowledge, stimulate energy, and promote improvement in ways that individuals acting in isolation could not achieve.

Leadership Capacity

Leadership in a SMART school looks and feels much different from leadership in traditional schools. In a SMART school, leadership is *not* about official positions of authority. Rather, it is about the school's or district's ability to engage the entire school community in broad-based and skillful participation in learning and improvement. In this sense, the real target is increased leadership *capacity*, which allows a school to create and fulfill a vision focused on student learning. Leadership capacity is achieved when there is a dynamic interaction of focus, reflection, and collaboration.

When a school or a district has high levels of leadership capacity, everyone takes responsibility for improvement of every aspect of the organization. Teams of teachers, support staff, administration, and even parents and students work together on system and process improvements, school improvement, and ongoing improvement of student results.

SMART schools have high levels of leadership capacity. One of the key characteristics of schools with high levels of leadership capacity is that leadership and learning are inextricably linked. There are some basic assumptions that support the link between leadership and learning:

- The opportunity to lead is inherently self-motivating.
- Everyone is capable of developing and exercising leadership.
- Leadership is expressed in a variety of ways.

- There are many domains within which leadership can be exercised.
- A school's culture either supports or diminishes the ability to develop shared leadership.

Though we distinguish *leadership* from the formal role of *leader*, leadership capacity is not intended to be a replacement of those in formal positions of leadership. In fact, one of the most important things a leader can do is to promote a different vision of leadership where everyone plays a role in improving the success of the whole school. A strong positional leader is most effective in building leadership capacity when he or she

- Engages others in the work of leadership
- Leads by example
- Has and adheres to a vision of success for all students and staff
- Acts with integrity and honor
- Is a learner, committed to continuously growing in knowledge and skill
- Facilitates the learning of others
- Makes difficult decisions on behalf of kids
- Is consistent, fair, and swift to act when values of the school community are compromised

Pulling the Pieces Together

This book is designed to address all aspects of the SMART school framework, though focus, reflection, collaboration, and leadership capacity are not explicitly highlighted elsewhere. Those principles are embedded in the methods, tools, and skills described throughout this book. You will find guidance on defining team roles, processes for working together effectively, and tools and methods for identifying and making improvements. Together, the chapters of this book provide both theory and practical advice on how to create SMART teams in SMART schools.

> **Predict the rough water and provide time to learn, reflect and shape. Get the people to say, "I helped build it. I feel safe here."**
>
> **—Patrick Dolan**

 A SMART school self assessment form appears on the CD-ROM.

Final Check: SMART

In SMART schools, teams of people consciously and continuously contribute to each other's learning. How would you rate your school's or district's performance in the following areas?

✓ Building relationships within the community

✓ Creating shared vision and goals

✓ Building collaborative and team skills

✓ Using data to inform decisions and practice

In which of these points are you the strongest? The weakest? Start thinking about what you can do to build on your strengths and become more proficient in your weaker areas.

Chapter 1
Setting the Stage for Collaboration and Teamwork

Productive collaboration does not come easily. Most of us have belonged to a team where everyone got along, but nothing got done. Sooner or later, busy people lose patience with teams that do not seem to accomplish much of anything. Productive collaboration takes both *purpose* and *skill* to be effective; teams need to be clear about why they exist (purpose) and have the ability to create and implement a plan for getting it done (skill). We can't create productive collaboration just by telling people to work together. Teams that have skill and purpose save time and develop effective solutions that can be implemented smoothly. Without skill and purpose, collaboration is a waste of time (yet, ironically, time is one of the most frequently cited reasons for why people do not collaborate).

This chapter discusses the components needed to add purpose and skill to collaboration, and ways that you can set the stage for productive collaboration.

Three Cornerstones of Productive Collaboration

The three cornerstones of effective collaboration and teamwork are **People**, **Task**, and **Process** (Figure 1.1). When all three are attended to and working in synergy, collaboration will be highly productive and enjoyable.

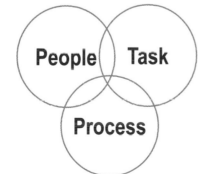

Figure 1.1 People, Task, and Process

Is Collaboration Worth the Effort?

Since the birth of the human relations movement in the 1920s, social scientists have been exploring the relationship between participation and productivity in the workplace. Social science researchers studied the structures and opportunities that people had to interact and to collaborate in their work.

The result? When people were taught the skills to work together collaboratively, they

- Had clearly defined and shared expectations as a group (task)
- Were given time and resources to engage in collaboration targeted at a specific task or outcome (process)
- Realized improved performance, higher quality solutions, greater innovation, and had happier workers

What could be better?

Source: Weisbord, M. (1987). *Productive workplaces: Organizing and managing for dignity, meaning, and community.* San Francisco, CA: Jossey-Bass.

People: Leadership, Commitment, Knowledge, and Skills

Teams operate on two levels:

1) The interests shaped by the skills and background of each individual member
2) The synergy created by the blending of members' knowledge and creativity

The concept that teams are comprised of individuals is important because sometimes people think they must give up who they are in order to be effective team players. Not true. In fact, high performing teams tap into the unique talents and skills of their individual members and value the diversity that those individuals represent.

Consider what it takes for us as individuals to be successful team members:

- We must be committed to developing skills that help us work effectively with others (communication, listening, conflict resolution, and participation).
- We must be committed to increasing our technical expertise or competence so that we can help the team make good decisions.
- We must be aware of our own behaviors and work-style preferences and their impact on others, so we can adjust our behaviors and help the group address the needs of *all* team members.
- We must bring our background and experiences to the table and share them. Helping our group tap into what people know and have done is an essential part of building a successful team.
- We must be willing to work together to become clearer about our common purpose and goals, to develop a shared sense of responsibility and commitment to achieving the group's mission and goals.

These conditions are the same for everyone on a team, and we cannot forget that effective teamwork is a balancing of individual and group needs. Creating an environment where team members can contribute their individual creativity to a collaborative effort increases the success rate of the team.

Task: Functions, Work Plans, Timelines, and Results

Teams exist for a purpose: they must accomplish certain goals within a given time frame. That is why an essential part of effective collaboration is organizing the team's tasks by identifying the team's function, and developing plans and timelines to fulfill those functions and achieve the desired results.

Much of Chapter 3 provides guidance on how a team can identify and organize its tasks. The basic principles are

- To be clear about the purpose and goals of the work
- To identify tasks that move the team toward those goals
- To clarify roles and responsibilities around those tasks
- To develop skills to work together effectively

Process: Decision-Making, Problem-Solving, Communication, and Meetings

Try to recall a major decision faced by a team to which you belonged. How did the team make that decision? Did your group talk about *how* it would make the decision before it was made? If the answer is no, you are not alone. Even when a committed group of skilled and highly motivated people come together around a clear and common purpose, conflicts often emerge if that group has not talked about *how* it will work together. In too many cases, team processes such as decision-making, problem-solving, communication, and meetings are informal or undefined.

Knowing what to expect as you set out to solve a problem or make a decision can help your team minimize conflict and confusion. A team that has not agreed on how it will solve problems or make decisions can easily get mired in unproductive conflict. Using well-defined collaborative processes is the best way to achieve *full* success as a team.

The Dynamic Interaction of People, Task, and Process

Both the beauty and the challenge of teamwork lies in the dynamic interplay of people, tasks, and processes. High-performing teams understand the complexities of this dynamic interaction and consciously manage the processes in ways that maximize the talents of the people to creatively and effectively complete their common tasks.

Is Teamwork Time Consuming?

Time is consistently identified as the most challenging barrier to teamwork in schools. Ironically, the effectiveness of teamwork in today's school environments has been limited by the confines of traditional systems that are not fundamentally designed to support it. Where, in the busy school day, can we find time not only to develop team skills, but also to use them in collaborative settings? Time—even more than money—is a school's most precious commodity, and effective teamwork takes time.

However, the perception that teamwork is time consuming is part truth, part fiction. Some of what we perceive to be time consuming is actually the "spin" put on teams and time. Here are some of the reasons teamwork is considered to be so time consuming:

- It is treated as an add-on, not as a different way to accomplish better results.
- Time is viewed as the enemy (We only have an hour to do this!) as opposed to being viewed as an ally (We have an hour together—let's see how much we can do).
- New learning always takes time. But because of the pressure to perform, teams seldom get past the threshold of the learning curve to a point where members can perform effectively together.
- What seems urgent almost always draws us away from what is most important. Thus, time tends to be

(continued on page 19 sidebar)

Successful teams continuously assess their own performance in all three spheres: people, task, and process. They expand their knowledge in each area—getting to know one another as individuals outside of the team environment, expanding their task knowledge and professional competencies together, learning new process techniques and applying them in new ways—as well as their collective understanding of how all three areas are working together.

Removing Barriers to Collaborative Learning and Improvement

Many schools would say that they are committed to the cornerstones of productive collaboration (people, task, and process), but there are many barriers that prevent them from acting on that commitment:

- Departments, units, and grade levels are defined as separate "chimneys of excellence."
- The school day is scheduled into fragmented units of learning.
- The school year is segmented and defined by contractual guarantees, leaving little flexibility for innovation or collaboration.
- Time for collaboration and teamwork is rarely built into the schedule of the day or year.
- The way in which people are recognized and rewarded for their work reinforces an individualistic approach.
- Space limitations make it difficult for people to work easily in groups.

Some less-obvious barriers present even greater challenges simply because they are not as visible. These include:

- Our mental models about teamwork
- Our skills in working as teams
- Policies and procedures that reinforce individual rather than collaborative approaches
- The inherent lack of structure that results when a team's purpose has not been clearly defined

Schools that have successfully implemented a collaborative approach have built structures for teamwork into their everyday lives and have made it a high priority. It is up to the leaders to create an environment that encourages teamwork. One method for doing this is to explicitly address the symbolic, cultural, and structural barriers to teamwork. Here is how your school can work to eliminate or reduce the impact of these barriers:

1. Expose and address structural and cultural barriers.

- Review the policies and procedures currently in place to see how they either encourage or hinder people working collaboratively.
- Explore the mental models, assumptions, and beliefs people have about teamwork.

2. Actively encourage and support teamwork.

- Celebrate team accomplishments.
- Model effective teamwork yourself.
- Sponsor staff development/skill building sessions for teams.
- Speak in terms of we.

3. Find and make time for collaboration and teamwork.

- Examine your priorities and shift how you spend your time so that your priorities get the most time and attention. As people become more skilled in working together, you will discover that you have more time to do productive, high-priority work.
- Manage meeting time more effectively.
  - Use the tools and methods described in Chapter 3 (see p. 64).
  - Challenge how faculty, department, and grade-level meetings currently work:
    - Is a meeting the best way to meet our objectives?
    - Is the agenda focused on the right purpose?
    - Are the right people involved?
    - Are we losing precious time because we're unprepared or waiting for someone?
- Hold a brainstorming session with staff where the topic is how can we use our time more effectively. Here's a list of ideas one school group brainstormed in just 5 minutes:
  - Combine individual planning time into team time.
  - Rearrange specials so that each grade is at specials together.
  - Create sectionals where support staff (custodial, food, bus, etc.) review safety or other issues with students.

(continued from page 18 sidebar)

devoted to managing crisis, leaving little time to address the root cause of the crisis.

- Educators have the do-it-all-to-perfection disease. Rather than testing new ideas on a small scale before full implementation, they want to get it *all* right and then implement on a full scale.
- Systems have limited capacity. Systems that weren't designed for teamwork are more limited than those that were. It's almost a Catch-22: The best way for systems with the least capacity to increase that capacity is to find time for collaborative efforts . . . yet they feel the most squeezed in trying to find that time.
- It takes time to make time. In SMART schools, educators and staff learn to use whatever time is available to them to make incremental gains. Doing less, but in focused and targeted ways, yields more in the long run.

Time is consistently identified as the most challenging barrier to teamwork in schools.

The Professional Learning Community

One powerful model for creating a learning organization focused on improvement is to think of one's entire school as a professional learning community (DuFour & Eaker, 1998; Newmann & Wehlage, 1995). In this model, the school becomes a community through the development of shared vision, mission, values, and goals. There is a clear priority placed on dialogue (see p. 87) as a learning tool. Assumptions, perception, beliefs, data, and interpretations are openly examined for meaning and for learning. As a result, professional learning communities are resilient in times of change because they never stop learning, changing, and improving.

- Move academic start time back one hour and plan meaningful activities for the students during that time, supervised by aides or other support staff.

 TIP

The important message from the brainstormed list above is not what the particular school identified as possible ways to use time, but that *any* school faculty with a desire to find time can do so if they put their minds to it. Collaborative teamwork is a perfect venue for sharing learning. As teams search for new and better ways of achieving their goals, individuals will be reading, researching, asking others for input, and studying the impact of their strategies.

4. Build in time for more formal learning.

- Create and value learning forums (study teams, action research teams, focus groups, community planning forums, etc.) as part of the real work of the school.
- Regularly use data to inform decisions.
- Create opportunities for diverse groups to come together to challenge assumptions, learn new perspectives, and share ideas.
- Encourage innovation teams to find new and better ways to meet emerging student needs.
- Embed staff development in real work, bringing successful past practices into alignment with emerging best new practices found in the field.

Final Check: Have You Set the Stage?

Teamwork will be more productive when the school environment supports collaborative efforts.

What has your school done to

✓ Encourage people to contribute their individual skills and talents to a collaborative effort? (*People*)

✓ Identify the work that teams need to accomplish? (*Task*)

✓ Help teams learn and identify the processes they will use to accomplish their tasks? (*Process*)

✓ Remove barriers that make it difficult or impossible for teachers, staff, students, parents, and other community members to work together? (*Process*)

✓ Make sure everyone is using time effectively so that people are able to participate fully in team efforts? (*Process*)

✓ Build formal learning into everyone's daily work? (*Process*)

Chapter 2
Structures for Teamwork

Collaboration occurs in a variety of ways, depending on the purpose or need that is driving the collaboration. For example, two teachers might meet over lunch to discuss a class exercise they both will be using. Collaboration here is brief and informal; creating a team would be more trouble and more time consuming than it's worth.

On the other hand, a principal or superintendent might want more structure if a department, school, or district is, for example, working to align curriculum, standards, and assessments. In such a situation, it is important that diverse points of view be represented. There is a lot of work to do, and the effort will likely take weeks or even months. The potential for conflict is also much greater. In short, the effort is more likely to be successful if the collaboration is more structured, and the best vehicle for structured collaboration is a team.

Schools that are making progress towards shared goals have created environments that support both formal and informal collaboration. This chapter focuses on the former, describing various types of team structures that schools have found useful. The key is to understand *why* you need a team and then create the type of team best suited for that purpose.

What Type of Team Is Appropriate?

Different types of teams serve different functions in a school or district. Two basic types of teams are **ongoing** and **ad hoc**:

- **Ongoing teams** manage and guide routine work or recurring tasks. Examples of ongoing teams include grade, subject, and departmental teaching teams, school leadership teams, and K–12 curriculum groups.
- **Ad hoc teams** come together around specific problems or challenges and then disband when that specific challenge is met. Examples include action research, accelerated process improvement projects, textbook adoption groups, and study teams.

Create a Team When . . .

- There is a clear purpose for the team.
- Informal collegiality will not accomplish the purpose.
- The resulting decisions or actions of the team will have broad impact.
- Several meetings will be required.
- Diverse points of view are needed and should be accommodated.

Ad hoc teams come together around specific problems or challenges and then disband when the challenge is met. Ongoing teams manage and guide routine work or recurring tasks.

Table 2.1 Characteristics of Ad Hoc and Ongoing Teams

Type of Team	Characteristics	Examples
Ongoing	▪ Exist for the duration ▪ Membership is relatively stable or rotated based on a long-range plan ▪ Have a broader, ongoing mission ▪ Often include members sharing similar perspectives or functions ▪ Members usually feel a strong allegiance to this team	▪ Grade, subject, departmental teaching teams ▪ School leadership teams ▪ Curriculum direction and alignment teams
Ad Hoc	▪ Have a beginning and an end ▪ Members may come and go ▪ Have a specific and usually fairly narrow mission and limited set of goals ▪ Often include members of various disciplines, functions, or perspectives ▪ Members often feel a first allegiance to other parts of the organization	▪ Curriculum/program improvement teams ▪ Problem-solving teams ▪ Action research teams ▪ Process improvement teams ▪ Study circles

Ad hoc teams and ongoing teams can be characterized differently (see Table 2.1).

The remainder of this chapter provides more detail about the following ongoing and ad hoc teams:

Ongoing	Ad Hoc
▪ Governance teams	▪ Steering teams
▪ School improvement teams	▪ Study teams
▪ System-level improvement teams	▪ Process improvement teams
▪ Departmental and unit teams	▪ Committees and task forces

Governance Teams

Purpose and Function

Governance teams can include school management teams, site-based decision-making teams, leadership teams, and faculty councils. Their primary purpose is to govern the school. Sometimes they act as mini school boards, setting school policies and allocating resources. In other cases, they are more managerial in function, making decisions that traditionally have been the responsibility of the school principal.

Your school and school district must determine the role and function of your school's governance team. Because governance is traditionally not a site/school function, the philosophy of the district will influence whether these teams even exist in your district. Where they do exist, their role (whether advisory or decision-making), and the scope of their influence (schedules, budgets, curriculum innovations, and staffing) will be shaped by the broader district vision of governance.

Characteristics

- Ongoing
- Meet regularly (quarterly or monthly)
- Meeting content fluctuates in response to situations that have arisen for which a policy or procedure was unclear or inappropriate. If their function is more managerial, their agendas will reflect schoolwide operational concerns.

Membership

- Led by a principal
- Includes teachers, support staff, and parents
- May also involve students, if a middle or high school governance team, especially if the role of the team includes making decisions about policies and procedures that address curricular offerings, behavioral expectations, and extra-curricular programs and events

Special Notes

Except for the team leader (typically a principal), members are usually voted onto a governance team by the constituents they represent, and serve set terms on a rotating basis.

Governance Teams

Purpose: Govern a school and provide strategic or managerial input

Membership: Principal, teachers, support staff, parents, and perhaps students

Meeting frequency: Quarterly or monthly

Meeting content: Varies according to whatever strategic or high-impact issues the school faces

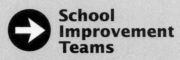

School Improvement Teams

Purpose: Continuously improve student learning

Membership: Teachers, parents, administration, support staff, and students when appropriate

Meeting frequency: Quarterly or more often

Meeting content: Changes predictably depending on the school year

School Improvement Teams

Purpose and Function

School Improvement Teams (SITs) focus on learning. Sometimes called School Effectiveness Teams (SETs), they are stewards of the school's mission, vision, and core values. They monitor achievement, climate, and satisfaction data to assure that the learning environment is producing results consistent with the school's stated goals.

A SIT is *not* an official watchdog of accountability nor is it responsible for achieving improved results. That is the work of everyone in the school. The SIT is responsible for identifying where gaps in performance exist and when, if at all, the core values, mission, and vision of the school are being compromised. It also monitors progress toward school goals. It may also identify processes that are in need of improvement.

Characteristics

- Ongoing
- Meet frequently throughout the year (quarterly or more often)
- Meeting agendas are influenced by the natural cycle of the school year. For example, at the beginning of the year, the team would review goals for the year, whereas in the spring it would review new test data.

Membership

- Like a school governance team, the SIT should be representative of the school population.
- The most effective SITs include teachers, parents, administrators, support staff, and students where appropriate.
- Leadership is often decided by the team or rotated on a scheduled basis (it is not necessary for the principal to be the SIT leader).

Special Notes

The SIT can serve an important role in monitoring and reinforcing the school's vision and core values by conducting climate surveys or sponsoring dialogues.

System-Level Improvement Teams

Purpose and Function

System-level improvement teams serve much the same function as school improvement teams except their scope is systemwide. Their purpose is usually defined around a specific interest such as curriculum, staff development, student services, community relations, or technology integration. These teams serve as stewards of the district's vision in that they help to design, improve, and coordinate the delivery systems that support school and district success in high-priority areas.

Characteristics

- Ongoing (because their mission is to continuously improve key aspects of the system in which they are working)
- Address both the content and the processes that affect their area of focus
- Typically meet quarterly

Membership

- The central office staff in charge of the area being studied usually convenes and leads the system-level improvement team.
- Typically limited to staff
- Involve representatives from each site and include various disciplines (content, grade level, student services, etc.)

Special Notes

In some cases it makes sense to include parents and community members in these teams. This is especially true when the outcome of the team's work is likely to require community support (in the form of referenda or a tax increase, for example) or involves any decision having significant impact on student learning (such as program additions/deletions or school closings).

System-Level Improvement Teams

Purpose: Improve systems, processes, and policies that have a broad impact throughout a district

Membership: Typically restricted to staff

Meeting frequency: Quarterly

Meeting content: Whatever key issues must be addressed in the area of interest

Departmental and Unit Teams

Purpose: Shape service and program delivery

Membership: All staff in a particular area (for example, content or discipline, grade level, department, or special area)

Meeting frequency: Weekly or even daily

Meeting content: Monitoring of ongoing issues and responding to new issues

Standard and Responsive Items on Departmental Agendas

- Standard items appear in every agenda. A typical grade-level team might review progress on curricular units, reactions to a teaching strategy that everyone agreed to try, and/or updates on classroom management practices.
- Responsive items are added to the team's agenda in response to current or unexpected problems or issues. For example, the grade-level team might want to address issues such as newly issued central office initiatives, changes in schedules, student concerns, or staffing decisions that affect their area.

Departmental and Unit Teams

Purpose and Function

Departmental and unit teams guide the work, monitor progress, and determine goals of the area they represent (such as the music department, fourth grade teachers, pupil services, or cross-grade/cross-curricular initiatives). These teams are responsible for service and program delivery and, as such, are much more hands-on than other ongoing teams. They manage the day-to-day services provided to students in their areas.

Characteristics

- Ongoing
- Meet weekly (or even daily) so that they can closely monitor implementation and shape day-to-day decisions
- Meeting agendas include both standard and responsive items (see sidebar)

Membership

- All staff within a particular area. (Even in large schools, regular departmental or unit meetings that include all staff are held for informational and decision-making purposes.)
- The team's leader can be appointed or elected.

Special Notes

- The principal is usually an *ex officio* member of a department or unit team by virtue of his or her responsibility as the instructional leader in his or her school. Therefore, communication strategies that keep the principal informed of key discussions and decisions are a vital element of the success of departmental and unit teams.
- In some districts, the department or unit leader receives additional pay, while in other districts leadership is rotated on a volunteer basis.

Steering Teams

Purpose and Function

Steering teams are typically created to launch major initiatives. They are aptly named: their purpose is to steer a program or process by advising a staff group or some other team on important aspects of design, planning for implementation, and building in strategies for evaluation. It is not appropriate for the steering team to do the actual implementation or evaluation. That becomes the work of other teams or individuals, depending on the nature of the program or process being implemented.

For example, a school might choose to engage in a strategic planning process. The role of the steering team in this case is to work with either the school's governance team or its school improvement team to design the process and to determine the budget, timelines, and participants for strategic planning to occur.

Characteristics

- Ad hoc: exist for as long as it takes to launch the initiative
- Disband when their tasks have been completed (even though the process or program the team was created to steer is ongoing)
- Handle start-up and planning
- Advisory

Membership

- People who represent the process or initiative the team will be asked to steer.
- If the process or initiative will have a broad impact, membership on the steering team should include broad representation.
- Include people with expertise in program development and evaluation.

Special Notes

Steering teams benefit from access to someone with budget-making authority. Because such teams are advisory (not a decision-making team per se), that person need not be a full-fledged member, but the team may need information about budget decisions that have affected or could affect the implementation of the process being steered.

Steering Teams

Purpose: Guide the launch of a major initiative

Membership: People representing the process or initiative being launched

Meeting frequency: As often as needed until the initiative is successfully launched

Meeting content: Developing plans and addressing start-up needs for the initiative

⬡ **Study Teams**
Purpose: Develop a deep understanding of a specified topic and share that knowledge with their school or district
Membership: No specific rules; people who will be affected by the issue or process being studied
Meeting frequency: Once a week or every 2 weeks
Meeting content: Sharing results of information gathered; determining areas for further research; synthesizing and interpreting research results

Study Teams

Purpose and Function

The purpose of study teams is to develop a deep understanding of an issue or process and then share that understanding with others in the school or district. Their specific purpose depends on the broader context in which they exist:

- If part of a needs assessment process within a school or district planning initiative, their focus is the organization or the community.
- If part of a school improvement process, their purpose is to learn about best instructional practices.
- They may also simply reflect a more collegial approach to shared learning in the context of collaborative action research or professional development around a particular topic.

Characteristics

- Ad hoc: Though the *learning* is ongoing, a given team usually disbands once it meets a well-defined objective, such as selecting a new teaching strategy, or completing a book.
- They exist to serve a broader purpose, so their work is incomplete until the study results are shared with others. For example, they may be part of a needs assessment process (results shared with a broader community of planners) or a professional development or action research study (results shared within their department, grade level, or unit).

Membership

- Individuals usually decide to participate based on interest.
- In some cases, membership is determined by who set and will be pursuing the goals. A school improvement study team, for example, would be researching best practices in instruction, and membership would depend on which area was being studied.

Special Notes

- Study teams usually have a process they agree to follow; sometimes they are required to complete their work within a specified time frame. In other ways, however, they tend to be less structured than other teams.
- Leadership on study teams is broad based, and stylistically they are often informal. For example, when a study team comes together to explore a particular topic through research, reading, or observations, its agenda may be just one item—dialogue.

Process Improvement Teams

Purpose and Function

Process improvement teams exist to improve any process in the school or system that, because of inefficiencies or unnecessary bureaucracy, is currently or has the potential to divert resources away from the district's core mission of student learning.

Characteristics

- Ad hoc
- Members structure their work around a well-defined improvement process (see Chapter 9).

Membership

- Membership should reflect people involved with the process to be improved.
- If the potential pool of members is relatively small, consider including everyone on the team.
- If there are far more people working on the process than can be included on the team, select representatives from different parts of the process. Ideally, process improvement teams have six to eight members.
- Example: If the Accounting for Activity Fees process is targeted for improvement, potential members include anyone involved in the process from the moment fees are collected until they are documented in the accountant's ledger. If the process has five main steps, select at least one person from each step to be on the team.

Special Notes

- The depth of study—and duration of the process improvement team—depends on the complexity of the issues associated with the targeted process.
- Consider using the Accelerated Improvement Process (p. 192), a highly structured process that accomplishes results in as little as 6 weeks, for most teams.
- If the targeted process has proven resistant to improvement, consider a more detailed improvement process (see p. 195).

⬢ Process Improvement Teams

Purpose: Improve a defined process that uses people or resources inefficiently or ineffectively

Membership: People representing various parts of the process to be improved

Meeting frequency: Once every week or two

Meeting content: Progresses along with the stage of improvement the team is in (collecting data, generating potential solutions, etc.)

Committees and Task Forces

Purpose: Achieve a narrowly defined objective (produce a product, implement an event) that varies by circumstance

Membership: Runs the gamut from voluntary to appointed depending on the issues to be addressed

Meeting frequency: Variable

Meeting content: Anything related to achieving the objective

Committees and Task Forces

Purpose and Function

Committees and task forces exist to achieve a predetermined product (a set of recommendations, a document or survey, etc.) or to implement a particular event (grandparents' visiting day, a class trip, or an all-school assembly). When the product or event has been successfully achieved, the team no longer has a purpose.

Characteristics

- Ad hoc: disband when the objective is achieved
- Focus is narrowly defined by the objective

Membership

- Often a function of personal interest
- Some task forces are created by boards of education because of sensitive political questions. In such cases, balanced membership becomes very important; the board or superintendent therefore usually determines who participates. The same may be true of a school task force that is convened by the principal or school governance team.

Special Notes

One of the challenging areas for committees and task forces is closure. Committees and task forces that were very clear about their specific objective and stayed on target with that objective find it much easier to end than those that didn't—the latter simply have a hard time knowing when they are done. To avoid needless continuation, create a charter that clearly specifies the team's purpose, tasks, timelines, and deliverables, followed by a plan that includes the team's exit strategy and projected completion date (see p. 41).

Supporting Ongoing and Ad Hoc Teams

Ongoing and ad hoc teams require different types of support. Ongoing teams usually have a clearer sense of their mission, so they usually do not need to work as much on purpose and goals as an ad hoc team. But because they meet regularly over long periods of time, ongoing teams can easily be distracted by non-vital work. It is particularly helpful for these groups to make sure the purposes and outcomes of their meeting agendas are tied to important work, not just *administrivia.* Ongoing teams also tend to develop strong inner-group cultures that act as barriers to newcomers. It is important for these groups to build in ways to be open to outside information; otherwise a kind of group arrogance can set in.

Ad hoc teams need to spend time early on defining their mutual interests, clarifying the team's mission, and establishing their processes for completing their tasks on time. Because assignment to an ad hoc team is frequently short-term and layered on top of already busy schedules, ad hoc team members (and others in their work group who are *not* on the team) tend to struggle more with issues around time, workload, and sharing responsibilities.

Ad hoc teams also need clear criteria for knowing when they are done with their work and may need help coming to closure when their tasks have been completed.

Final Check: Is the Right Structure in Place?

✓ We have concluded that a formal collaborative structure is the best way to address an issue or meet a particular need.

✓ We have matched our purpose to the appropriate type of team.

✓ We have selected appropriate members.

✓ We have support mechanisms in place.

✓ Our ongoing teams have a means for identifying and including new members.

✓ Our ad hoc teams have a means for closure.

> Experience is something you don't get until just after you need it.
>
> —George Carlin

Chapter 3
The Basics of Effective Teamwork

To effectively support school or district learning goals, teams must not only learn new skills and methods, but also manage the interactions and development that are a normal part of team dynamics. This chapter discusses a broad range of roles, principles, methods, and techniques that go into making an effective team.

Start-Up Basics

There are seven tasks that help get a team off to an organized, efficient start:

Identify the WHO
1. Identify team members.
2. Identify the sponsor and stakeholders.
3. Define team member functions.

Identify the WHAT and WHY
4. Identify group goals.

Define the HOW
5. Plan the work and develop a charter.
6. Discuss the assumptions about teamwork.
7. Agree on guidelines for group behavior.

1. Identify Team Members

Who should be on a team depends on what the team needs to accomplish, and therefore what knowledge, experience, and authority should be present on the team. You can use the guidelines given in Chapter 2 to get you started.

> The team is the cornerstone of the learning organization. What really matters is how people make decisions and take action—how the team thinks and acts together.
>
> — Peter Senge

Seven Start-Up Tasks

Identify the WHO
→ **1. Identify team members.**
   2. Identify the sponsor and stakeholders.
   3. Define team member functions.

Identify the WHAT and WHY
   4. Identify group goals.

Define the HOW
   5. Plan the work and develop a charter.
   6. Discuss the assumptions about teamwork.
   7. Agree on guidelines for group behavior.

Team membership can be decided in a variety of ways. The team's purpose should also provide guidance on how team members are selected. Members might

- **Volunteer:** Choose this option when a high level of team member interest is of primary importance.
- **Be elected by peers:** Choose this option when representation is of primary importance.
- **Be appointed by the principal, superintendent, or board:** Choose this option when the stakes are high.

Parent and Community Involvement

The trickiest consideration may well be whether to involve parents and community members on school and district teams. Having those stakeholders represented provides a number of benefits:

- Broader perspectives and new ideas
- Diverse expertise, which contributes to better results
- Strengthened commitment to the team's recommendations
- Enhanced communication
- Stronger school-community relationships

What is in question for many school teams is how best to involve parents and community members. Some will argue that the challenges are greater than the benefits warrant. But that's usually because the parents and community members are viewed as invited guests rather than as true members of the team. As a result, the dynamics of the team are compromised and there is a pervasive tension that keeps the team from becoming truly effective.

The team can manage this dynamic by how it chooses to involve these members. Three of the most obvious and easiest remedies have to do with roles, logistics, and language.

Roles for Parents and Community Members

When parents and community members either volunteer or accept an invitation to be a part of a school team, they will have the same kinds of questions about their roles and their involvement as any new member would. They are likely to wonder such things as

- What perspective am I expected to bring? (Am I here as the parent of my child or as a representative of a parental point of view?)

- Am I an equal member of this team with the right to share my opinions even though I've never been a professional educator? Do I have a vote?
- Will I be expected to do work between meetings and attend all meetings?
- What kind of commitment am I making? For how long?
- What happens if I disagree with the team? Will my child suffer any consequences?
- Do I have anything unique or valuable to offer?

There is only one way to find the answers to these questions and that is to talk about them. Early on in the team's formation, parents and community members may not feel comfortable asking these kinds of questions, so it's important that the team be proactive in addressing them as a part of the start-up process.

Logistics of Parent or Community Member Involvement

Logistics include both where the meetings are held and when the meetings are held. Making a concerted effort to hold meetings at times and places that are accessible to a variety of parents and community members sends an important message that their involvement really is important. This may mean making some compromises on the part of school staff, but in the long run, the results will be worth it.

Language: Watch the Jargon!

Like most disciplines, education has its own language. Even within the educational system, the language is different from one discipline to the next. This use of specific language is intimidating to those outside of the system. The team should take time during the first couple of meetings to identify terms that are likely to cause confusion and work as a group to develop agreed-on definitions, especially if team members come from different disciplines, grades, schools, etc. That way, individuals who may not know the meaning of the terms do not feel left out or uninformed.

2. Identify the Sponsor and Stakeholders

The work of every team ultimately affects more than just the people serving on that team, and its work is affected by others outside the team. To operate efficiently and effectively, a team needs to know who has authority over or ultimate responsibility for its actions (the **sponsor**), and what people are interested in and likely affected by the team's work (the **stakeholders**).

Seven Start-Up Tasks

Identify the WHO
1. Identify team members.
→ **2. Identify the sponsor and stakeholders.**
3. Define team member functions.

Identify the WHAT and WHY
4. Identify group goals.

Define the HOW
5. Plan the work and develop a charter.
6. Discuss the assumptions about teamwork.
7. Agree on guidelines for group behavior.

The sponsor is typically an administrator (principal, central office administrator, etc.) who has the authority to allocate time and resources for the team and to approve (or deny) its solutions and actions. High-performing teams keep their sponsors informed of progress and use their sponsor as a resource for overcoming barriers and as a communication link to the district administration.

Though stakeholders have little formal authority over a team's work, their support and buy-in can make implementation go much more smoothly. Conversely, if left out of the loop, stakeholders can easily become obstacles to implementation. Typical stakeholders come from the following groups:

- Parents
- Community members
- Board members
- Principals
- Central office administrators
- Teachers
- Other school staff
- Students or graduates

3. Define Team Member Functions

Every person on the team has an important function to perform in achieving its mission and accomplishing its goals. In high-performing teams, leadership is shared; everyone accepts responsibility for making sure the team's work goes well. Different members, depending on their particular knowledge or experience, lead the group when their expertise is needed.

There are three team functions that every team should clearly identify:

- Team leader
- Team members
- Team facilitator

1. **Team leader:** The person responsible for seeing that the team accomplishes its work. This person does not *do* all the work him- or herself, but provides the guidance, support, and structure that

---

Seven Start-Up Tasks

Identify the WHO
1. Identify team members.
2. Identify the sponsor and stakeholders.
→3. **Define team member functions.**

Identify the WHAT and WHY
4. Identify group goals.

Define the HOW
5. Plan the work and develop a charter.
6. Discuss the assumptions about teamwork.
7. Agree on guidelines for group behavior.

allows *all* members to contribute and keeps a team moving forward. The team leader shapes meeting agendas to ensure critical issues are addressed at appropriate stages in the project or effort, using initial meetings to identify goals and define team roles and ground rules, for example, or scheduling regular reviews so that the team can check on and improve its work.

Team leaders also link the team with the rest of the school, district, or community:

- They apprise the sponsor of the team's progress and seek support and guidance from that person as needed.
- They make sure that the team communicates its progress to all the stakeholders interested in its work.

2. **Team members:** The people who carry out the work of the team. A team member's responsibility is to participate fully in all the team's work by

- Participating fully in team meetings
  - Attend meetings
  - Voice opinions during team meetings
  - Offer input and advice based on past experience and expert knowledge
  - Volunteer to perform specific meeting roles (see p. 64–65)
- Carrying out assigned or volunteer tasks on time (and communicating with the team leader when tasks cannot be completed on time)
- Being open to learning from others

3. **Team facilitator:** Many teams have a special advisor who is an expert in group dynamics and collaborative methods and tools. This person, called a facilitator, makes sure the group works together as effectively as possible. He or she can help structure team activities to achieve desired goals, provide alternative discussion techniques when the team is stuck, help the group work through conflict, and so on. In short, the facilitator's job is to make it easier for the group to be successful. Some teams have a full-time facilitator who works closely with the team leader and attends all meetings; others have a facilitator available on call to provide assistance when needed.

Note: The facilitator is usually *not* a team member in the sense that he or she would carry out the team's work (gathering data, studying

When to Have a Team Facilitator

A team facilitator can be very helpful in the following situations:

- When the school is going through a school improvement planning process
- When there is conflict and strong disagreement in the team
- When a team is stuck or floundering
- When there is a mix of strong personalities on the team
- When starting a team

Where Do Goals Come From?

Where do goals come from? Ideally, your school or district will have begun its own broad-based school improvement effort, identifying both a long-term vision and immediate needs. The team's goals would then derive from what the school or district identified as its priorities. If that work has not been done, there must still be some background information about your team's purpose or else it would not have been started in the first place. Review any meeting notes, data, surveys, etc., that provided the impetus for the team.

Use your team goals to monitor effectiveness. You can do this informally by simply asking the question, "Is what we're doing contributing to progress towards our goals?" Or you can chart formal data that provide objective measures of success.

issues, making decisions, and so on). Rather, the facilitator is best described as an impartial observer who is there to help the team accomplish its work. Since the facilitator is outside of the team's work, it is not critical that he or she has content knowledge associated with the team's mission.

Not every team has the luxury of having a skilled facilitator. But *all* team members can acquire basic facilitation skills, particularly those that help a team hold effective and efficient meetings (see p. 46). If your team runs into situations where those basic skills are inadequate to help you through a difficult period, there are a number of places to look within the school district or community for an objective person who can help facilitate. In particular, don't overlook the potential of skilled facilitator volunteers from among the following groups:

- Support staff (secretaries, instructional aides, maintenance, or custodial staff)
- Parents
- Community members
- High school students

4. Identify Group Goals

Goals directly related to a team's mission keep it focused and on task. Team goals can address both desired results (improve third grade reading) as well as how the group will work together (resolve conflicts quickly and with respect). What's most important is that

- The goals collectively lead to the accomplishment of the team's mission
- Everyone on the team is involved in developing the goals and the tasks meant to achieve them. Developing goals collaboratively helps to ensure that all team members understand and are committed to achieving them

Any goal is better than no goal at all, and SMART goals are better still. Use the SMART guidelines (p. 4) to define goals that are *Strategic* and *Specific, Measurable, Attainable, Results-based,* and *Time-bound.* Building those characteristics into your goals helps make sure the team sets realistic goals that it can measure and attain.

5. Plan the Work and Develop a Charter

The best intentions of a team are often lost through ill-planned implementation strategies. All the work of the group will be rendered useless if careful thought is not given to how the group will organize the tasks it needs to accomplish. School-based projects or initiatives can be especially difficult to plan because they

- Are multi-faceted
- Affect a broad range of stakeholders both inside and outside of the school
- Carry some emotional and/or political baggage with them

This is why a good project-management strategy is needed by all SMART teams.

Given limited time and a bias for action, teams often jump headfirst into doing the work. In the long run, this kind of approach can lead to duplication of effort or missed opportunities. Instead, take time early on to get organized.

- Make sure everyone understands the scope (size), overall expectations, and time frame for the group's work.
- Divide the work into manageable pieces.
- Define specific goals and benchmarks for each task.
- Assign individual or small group responsibilities based on member interest, skills, and knowledge.
- Schedule tasks and time frames for review.

Simply completing the team charter document (Figure 3.1) together will help the team get organized. The charter document is a good place to start with defining the parameters of the project. Once the team is clear about what it needs to accomplish and the amount of time it has available to do it, the members can attach names to the various tasks, roles, or responsibilities. This is where the match between interests, skills, and experiences of the team members and needs, roles, and responsibilities of the project becomes critical. If the team has done its start-up work, this should not be a difficult exercise.

Using a standard format for chartering the team can help the group get organized and assure that everyone is literally on the same page when it comes to the work of the group.

Seven Start-Up Tasks

Identify the WHO

1. Identify team members.
2. Identify the sponsor and stakeholders.
3. Define team member functions.

Identify the WHAT and WHY

4. Identify group goals.

Define the HOW

→ 5. **Plan the work and develop a charter.**
6. Discuss the assumptions about teamwork.
7. Agree on guidelines for group behavior.

 A template of a team charter appears on the CD-ROM.

Team Charter

Team Members (List all members.):

_____
_____
_____
_____
_____

Mission (A brief statement of purpose that includes specific end results or outcomes.):

_____
_____
_____
_____
_____

Tasks to Complete (A sequential list of activities that the team will use to achieve the end results/ outcomes provided in the mission.):

_____
_____
_____
_____
_____
_____
_____

Timeline (Either phases or a specific timeline that the group will follow to achieve its mission. Ad hoc groups will most likely have a stated date for completion; ongoing groups will have a timeline that targets incremental progress within specified time ranges.):

_____
_____
_____
_____
_____

Figure 3.1 Team Charter

Scheduling Work

Two tools that are useful for scheduling complex projects are the Activity Network Diagram (AND) and the Gantt Chart (see pp. 110–112). Both of these tools allow the team to work together to create a schedule that illustrates the sequence of tasks as well as which tasks might be accomplished simultaneously. The AND allows the team to discover the most efficient path and the most realistic schedule for the completion of the project.

The Gantt Chart is similar to the AND in that tasks are scheduled both sequentially as well as simultaneously and are plotted on a horizontal calendar of time ranges. They are easier to create than AND charts (and a standard format exists for some software programs), but they cannot show which tasks are specifically dependent on others because there are no connecting arrows between the tasks, as there are in an AND chart.

Determining Roles and Responsibilities

A key aspect of planning work is deciding *who* is responsible for *what*. A special type of flowchart called a deployment flowchart (see p. 100) can help you visually depict which individuals or groups are assigned what responsibilities once the tasks have been scheduled.

6. Discuss the Assumptions About Teamwork

To fully appreciate the value of teams and their complexity, it is helpful to understand the underlying assumptions that influence a team's performance:

- Teams exist for a purpose; they are a means to an end that cannot be as effectively achieved by individuals working in isolation.
- Skillful teamwork doesn't just happen; teams must work at becoming effective.
- Team development is a journey, not an event; team development is dynamic.
- Teams move through predictable stages of development, though each is manifest in unique ways because each team is unique.
- Team development becomes increasingly complex and dynamic as teams mature, requiring increasing levels of personal effectiveness, skill, and trust on the part of the members.

Seven Start-Up Tasks

Identify the WHO
1. Identify team members.
2. Identify the sponsor and stakeholders.
3. Define team member functions.

Identify the WHAT and WHY
4. Identify group goals.

Define the HOW
5. Plan the work and develop a charter.
→ **6. Discuss the assumptions about teamwork.**
7. Agree on guidelines for group behavior.

Sharing these assumptions within a team

- Sets the expectation that the team is there to accomplish real work (*while* having fun!)
- Helps people accept that teamwork involves specific skills that must be learned and improved
- Eases the pressure to be perfect from the beginning

When these assumptions and expectations are discussed in a group, members often indicate a sense of relief in knowing that there's more to teamwork than they had thought.

7. Agree on Guidelines for Group Behavior

Ground rules help a group take ownership of its collective behavior, articulate its concerns, and take action on those concerns by establishing their own norms of conduct as a team. Ground rules are often established early on in a group's development, but may also be developed after several meetings, by which time the group will have a better sense of its normal dynamics.

Creating Ground Rules

Creating ground rules as a whole group increases the odds that people will follow them. There are several methods you can use. For example:

1. **Pose open questions to the group and then discuss the answers.** Use the following questions as discussion starters for talking about how the group wants to function. You might write down answers to the questions on a flipchart or whiteboard, for example, and then have your team discuss what themes appear in their answers.
   - The Cotter Question[1]: What could this group do to assure that this team fails?
     (This question usually generates some laughter, but after the group begins to really think about it, they discover that some of their previous team experiences were bad enough to have been planned that way. Had they thought through the behaviors that they wanted to avoid, those experiences would have been quite different.)

---

[1]Named for its creator, Maury Cotter, University of Wisconsin, Office of Quality Improvement.

Seven Start-Up Tasks

Identify the WHO
1. Identify team members.
2. Identify the sponsor and stakeholders.
3. Define team functions.

Identify the WHAT and WHY
4. Identify group goals.

Define the HOW
5. Plan the work and develop a charter.
6. Discuss the assumptions about teamwork.
→ 7. **Agree on guidelines for group behavior.**

- What makes a team successful?
- What drives you crazy about meetings?
- If you had the chance to create the perfect team experience, what would it be like?
- It's okay to _____; It's not okay to _____.

2. **Have the group discuss various categories of behavior.**
   Another process for creating ground rules is to identify categories of behavior and ask people to write one idea per category on self-stick notes and post their ideas on a flipchart. Then discuss which of the ideas the group would like to adopt as its own.

Typical ground rule topics and some examples are shown in Table 3.1.

Suggestions for Using Ground Rules

- Create them as a team.
- Review them often.
- Discuss them with new members.
- Keep them visible at all times.
- Confront behaviors that violate them.
- Revise them as needed.

Table 3.1 Ground Rule Topics and Examples

Ground Rule Topics	Examples
Attendance	All members agree to attend every meeting. When someone cannot attend, that person agrees to contact the team leader 24 hours in advance of the meeting if possible.
Participation	There should be no substitutes for team members. Members should participate fully both inside and outside meetings.
Interruptions	We will attend meetings as though we had driven 100 miles to attend. We will allow interruptions for emergencies only.
Preparation	We will come to all meetings with assignments completed, prepared to productively contribute to discussions and decisions.
Timeliness	We will start on time if at least 80% of the team is here. Since schedules are so important, we will stop all discussions 5 minutes before the meeting ends so that we can decide on next steps and how to handle unresolved issues.
Decision-making	We will discuss the best decision-making model for each situation. We will support decisions made by the group.
Conflict Management	We will deal with conflicts in the group directly, respectfully, and immediately.
Communication	We will keep accurate meeting records and share them with team members within 3 days following the meeting if at all possible.
Meeting Practices	We will have an agenda for every meeting and commit to following it.
Jargon Cops	At each meeting we will appoint one person to pay attention to jargon. Violators will throw 25 cents into the treat fund.

Skills and Methods of Effective Teamwork

For teamwork to be productive, team members must be deliberate in determining how they will work together and in developing their collaborative skills. Here are five areas that, if attended to, will increase a team's likelihood for success:

1. Communication
2. Decision-making
3. Conflict management
4. Use of data
5. Cohesiveness

Team Skills

→ 1. **Communication**
2. Decision-making
3. Conflict management
4. Use of data
5. Cohesiveness

1. Communication: Pay Attention to What Is Said, and How

Communication in high-performing teams encompasses a broad range of formal and informal ways for people to exchange ideas and information. The underlying theme is that all communication is open and honest. People feel free to express their thoughts, feelings, and ideas, knowing that they will be heard and considered without criticism. They view communication as a vehicle for building relationships, staying informed, obtaining input and feedback on the group's work, and maintaining a level of professional respect that keeps the team confident in its work and its members.

Four types of communication are particularly important in teamwork:

- Sharing
- Discussion
- Dialogue
- Active Listening

Sharing Information About the Team's Work

Ways to build communication into your team's everyday work are shown in Table 3.2.

Table 3.2 Information Sharing Techniques and Examples

Information Sharing Techniques	Examples
Maintain accurate records of meetings.	• Post logs of decisions and to-do lists in a common space.
Check in with team members between meetings.	• Ask, "I was wondering how your research on criterion-referenced tests was going. Do you need any help?"
Share information about team discussions and decisions with colleagues outside of the team.	• State, "We're developing some really terrific rubrics for the first-grade art students that I think will be helpful in other grades as well."
Invite feedback as a normal course of interaction on the team.	• Ask, "I decided to do _____. What do you think? Did I miss anything?"
Use different ways of communicating to accommodate the different ways in which people listen and learn.	• Write discussion points on a flipchart in clear view of the group. • Use a round-robin method of sharing opinions so that the talkers don't overshadow others in the group. • Provide written documentation for those who learn better by reading.

Discussion Skills

Much of a team's work happens through discussion. On a personal level, a basic discussion skill is being able to express ideas clearly. As a team, discussion skills include techniques that stimulate thinking in the group and help guide the discussion into productive pathways.

For example, a few skills that any team member can use during a discussion are shown in Table 3.3 on the next page.

Dialogue: Balancing Advocacy With Inquiry

Dialogue is a special way of talking together. Its purpose is to *explore meaning*—to create mutual understanding, not necessarily to come to an agreement, a decision, or a solution. Dialogue is a balancing act—balancing speaking and listening, reflection and assertion, advocacy and inquiry.

Table 3.3 Discussion Skills and Examples

Discussion Skills	Examples
Leading Introduce new topics and keep the discussion moving.	• "The next agenda item is about the alternative class schedules we've been exploring. . . ." • "Has everyone had a chance to give their opinion? Are we ready to make a decision yet?"
Innovating Introduce new ideas and strategies. Push the group to think differently —outside the box	• "Let's think about entirely new ways to evaluate how well the fourth graders are doing on their science projects. Has anyone worked with rubrics before?"
Summarizing Restate key discussion points and review decisions to make sure there is a common understanding about decisions and their consequences.	• "It sounds like we've agreed to do a pilot study in Ivan's class before doing anything else. Is that right?"
Clarifying Identify when there is confusion and clarify the points of misunderstanding by restating the issue or asking clarifying questions.	• "I think we're confusing two different issues here. . . ."
Advocating Challenge the underlying assumptions and unstated biases that keep the group from moving toward innovative solutions.	• "Do we know for sure that we can't hire a part-time aide to monitor classes twice a month while we hold our meetings? Has anyone asked?"
Resourcing Bring new information and strategies to the group to help members learn and grow.	• "I just learned this great technique for integrating art and history content . . . "
Integrating Merge disparate conversations, ideas, and concepts together into an integrated whole.	• "The problems we're talking about remind me of the discussion we had last week about . . . "
Initiating Initiate new models of working together and work to implement them.	• "Let's do a map of our history curriculum to see if we're missing anything important. Here's a process we can use. . . ."

Advocacy is making one's own thinking or point of view known and visible to others. Advocacy includes stating your assumptions, describing your underlying reasons for your assumptions, and talking about how you feel about the topic or issue, being careful to distinguish the data from your own interpretation of the data.

Inquiry is asking others to make their thinking, perspectives, assumptions, and feelings visible. Inquiry involves asking for and then listening deeply to someone else's point of view and seeking to understand why he or she sees the situation in that way.

Consider the examples shown in Table 3.4.

Table 3.4 Advocacy and Inquiry

What the Person Says . . .	Interpretation
"I'm convinced that our students are not being challenged to their fullest potential. Too many students have a lot of ability, but don't go on to take more rigorous classes at the high school. That frustrates me."	The person is stating an opinion—*advocating* a particular position.
". . . Does anyone else have that same feeling? What do you think is happening? Is my reasoning flawed?"	The person then opens the discussion for dialogue by making an *inquiry* of the group.
"The data show a trend downward in the numbers of students electing advanced placement classes. At least that's how I read the chart."	The person returns to *advocacy* and uses data to support the statements.
"What else could the data be telling us? Are there other interpretations or possible reasons?"	. . . And again creates an opportunity for true dialogue by making an *inquiry*.

Source: Senge, P., Ross, R., Smith, B., Roberts, C., & Kleiner, A. (1994). *The Fifth Discipline Fieldbook*. New York, NY: Doubleday.

Nature has given men and women one tongue, but two ears, that we may hear from others twice as much as we speak.

— Epictetus

Active Listening

Advocacy and inquiry are two skills that team members can use to articulate clearly when they speak. The complementary skill is active listening.

On the one hand, listening does not seem to be all that difficult. But active listening—where you really *hear* and *understand* what someone else is saying—is hard work. Why? In part, because we usually listen just long enough to hear what we need to fuel our next point of disagreement (or agreement). This is especially true when we feel pressured by time, by other stresses in our lives, or by the need to be heard because no one is listening back. Some of the more common barriers to listening include

- Stress
- Emotions
- Preoccupation
- Bias
- Physical state
- Closed mind
- How we feel about the speaker
- Lack of interest in the topic

Changing our listening habits isn't easy—it takes commitment and effort. If you want to become a better listener, begin by thinking about the benefits of listening:

- Builds trust
- Creates understanding
- Reduces erroneous assumptions
- Clarifies meaning
- Builds relationships

If these are the outcomes you desire, then ask yourself these questions:

- Under what conditions or circumstances am I an effective listener?
- When don't I listen effectively?
- What would I expect someone else to be like when listening to me?
- When I'm not really listening, what am I doing instead?
- What gets in the way of my being a good listener?

There are ways to turn passive listening into active listening. Active listening means that the listener is providing some sort of feedback to the speaker during the communication. There are three strategies for active listening:

1. Paraphrasing
2. Perception checking
3. Probing

Paraphrasing is nothing more than a reality check on the listener's understanding. Here's how to do it:

- Listen without distraction. Tune in to both text and subtext (tone of voice, choice of words, pacing, body language, etc.).
- Briefly summarize what you heard and understood *in your own words* (you don't want to sound like a parrot).
   "What I hear you saying is . . . "
   "If I understand correctly, you . . . "
- Check the accuracy of your paraphrasing.
   "Did I catch what you're saying?"
   "Am I understanding what you're feeling?"

Paraphrasing improves mutual understanding about what is being said and provides an opportunity to correct or clarify any potential misunderstandings. Note that *paraphrasing is not the same as agreeing with the speaker.* In fact, good paraphrasing should bring no judgment or evaluation with it, and that's just fine. The need to be *heard* and *understood* far exceeds a person's need to have someone agree with him or her.

Perception checking is similar to paraphrasing, except that it involves a level of interpretation that paraphrasing does not. In paraphrasing, the listener simply repeats or summarizes what has been heard. In perception checking, the listener draws a conclusion or makes an interpretation and then checks with the speaker to make sure that he or she is accurate. For example:

"It sounds like you're really frustrated with this project, is that correct?"

"This doesn't seem like a good time to talk, am I right?"

"With everything you've described, it sounds to me like you're pretty overwhelmed."

> Listen with your heart as well as your mind.
>
> —Anonymous

A perception check describes what you think the other person is feeling, but does not express disapproval or approval.

Probing is a strategy for taking the conversation deeper. The purpose of probing is to

- Expand on ideas
- Go deeper in understanding
- Get clearer about meaning
- Unearth assumptions
- Explore applications

It's important to remember that the speaker sets the stage in terms of content and initial depth of the conversation by what he or she offers. The role of the active listener is to probe into the meaning that has been initiated by the speaker, not to take the speaker in another direction. Also, take care to watch for signs that the speaker may not be comfortable going deeper, especially if the content of the conversation is personal. In that case, the listener should get permission from the speaker to probe further.

Here are some examples of probing:

> *"Do you mind my asking, what led you to that conclusion?"*
>
> *"If you don't mind telling me, what do you think were the most critical factors that influenced you in this situation?"*
>
> *"Tell me more about that if you're comfortable doing so."*
>
> *"So what do you think that means?"*

Generally, whether paraphrasing, perception checking, or probing, there are some things to keep in mind when working on improving your listening skills:

- Stop talking.
- Don't interrupt.
- Always listen patiently; don't be afraid of silence.
- Listen for changes in tone and volume.
- Listen to what is not being said.
- Refrain from any reactions or comments that would indicate judgment, disagreement, or evaluation.

- Indicate understanding.
- Be interested.
- If you don't have time, say so.
- If you don't understand something, say so.
- Try not to be influenced by your feelings or biases about who is talking.
- When the content of the conversation is personal, find a quiet space and limit interruptions if possible.
- Check your tendency to hear only what you want to hear.

2. Decision-Making: Decide How to Decide

There are a lot of different ways to go about making a decision. Since a team is a collaborative effort, decision-making in the team also needs to be collaborative. The key to good collaborative decision-making is for the team to be explicit about its decision-making process—selecting the right decision-making process for the need.

Collaborative decision-making is highly effective when

- Decisions require diverse, creative ideas
- Many perspectives are needed to understand the issue or problem
- A fundamental or significant change is likely
- Many people or groups share the same problem

The first step in collaborative decision-making is assessing what outcomes your team needs as well as what authority it has (see the sidebar, "What Do You Have the Authority to Decide?" on p. 54). Then, establish norms for how decisions will be made so you can avoid some of the inevitable conflicts that groups experience when they must finally make a decision.

Four Decision-Making Options

The following is a list of four possible decision-making options. Which option you use depends on the situation:

- **Consensus Decisions**—All members of the team agree to support the group's decision, even if the selected option is not their first preference.

Team Skills

1. Communication
→ **2. Decision-making**
3. Conflict management
4. Use of data
5. Cohesiveness

Goals of Group Decision-Making

Ideally, team members should feel their team is making high-quality decisions, and that they have the group's acceptance and support to carry out those decisions. That is the essence of collaborative decision-making.

What Do You Have the Authority to Decide?

Let's be practical here. Your team only exists because someone with the authority to allow it to exist thinks it's okay for people to use their time in that way. For school-based teams, that person is likely to be a positional leader (principal, department chair, or unit leader) or the School Improvement Team that's overseeing a process. For other teams, it may be a central office administrator, the superintendent, or even the board.

We've all been in situations where we put a lot of time and effort into making a decision only to hear the positional leader say, "Thanks for your input. I'll take it under advisement." So before your team spends a lot of time deciding how you'll make decisions *within* the team, you need to be clear about what decisions the team as a whole is authorized to make. That means working with the authority to be clear about what he or she or they want out of the team. For example, are you supposed to

- Study an issue and come up with options?
- Make a recommendation?
- Make the decision?
- Implement the decision?

You'll also need to know what criteria or limits the authority has placed on the team's outcomes. Here's an example: To study the textbook ordering process and devise and implement a new process as long as it can be

(continued on page 55)

- **Voting**—Group members vote on various options.

  Majority vote: For an option to win, it must receive at least 51% of the votes, or a two-thirds majority.

  Most votes: The option with the most votes wins, even if it doesn't have a majority.

- **Consultative Decisions**—The team or one member of the group makes the decision in consultation with others.

- **Command Decisions**

  Decision by authority: The decision is made by a person with positional or delegated authority.

  Expert decision: The group determines that the decision can best be made by someone with expert knowledge in a particular area (who need not necessarily be a member of the group).

The first two options—consensus and voting—involve all team members in the decision. The latter two provide alternatives that can be used either when it is not necessary for the whole team to be included or when an individual has the specific authority or job requirement to make a decision.

Consensus Decisions

When the group's primary concern is that *every team member* is comfortable with the decision, the best decision-making mode is **consensus**. Consensus means that everyone agrees to support the decision, *publicly and privately*, once the decision is final. It does not mean that the selected option is everyone's first choice. The key consensus question is "Can we live with this decision?"

Your team will reach consensus only when everyone involved in making the decision is satisfied that his or her concerns have been heard and considered. That's why consensus decisions are typically preceded by

- Extensive dialogue where people get to voice their opinions
- A thorough investigation of all aspects of the decision (both positive and negative)
- A weighing of all the options (not just a favored few)

It's probably obvious from this description that consensus decisions take more time up front than the other decision-making options discussed later. But this up-front investment has a huge payoff down the road in smoother implementation. The higher the stakes, the more desirable consensus becomes.

Use consensus decision-making when

- Full support and commitment are needed to successfully implement the decision
- Many people will be affected by the decision; many will be responsible for implementation
- The decision affects or may change the core processes of those involved

See pages 94–95 for a consensus decision-making process.

Voting

When the group needs a more expedient approach due to time constraints or decides that it is not critical to have all people totally committed to the decision, it may elect to conduct a vote. The team will have to decide whether to keep going until one option has a clear **majority** (either 51% or two-thirds of the votes) or whether the option with the most votes will win no matter what (if Option A receives 40% of the votes, option B receives 35%, and option C receives 25%, then option A wins).

Because as many as 49% of the team could be on the losing side in a majority vote, you have to be very careful when using this decision-making mode.

Voting is appropriate when

- The stakes are low
- The group is very large
- Time is of the essence
- Commitment to the decision is less important than getting on with the task

(continued from page 54)

completed by August 1 and requires no new equipment purchases.

If you are not given any decision boundaries or criteria up front, have your team write down what authority you think you have and then check with the positional leader.

Most of the important decisions a team faces should be made by consensus because such decisions will receive support by the entire group. However, school teams work in the real world, and sometimes a decision has to be made whether or not the group has reached consensus. Have your group discuss under what circumstances it will be okay to use a different decision-making strategy even if consensus was the goal (after a certain amount of time or after a certain number of attempts at reaching consensus, for example). Use caution here: Make sure there is a legitimate reason for abandoning the attempt to reach consensus. Don't give up too easily or you'll erode the group's trust that its input is valued.

Tips for Enhancing the Consensus Process

- Don't try to force compromises.
- Don't avoid tough discussions or you'll never reach a point where everyone feels their concerns have been heard and dealt with.
- Be careful not to rush to decision; people need time to weigh alternatives before they can put their full support behind one option.
- Seek ways to combine and recombine various positions.
- Don't *vote* for the final decision; consensus means *everyone* agrees to support the final choice.
- Do whatever you can to equalize participation, especially if there are individuals who have positions of authority over others in the group.
- When you think you're close to consensus, have someone write a clear statement of the impending decision. Then ask group members if they understand and support that statement and make any agreed-on changes.

 TIP

If your team has a lot of options from which to choose to make a final decision, use the decision matrix (page 93) to help you narrow down the list to the best alternatives.

Consultative Decisions

Consultative decisions allow for broader input, but are made by one individual or a smaller subgroup of the team after they have sought advice, input, or expertise from others or done research. Consultative decisions are best used when

- The whole team does not need to be involved in making the decision
- The group trusts an individual or subset of the team to make reasonable decisions
- The group understands and accepts the fact that the group as a whole is not the final decision maker
- Outside input will enhance both the decision and commitment to implement it
  - Advice from an expert—someone with specialized knowledge—is needed
  - Making an overt attempt to consult available research will enhance the decision
- One individual cannot know all facets of the decision or its potential impact
- The decision is likely to have vastly different consequences for different people, and all groups should be consulted before a decision is made. For example, if a decision would make life great for custodians, but add to the secretaries' workload, consult with both groups to make sure you understand their needs and the consequences of the team's decision
- The decision is an interim step or prerequisite for other decisions that the team *will* make as a whole

Command Decisions

The last decision-making options are referred to as command decisions because they are made by one individual who has the formal or official authority, knowledge, power, or status to make the decision. If that person is someone not on the team (the principal or school board leader, for instance), the team is, for all intents and purposes, just making a recommendation to that person. But the team could also defer to one of its members for particular decisions. For example: "Functionally, all of our software options seem like they will work. Since Dave knows more about software compatibility than anyone on the team, let's let him make this decision, then we can build from there."

Sometimes you may not have a choice about when to use a command decision, such as when your principal, school superintendent, or school board is simply asking your team for recommendations. Within the team, however, you can use command decisions when

- Relatively quick action is needed; the consequences of not acting immediately could be dire
- It's the law
- The decision is consistent with an already defined plan of action
- The decision is objective and follows the strategic direction of the organization
- There is little room for movement, leeway, or options
- The leader is willing to accept full responsibility for the result
- The team agrees to allow one individual to make decisions

3. Conflict Management

High-performing teams establish processes and norms around conflict management. They understand that conflict and disagreement are natural, and deal with them in productive ways. The emphasis is on *resolving issues*, not on criticizing personalities. Diversity of opinions is viewed as a strength of the team. Individual members take responsibility for their own actions and commit to being flexible and sensitive to the needs of others when conflicts arise.

Conflict Management Techniques

1. **Taking preventive actions**—To prevent problems from appearing later on, identify group norms and expectations and agree on consequences for violating them.
2. **Defining a process for resolving conflicts**—Agree as a group on what the team will do to address conflicts when they arise. Here is one possibility:
   - Set or review ground rules for respectful resolution.
   - Define the issue in terms of the group's task or mission, not based on individual positions or preferred solutions.

Inform Your Team of Consultative and Command Decisions

By definition, consultative and command decisions are usually made by only one person (who may or may not be on the team) or by a small subset of the team. Though they will have no say in such decisions, team members still need to know the outcome. Provide them with a description of the decision, plus a brief summary of why that particular option was chosen.

Team Skills

1. Communication
2. Decision-making
→ **3. Conflict management**
4. Use of data
5. Cohesiveness

Respectful Conflict Resolution

Once teams learn how to resolve conflicts respectfully, trust increases, making it easier to resolve future conflicts (see Figure 3.2).

- Understand that emotions are a part of conflict resolution. Allow people to have their say (vent).

  Example: *"It sounds like you have strong feelings about this. Could you say more about why you feel that way?"*

- Work to de-escalate the conflict and emotions by listening actively, acknowledging people's feelings, and reframing the conflict around issues, not personalities.

  Example: *"I'm hearing that you think people aren't contributing equally to the team. Is that right?"*

- Move into productive resolution of the conflict using an agreed-upon process.

- If the group doesn't already have one, define a ground rule for how to deal with conflict. Following your own ground rules is a good way to build and sustain trust.

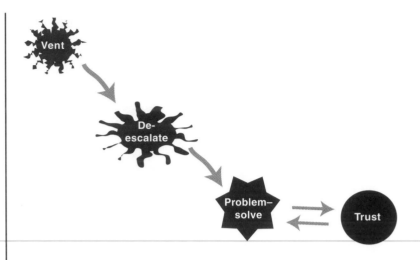

Figure 3.2 Respectful Conflict Resolution
Note. Copyright © 2001 by QLD, LLC. Reprinted with permission.

- Allow each person to state his or her point of view on the issue and listen actively.
- Brainstorm solutions.
- Select a solution (assess potential consequences).
- Plan for implementation.

3. **Using consensus-building methods**—Throughout the process of problem-solving, periodically check for levels of consensus and work to build understanding and support for the group's decisions. (See consensus decision-making on p. 94.)

4. **Changing the channel of communication**—If your group appears to be stuck in one way of thinking about an issue, switch the modality of its communication.

   Example: *Stop a fruitless discussion to allow for 5 or 10 minutes of silent, individual reflection during which people write down their individual thoughts. Follow this silent period with an open brainstorming session to introduce new perspectives.*

5. **Role playing**—Each person on the team is forced to take on a role or point of view other than their own and discuss the issue from that new point of view.

6. **Facilitating dialogue**—Balance advocacy and inquiry (p. 88) as a way to explore the meaning of an issue without the need to find a solution or answer in the immediate future.

Giving effective feedback means being...

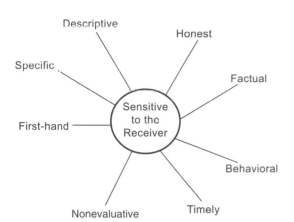

Receiving feedback effectively means...

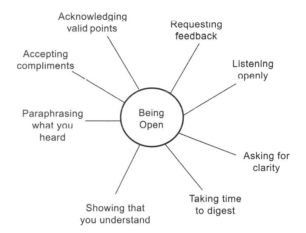

Figure 3.3 Giving and Receiving Effective Feedback
Note. Copyright © 2001 by QLD, LLC. Reprinted with permission.

7. **Using direct confrontation and feedback**—When the situation warrants, the group will stop what it is doing and deal directly with the conflict. This requires an enormous level of trust. The group essentially identifies all of its individual and collective issues, places them openly on the table, and takes time to respectfully consider each person's perspective and needs related to the issues.

Giving and Receiving Feedback

Teams that are skilled in conflict management know how to use feedback for learning. Giving effective feedback takes skill and sensitivity. Receiving feedback effectively requires an open, non-defensive posture. Both require trust. Effective feedback is descriptive, specific, first-hand, nonevaluative, timely, behavioral, factual, and honest (Figure 3.3). See Table 3.5 (p. 60) for more information on and examples of the characteristics of giving effective feedback.

The first rule of receiving feedback is that you are under no obligation to agree with the speaker! Your role as the *receiver* of feedback is to listen and make sure you understand what the speaker is saying. In addition, you should take time to digest the feedback, acknowledge the speaker's valid points, accept compliments, paraphrase what you hear, show that you understand even if you don't agree, ask for clarification as needed, and request feedback. See Table 3.6 (p. 61) for tips and examples on receiving feedback.

Table 3.5 Characteristics and Examples of Effective Feedback

Characteristics of Effective Feedback	Examples
Descriptive: Describe the situation or behavior in observable terms.	Instead of saying, "You're very hostile to staff . . . " Say this: "When you use language like 'incompetent' and 'insensitive' to describe the staff . . . "
Specific: Be as specific as possible. Avoid using terms such as "always" or "never."	Instead of saying, "You are always interrupting me . . . " Say this: "When you interrupt me as you did just now . . . "
First-hand: Make sure that you have observed or experienced the behavior first-hand and that the feedback is not based on rumors, gossip, or suspicions.	Instead of saying, "Everyone appreciates how you . . . " Say this: "I noticed in the meeting that you often helped us get back on track . . . "
Nonevaluative: Don't use words that are judgmental in nature, such as "unacceptable" or "bad."	Instead of saying, "You talk too much" (a judgment), simply inform the individual of the specific behavior you are observing. Say this: "When others are speaking, you interrupt them."
Timely: Provide feedback as close in time to the occurrence of the behavior as possible without doing so publicly if the feedback is not positive.	Talk to the person in private as soon as possible. When giving feedback, it is unfair to dredge up past occurrences ("Two months ago you did the same thing!").
Behavioral: Stick to specific behaviors that can be observed and repeated or changed; do not make inferences about someone's attitudes, mannerisms, or tone.	Do not comment on someone's appearance, voice, or mannerisms. Do comment on what people do or say that affects the group strongly (positive or negative).
Factual: Provide facts whenever possible to substantiate your concern or your delight.	Describe specific occurrences (if recent).
Honest: Be honest without being brutal.	Instead of saying, "You're a real procrastinator . . . " Say this: "This is the third time you've come unprepared. Are you over-extended or unclear about what to do?"

Table 3.6 Tips and Examples for Receiving Feedback

Tips for Receiving Feedback	Examples
Listen openly: Try to put yourself in others' shoes to understand a different point of view. Be open to the fact that someone else may be interpreting things very differently than you. It would also provide an opportunity to learn how others are perceiving the situation and give you a chance to help them see it differently.	Just listen! This can be tough if the feedback is negative, but remind yourself that your only obligation is to listen.
Take time to digest: Give yourself time to think about what you are hearing. Your immediate reaction might be unnecessarily defensive. Taking time will allow you to take some of the emotion out of the interaction.	"Thanks. You've given me something to think about."
Acknowledge valid points: Whenever you agree, say so and acknowledge that you are aware of this behavior.	"I know I talk too much sometimes. I appreciate you helping me get better at listening."
Accept compliments: Thank the person for compliments—no need to argue whether you agree since it's obviously a perception that the person giving the feedback believes to be true.	Instead of saying, "It was nothing," say, "Thank you."
Paraphrase what you heard: Summarize what you heard the person telling you.	"You're saying you think it's disrespectful of me to keep my cell phone turned on during meetings. Is that right?"
Show that you understand even if you don't agree with the speaker's interpretation: Provide an example or application of what you are hearing to illustrate that you not only heard, but also understood.	Someone shares a concern about your lack of participation in meetings and wants you to be a meeting facilitator at the next meeting. If you are not comfortable taking a facilitation role, you should acknowledge that the person would like you to be more involved, and suggest that in the future, you would be most comfortable participating as a timekeeper or scribe.
Ask for clarification: Whenever you don't clearly understand what someone means, ask for clarification or an example.	"I'm not sure what you mean by saying I 'take my responsibilities too lightly.' Could you give me an example?"
Request feedback: The best defense is a good offense. If feedback truly is for learning, show that you're interested in learning and improving by inviting feedback from others on a regular basis.	"I'm not very confident in my role as meeting facilitator. How do you think I did today? Do you have any suggestions for what I could try next time?"

Team Skills

1. Communication
2. Decision-making
3. Conflict management
→**4. Use of data**
5. Cohesiveness

Five Data Collection Ground Rules

1. Keep it simple. Stay focused.
2. Let the data do the talking.
3. Handle with care—data are not for saying "gotcha."
4. Use the right tool for its intended purpose.
5. Start with a question, a theory, a hunch, or a need to know. Then collect the data.

Data Tools Chapters

For more information about gathering, analyzing, and interpreting data, refer to the following chapters in this book:

Chapter 4: Group Process and Planning Tools (p. 85)

Chapter 5: Tools for Understanding Perceptions and Opinions (p. 115)

Chapter 6: Tools for Understanding Problems and Improving Results (p. 133)

Chapter 7: Tools for Measuring Student Performance (p. 163)

4. Use of Data

As educators we certainly know how important it is not to reduce students to numbers and statistics; until recently we've mostly relied on our intuition and experience to tell us whether we're being effective. But the days are long gone when an educator's best judgment is enough proof that what's been taught has been learned. Effective teams place a high priority on basing decisions on data.

That doesn't mean that data are the *only* input into a team's decisions. Dr. W. Edwards Deming, a renowned statistician and management expert, spent much of his life trying to convince people to use data more often when making decisions. But even he knew that hard facts and measurable figures show only part of the picture. He cautioned us not to rely too heavily on "visible figures, with little or no consideration of figures that are unknown and unknowable." The message: Yes, we should collect data, but we shouldn't throw our judgment, intuition, and experience out the door (Deming, 1982, 1993).

The key is to think of data as a learning tool: We use data to test theories or ideas. Trying to understand theory without knowledge of its application is meaningless; to apply models and strategies void of a well thought-out theory is equally meaningless. Cumulative and continuous learning occur when theory contributes to application, and application either substantiates or modifies the theory (Deming, 1982, 1983).

The data-logic chain (Figure 3.4) illustrates this continuous learning or improvement process. A pursuit into learning begins with a need to know something, a theory, a hunch, or a question that has come to us through some natural flow of **logic**. Then we test that theory by looking at **data** from the real world (by making observations, gathering information, measuring, or testing some aspect of our theory). What we learn from the data leads to new ideas, and a new set of questions, for which we need to gather more data, and so on.

Later chapters in this book describe a variety of tools and methods that school teams can use to gather and interpret data. The first thing to know about data tools is that they are like any other kinds of tools: Each has its own special purpose. You'll almost never need *all* the tools at once. The key is knowing which tool to use for which purpose.

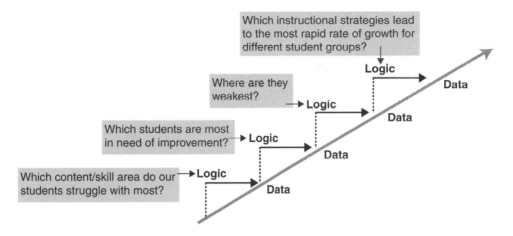

Figure 3.4 The Data-Logic Chain: An Alternative Process for Improvement

Note. Copyright © 2001 by QLD, LLC. Reprinted with permission.

5. Cohesiveness: Becoming a Group

Group cohesiveness happens when team members have a strong sense of belonging to the group and a commitment to its actions. The climate during meetings is comfortable and informal. People share the risks and benefits of their collaborative efforts, trusting their team colleagues to treat them with respect (and vice versa). Like trust, group cohesiveness doesn't appear overnight. It is something the group must work to attain. It is also difficult to measure or observe—but groups know when they have it or do not have it. Group cohesiveness is characterized by mutuality, shared vision, common purpose, and interdependence of members.

Cohesiveness naturally arises when a team works together to effectively solve problems and implement improvements. Techniques for building cohesiveness include spending time in meetings getting to know each other, spending time talking about the team's mission and the school's vision and core values, celebrating small successes and progress, and developing a team identity. These techniques are described in Table 3.7 on the following page.

> **Team Skills**
>
> 1. Communication
> 2. Decision-making
> 3. Conflict management
> 4. Use of data
> →5. **Cohesiveness**

Table 3.7 Techniques for Building Team Cohesiveness

Techniques for Building Cohesiveness	Examples
Spend time in meetings getting to know each other personally: This need not be anything too elaborate. Use simple warm-ups, ice beakers, or check-ins where people share something personal about themselves.	Have a brief warm-up where people share where they were born, something about their family, or a favorite hobby.
Spend time talking about the team's mission, the school's vision, and core values: This helps team members develop a sense of shared purpose and see that they are helping their school or district achieve its vision.	At the team's first meeting, ask members to describe how the team's mission does or does not support the school's vision. (If you find significant discrepancies, take that information to your positional leaders for discussion. Perhaps the team's mission should be focused on a higher school priority.)
Celebrate small successes and progress: It's easy for team members to get discouraged when working on a long or complex project. Celebrating progress can provide a needed boost in morale.	"We're having a pizza lunch today to celebrate completion of our plan!"
Develop a team identity by creating a team name, logo, mascot, or saying: Be sure the team name reflects its unique mission or personality.	One team that worked on enrollment called themselves the High Rollers. Teams with strong identity often use a team name on their meeting agendas and notes and in conversations ("I have a meeting with the High Rollers over lunch today").

Managing Team Meetings

Much of a team's collaborative work time will be spent in meetings (though equal emphasis should be placed on what happens *between* meetings). Your meetings will be more effective if you have clearly defined meeting roles, use PDSA (Plan-Do-Study-Act) to plan, conduct, and improve the meetings, and keep useful meeting notes.

Functional Roles for Effective Meetings

Think about meetings you've attended that went well and those that were a waste of time. In all likelihood, a big difference in the effective meetings was that people had specific responsibilities to manage different aspects of the meeting.

- **Meeting leader:** The meeting leader's job is to guide the group through the agenda. He or she
  - Starts the meeting on time
  - Describes and guides the check-in

- Introduces each agenda item in turn, describes the desired outcome, describes what method will be used for that item (discussion, report, etc.), and states how much time is allotted for that item
- Helps guide the discussion by asking participants to contribute
- Leads group activities associated with any agenda item (such as brainstorming and multivoting), or finds volunteers to perform that function
- Involves the group in summarizing decisions, actions, and questions about each agenda item so that the group can move to the next item
- Closes the meeting and conducts the check-out/meeting evaluation

The meeting leader is *not* responsible for doing all the talking or making all the decisions at the meeting—in fact, the exact opposite should occur.

- **Timekeeper:** The timekeeper's role is to help the team make deliberate decisions about how it spends its limited meeting time. For example, a timekeeper should alert the group when it is getting close to the time limits set for each agenda item and ask the team to decide whether to continue the discussion or move on.

  Example: *"We have another 5 minutes allocated for this discussion, but it doesn't look like we're close to making a decision. Should we continue the discussion now and move another agenda item to the next meeting, or defer this discussion to later?"*

  Managing time in this way prevents the team from running out of time. *"Our time is up and we still have three issues to discuss!"*

- **Record keeper:** The record keeper maintains a record of the key decisions made, issues left unresolved, and a summary of the discussions on each agenda item. He or she should use a standard, concise format developed by the team.

- **Scribe:** The scribe keeps a visual presence of the discussion in front of the group by recording brainstorming or other verbal contributions on the flip chart or overhead.

Coordinating the Meeting Leader and Team Leader Functions

When a team first begins to meet, the team leader is often also the meeting leader. But rotating the role of meeting leader is a great way to build shared responsibility within the team. The two functions can easily be separated:

- The meeting leader guides the *meeting:* moving the group through the agenda, making sure the group starts and ends on time, etc.
- The team leader guides the *team,* part of which includes doing the prework needed to make sure meetings will be effective (distributing the agenda and communicating with meeting participants ahead of time to make sure they are prepared).

The meeting leader needs to know what is expected from each meeting, so he or she usually works closely with the team leader to develop the agenda.

Rotating Meeting Roles

One of the most common complaints about meetings is that people do not feel involved. Getting people more involved can make the team more effective, increase ownership in both the outcome and the process, relieve the team leader from having to do all the work, and allow him or her to fully participate as a team member. One way to increase participation is to rotate the meeting roles. At the end of each meeting, ask for volunteers for each role at your next meeting. Or if your team prefers, identify a more formal rotation that will have everyone playing each role eventually.

How the Meeting Roles Work Together

- The meeting leader checks in with the timekeeper to make sure the agenda will be completed in the time allotted.
- The record keeper uses the scribe's flipchart notes to construct meeting documentation after the meeting.
- The meeting leader checks with the scribe to make sure everyone's ideas are being recorded accurately.

Facilitation in Team Meetings

When meetings are going well, people are engaged in the content—paying attention to the *what* of the meeting. However, every team runs into situations where it helps to have someone paying attention to the *how*: the methods the team is using to conduct the meeting. The skill associated with guiding *how* a team works together is called facilitation.

Even if your team has access to an expert facilitator (see p. 39), every team member can and should develop some skill with basic facilitation. For example, if the team is stuck on a particular discussion point or issue, any team member could suggest that the team take a break, or even lead the team through an activity that lets them address the issue through a different approach. (Use the list of meeting techniques that increase cohesiveness on p. 64 to help identify some alternative methods.) This way, team members take on a shared responsibility for making sure the team is using the most effective methods for achieving its goals.

Facilitation also includes paying attention to participation, making sure that all members have a chance to contribute, perhaps by using structured discussion techniques (such as round robins) when appropriate. The more that your team members become familiar with alternative group methods, the more effective you will be.

However, there are times when having access to a trained facilitator is invaluable: when dealing with particularly challenging issues or situations, for example. Usually it is easier for a neutral third party to guide discussions and help the group work through strong conflict than it is for someone on the team.

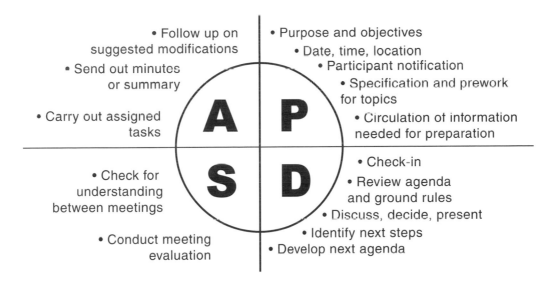

Figure 3.5 PDSA Meeting Wheel

The Meeting PDSA Process

Meetings are a process and, as such, can be improved like any other process using the PDSA (Plan-Do-Study-Act) continuous improvement model (Figure 3.5).

Planning a Meeting

There is no greater time-waster in schools (or any organization for that matter) than unproductive meetings. Hundreds of thousands of hours are spent in meetings each year. Yet we rarely take the few minutes it requires to plan for meetings to go well. Too frequently, people come to meetings not knowing what to expect, who will be there, why the meeting is being held, what their particular role is supposed to be, or how long they are being asked to commit. Meetings that have not been carefully organized or communicated waste valuable time and typically do not accomplish half of what could be accomplished if planning had been done.

Who Plans the Meeting?

Typically, the team leader is responsible for making sure that the planning for a meeting occurs. If the team leader is also playing the role of meeting leader, he or she may do the planning alone (or in consultation with others). If a team rotates its meeting leader role, the team leader should work with that person to do the planning.

It's Okay Not to Meet

Sometimes after defining the purpose and objectives for a meeting, the planners realize that a meeting is not the most appropriate way to accomplish those objectives. For example, if the primary purpose of the meeting is to share information, there are many ways to accomplish this without bringing people together all in one place. If, however, there is a need to have discussion or seek input on a particular item, then perhaps a meeting is warranted. Early planning should help determine if and when a meeting should take place.

Four Elements of a Meeting Plan

1. **Purpose and objectives:** The planning phase begins with clearly stated purpose and objectives for the meeting. This will help the planner(s) determine what needs to be discussed or decided, and approximately how long the meeting should take. Sharing the purpose and objectives with participants helps them know why the meeting is being held and how they personally can contribute. Additionally, a detailed plan can help the meeting planner(s) identify whether the whole team needs to be present at the meeting and whether other non-team members should be invited.

2. **Logistics:** Ongoing teams should standardize the meeting dates, times, and place so that people can spend their thinking energy on the content of the group's work and not on the logistics of the next meeting. For example, a school improvement team might decide to meet once a month on the third Tuesday from 3:30–5:00 in the library. That meeting then becomes a part of each member's normal course of business, and other activities and committees can be scheduled around it.

   For ad hoc team meetings or periodic meetings, the planner(s) should again think about the purpose and the participants of the meeting before selecting the time, date, and location. If the meeting is to include parents and community members, it may need to be held outside of normal school hours. The location and meeting environment are especially important if the meeting will require small group work, audio-visual presentations, flowcharting or other group process work, or if a large number of participants are involved. Let people know the meeting logistics well enough ahead of time so that they can plan appropriately (for some participants that might mean months in advance, depending on the nature of their work or family schedules). Before finalizing a date, consider scheduled school and community events and holidays that might coincide with—and therefore compete with—attendance at this meeting.

3. **Agendas:** The meeting agenda is a written plan for how the meeting will happen and what the meeting is expected to accomplish (see Figure 3.6 on p. 70). Every meeting, no matter how short or how simple, should have an explicit agenda that communicates

   - The meeting purpose
   - What will be covered
   - How much time will be needed
   - Who will be involved

   When circulated prior to the meeting, the agenda is used by the participants to plan ahead and come to the meeting prepared. If constructed by the participants at the time of the meeting, the agenda is used to help the group agree on its most important work. Finally, the agenda is used throughout the meeting to keep everyone focused, on task, and on time.

4. **Communication strategy:** An essential element of a meeting plan is how you will inform people about the meeting, its purpose, and their role. You need to decide *how* to communicate with team members (via e-mail, hard copy memo, personal communication, etc.), who will do the communicating, and when it will happen. Be thorough in this communication *before* the meeting so that people can come prepared to participate fully. They should know what topics will be discussed and whether decisions will be made at the meeting. There should be an agenda, an information packet with key pieces of data or background material, and a list of invited participants. If any individual is going to be asked to take responsibility for any part of the agenda (such as leading a discussion or making a presentation), they deserve a personal call or visit to discuss the nature of the expectations for their involvement. This visit should allow them plenty of time to prepare in advance of the meeting.

Constructing an Agenda

To save time, it helps if your team uses a standard agenda format for all meetings. Constructing the agenda simply becomes a process of filling in the appropriate content items. Put the group's most important tasks or items first. Then, if time runs short, the group will have at least accomplished its most important business. Create the agenda for the *next* meeting at the end of the group's current meeting. This assures that everyone is involved in setting the agenda and knows what each person's role and responsibilities will be between meetings and at the next meeting.

The 30+ Minute Meeting Series (Appendix, p. 261) shows sample agendas that can be used by the whole staff, by grade level teams, or by departments.

 A template of a meeting agenda appears on the CD-ROM.

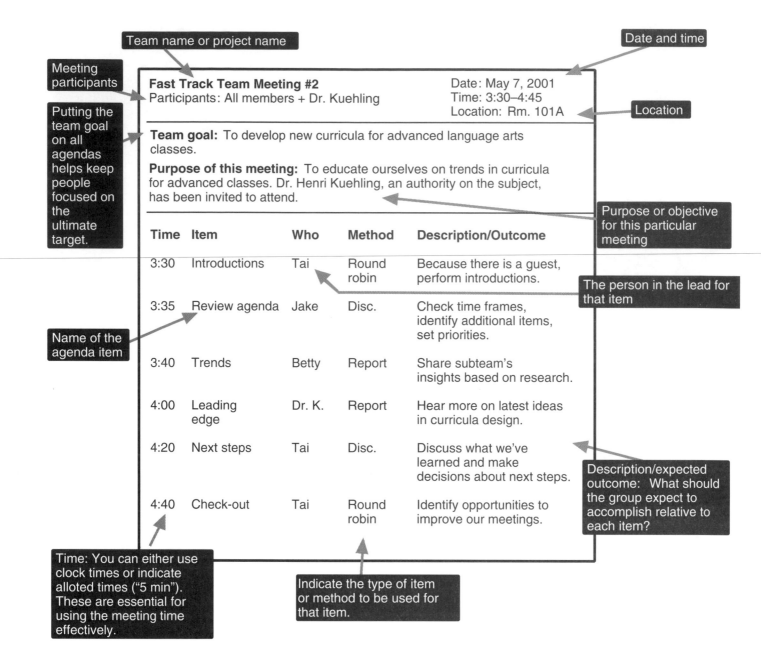

Team name or project name

Date and time

Meeting participants

Putting the team goal on all agendas helps keep people focused on the ultimate target.

Fast Track Team Meeting #2
Participants: All members + Dr. Kuehling

Date: May 7, 2001
Time: 3:30–4:45
Location: Rm. 101A

Location

Team goal: To develop new curricula for advanced language arts classes.

Purpose of this meeting: To educate ourselves on trends in curricula for advanced classes. Dr. Henri Kuehling, an authority on the subject, has been invited to attend.

Purpose or objective for this particular meeting

Time	Item	Who	Method	Description/Outcome
3:30	Introductions	Tai	Round robin	Because there is a guest, perform introductions.
3:35	Review agenda	Jake	Disc.	Check time frames, identify additional items, set priorities.
3:40	Trends	Betty	Report	Share subteam's insights based on research.
4:00	Leading edge	Dr. K.	Report	Hear more on latest ideas in curricula design.
4:20	Next steps	Tai	Disc.	Discuss what we've learned and make decisions about next steps.
4:40	Check-out	Tai	Round robin	Identify opportunities to improve our meetings.

The person in the lead for that item

Name of the agenda item

Description/expected outcome: What should the group expect to accomplish relative to each item?

Time: You can either use clock times or indicate alloted times ("5 min"). These are essential for using the meeting time effectively.

Indicate the type of item or method to be used for that item.

Figure 3.6 Standard Meeting Agenda Format
Note. Copyright © 2001 by QLD, LLC. Reprinted with permission.

70

Doing the Meeting

Conducting the meeting should involve following the agenda that the planners developed:

1. Check-in
2. Review agenda and ground rules
3. Discuss/decide/present
4. Identify next steps
5. Develop next agenda

The designated meeting leader guides the team through the meeting, moving through the agenda item by item while also paying attention to pace and participation.

1. Check-In

The first item on many agendas is a **check-in**. A check-in signals the official start of the meeting. Each individual makes a brief statement (5 to 15 seconds) about his or her current frame of mind. The check-in helps people

- Settle into the meeting
- Get focused on the meeting
- Mentally and audibly discard distractions
- Learn and be sensitive to others' situations at the time of the meeting

The check-in can be conducted in a variety of ways:

- **Round robin:** Move around the table and allow each person to speak in sequence.
- **Pair and share:** Have people check in with the individual next to them and then share the other person's check-in.
- **Bean bag:** Have a bean bag or some other small and soft object at the meeting. The person holding the bean bag has the floor, states their check-in, and then passes it on to someone else at the table until each person has had a chance to speak.
- **Speaker picks:** The first person to check-in gets to name the next person to speak.
- **Large group check-ins:** When the group is quite large, it may take too much time to have everyone check in to the whole group. In this case, have people gather into small groups to check in with each other. Then have one person from each group give a summary or make a statement that reflects the general tenor of the group.

The Usefulness of Check-Ins

Here are some examples of the kinds of things that might be helpful for a team to learn during a check-in:

- "I was up until 3:00 this morning with a sick child." (This person might be impatient, sleepy, or even uninvolved during the meeting.)
- "I have a meeting with a parent right after this meeting and would love it if we could finish just a little early today." (This person may not be as tolerant of off-task behavior or may be preoccupied with the parent meeting.)
- "I've been looking forward to this meeting, especially the chance to finally decide on the curriculum project participants." (This person will be disappointed if the agenda item dealing with curriculum is not addressed or decided.)

Simple Rules for Check-Ins

- No discussion, comments, or conversations are allowed during check-in.
- Keep the check-in short and moving along.
- It is okay for someone to pass rather than make a statement.

Energizing Your Meetings

Each of us comes to the team with our own particular needs as a learner and participant. And yet the vast majority of meeting time is spent in one mode of interaction—discussion. For individuals who are most comfortable expressing themselves or learning from their verbal/auditory channels, this traditional meeting format is just fine. But that usually doesn't include everyone in the group. Unfortunately, by limiting the interaction to talking, those who learn best through their visual or kinesthetic channels don't fully contribute. The net effect is that we don't gain the full benefit of those people.

Kinesthetic aids help keep participants physically engaged and actively involved in the meeting. These can be actual objects (small, quiet toys or manipulatives) or processes that engage people in physically active ways.

Small objects that people can play with during the meeting can help some people clarify what they are thinking before having to express it verbally. Using the kinesthetic channel helps some people release thoughts from deeper in the subconscious mind, allowing for a more free-flowing expression of ideas. Having something to hold onto or to manipulate during a meeting can also help to keep people from becoming sleepy, especially if the meeting is all talk.

Processes that engage people in a physical activity or some form of creative expression help individuals and groups break out of habitual

(continued on page 73 sidebar)

2. Review Agenda and Ground Rules

After the check-in, review the agenda and ground rules. This is especially important if there are new people at the meeting.

Reviewing the agenda is another way to achieve focus. It brings everyone's attention to the content of the meeting and provides an opportunity for people to ask for clarification, contribute new items, or discard items that may no longer be necessary. Reviewing the agenda as a whole reminds everyone about the meeting purpose, content, and length. This is important because it helps the group self-regulate. In the process of reviewing the agenda, the group may discover that not enough time has been devoted to a certain item or, conversely, that something has happened since the previous meeting that will make an item less time-consuming (perhaps new information has surfaced or a decision was made).

 TIP

> During the agenda review, identify a flex item or two on the agenda. A flex item is something that the entire group agrees may be eliminated, postponed, or dealt with in a different way if you run out of time at a meeting.

Reviewing ground rules reminds people of the norms they have agreed to follow. It's not necessary to review them at every meeting, but revisit them periodically, particularly whenever the group senses that it is swaying from its ground rules or if new behaviors emerge as the group develops.

3. Discuss/Decide/Present

This is the meat of the meeting. Devote the majority of the group's time to working on the content and tasks identified on the agenda. An underlying goal is to ensure that all members have a chance to participate and contribute (see the sidebar "Energizing Your Meetings" for tips on how to make this happen).

As each agenda item is completed, have one person summarize key discussion points, decisions, and action items. This summary process helps the group expose discrepancies in how the members were interpreting a decision.

4. Identify Next Steps

One strategy that helps the group feel like it is truly making progress is to have an agenda item devoted to planning the group's next steps. This not only has a positive psychological effect, it also keeps the group focused on its future work. Identification of next steps and assignments to be completed between meetings will enhance the group's productivity.

5. Develop Next Agenda

Developing and recording topics for the *next* meeting agenda at the end of the current meeting helps the group in a number of ways:

- People feel more ownership in the future agenda.
- Everyone knows what to expect and can better plan for their participation.
- It is another way to communicate that the group is making progress.
- It helps the meeting planners construct the next agenda.

Studying the Meeting Process

There are two ways to study or "check" a meeting:

- Conduct a check-out.
- Conduct a formal evaluation.

A **check-out** is conducted just like the check-in, one person at a time, except here the focus is on what just happened in the meeting. A check-out can serve as a meeting evaluation, an opportunity to identify improvements, or a means for individuals to have their final say. It is *not* a time to bring up new items, to challenge decisions, or to rehash meeting topics. The same rules apply as with check-ins.

In addition to checking out, which is an informal evaluation process, groups may want to conduct a **formal meeting evaluation**. This allows them to track their work progress and their growth as a team. The evaluation can be written or conducted as a structured group process. For example, on a flipchart draw a line down the middle of the page with a + on the left side and a − on the right side. Ask each person to think of one strength of the meeting and one thing that could be improved. Record the group's responses on the appropriate side of the line.

(continued from page 72 sidebar)

patterns of thinking. They force the mind to consider alternative ways of thinking about a problem or solution. Kinesthetic processes include:

- Drawing a picture of a situation rather than simply telling about it
- Brainwriting—Writing down brainstormed ideas before collecting them as a group
- Role-playing a situation or a potential implementation strategy
- Walk-abouts—Displaying the group's work on chart paper posted around the room and having people walk around the room, writing comments, suggestions, or compliments on self-stick notes, posting them as they go
- Constructing artifacts or models
- Writing and presenting a solution via a poem, song, or skit

Examples of Useful Check-Outs

- "This was a good meeting. We stayed on time and accomplished everything we set out to do." *(evaluation)*
- "I thought we spent way too much time on the bus situation." *(evaluation)*
- "I would suggest that the next time we get together, someone be responsible for watching the time, so we don't end up hurried at the end." *(suggested improvement)*
- "I just want to say I'm really glad we decided to go with the reading goal." *(individual commitment)*

 Templates of a meeting evaluation form and a meeting skills self-assessment appear on the CD-ROM.

Tools and Methods for Managing Tangents

Occasionally, a group finds itself straying off the agenda into completely different topics. This happens for a variety of reasons and may even be productive at times, but it's something that the group should monitor and manage. Here are some strategies for handling tangents:

Parking lot or issue bin—Post a flipchart page on the wall at the beginning of every meeting and label it the Parking Lot or Issue Bin. When the group begins to go off on a tangent, write the issue on the chart paper. Then, get back on track. At the end of the meeting, revisit the page and discuss how to handle the issues listed there. There may be some tangents that deserve time and attention on the next meeting agenda.

Identify a tangent cop—If you don't have a facilitator, appoint one person at the start of every meeting who can help the group be aware when it is going off task. That person has the authority to call the group back to task.

Egg timer—If the group agrees it is necessary to clarify or explore a non-agenda issue, first agree on how much time to devote to the discussion. Use an egg timer or timekeeper to notify the group when time is up. If the issue isn't resolved, the group must decide whether to change the agenda to allow for more discussion (at the expense of other agenda items) or to table the discussion for the time being.

Alternatively, you could focus on a few specific issues the group would like to improve, such as the following:

Topics	Sample Questions
Balance of participation	• Did you feel like you had a chance to voice your opinions and to participate?
Timeliness	• Did we manage our time effectively? • Did we start and end on time?
Success in meeting the objectives	• Did we meet our objectives?
Focus	• Did we stay on focus? Did we allow too many side discussions?
Adherence to ground rules	• Which ground rules, if any, did you think were violated?
Clarity of decisions made	• Do you think we're clear on what decisions were made? Do you think we all share a common understanding?
Logistic concerns	• Did the meeting space work well?

Action: What to Do Between Meetings

The action part of the PDSA cycle is absolutely critical to the team's success. If people are well informed, have been active participants on the team, and are committed to the team's task and purpose, action should not be a problem. However, if people are over-committed or unclear about the work expected of them, the group can become stuck. Future meetings will be a waste of time if people come unprepared.

In between meetings, help your team

• **Check for understanding:** Checking with people between meetings is a good way to keep momentum and to correct miscommunications. The team leader can simply e-mail, call, or stop by to meet with a few team members and ask for their understanding about what took place or was decided during the meeting. This is also a good way to support people in completing their assignments and to communicate the importance of what they are doing.

- **Act on ideas for improvement**: Follow through on decisions, modifications, or improvements that were identified or suggested at the meeting.
- **Carry out assigned tasks**: It is each individual's responsibility to carry out their assigned tasks and to ask for assistance and clarification if needed. A good team leader will provide gentle reminders and helpful suggestions as a way to support the work of the team.
- **Send out minutes or summary**: Circulate the meeting record or summary of key points and decisions as soon after the meeting as possible.

Meeting Records

Meeting records are essential to effective teams because they document key meeting activities. A meeting record is *not* the same as detailed meeting notes; typically they are brief (1- or 2-page) summaries of decisions, actions, assignments, and issues.

Use a standardized format to make meeting records easy to complete and read. Here are some suggestions:

- Put the times, dates, and location of future meetings on the first page for easy access.
- Identify meeting participants and their roles for the upcoming meeting on the first page.
- Keep track of key discussion topics and decisions made.
- Keep track of assignments and who is responsible as a part of every record.
- Keep track of side issues that come up during the meeting. Address them as necessary.
- Put the meeting record as a template on your laptop and fill it in as you go. Then it's ready to be sent electronically or printed for distribution immediately after the meeting.
- If distributing hard copies, use a bright color for the front page that is the same every time. That way, it will stand out in the mailbox and people will automatically know that it is the meeting record for that particular team.

 A template of a meeting record appears on the CD-ROM.

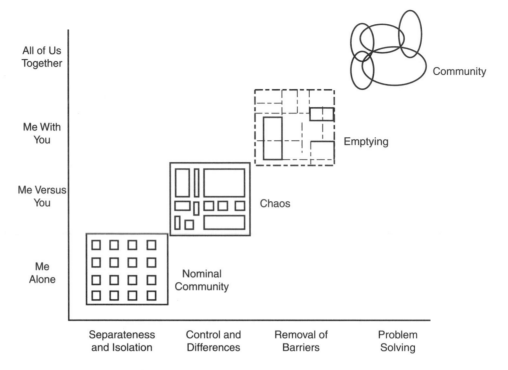

Figure 3.7 Team Growth and Development

Note. Developed by the University of Wisconsin—Parkside. Reprinted with permission. Based on work by M. Scott Peck in *The Different Drum*, 1987, New York: Simon & Schuster.

Team Growth and Development

No matter how perfectly everyone on a team gets along, or how skilled they are at group processes and team skills, every team will go through stages as it develops into maturity (Figure 3.7):

1. Forming or Nominal Community
2. Storming or Chaos
3. Norming or Emptying
4. Performing or Fully Functioning Community
5. Transforming

Understanding these phases and helping teams move through them is essential to making teams fully functional.

Stage 1: Forming or Nominal Community

Description: An orientation period when members are anxious about what their team will be like and preoccupied by the question of how and if they fit into the team.

Key tasks: The whole team addresses the issues of goals, expectations, membership, and tasks to be done.

Characteristic group behavior: This stage is characterized by conflict avoidance. The group emphasizes similarities and ignores or glosses over differences and disagreements. Nominal teams—groups that are teams in name only—tend to look for easy answers, quick fixes, and external solutions. They discuss issues in a general way, but people tend not to share their individual experiences or the impact events have on them. Denial is common.

Example: A new math initiative is about to be launched and a K–12 team of teachers and parents is convened to oversee a pilot study of the new program. At the first meeting, team members are confused about their task—both its scope and purpose. They do not know each other, but are polite and engaging. Some may be wondering why they were selected for the team. Team members are anxious to get started, but may not know what to do first. Not everyone has the same level of familiarity or comfort with the new program.

In the forming stage, members are anxious about what their team will be like and preoccupied by how they will fit in.

Some people find the forming stage exciting; others just find it frustrating. Roles are changing; people are learning new skills; there is a rapid learning curve. The people who have the easiest time during this stage are those who have faith in a collaborative philosophy and are personally committed to helping their team succeed. These people look for small successes, even at this early stage; share their excitement about the little victories; and praise the efforts of colleagues. They don't dwell on failures (which are inevitable), and they don't find reasons for why this collaborative effort will never work.

In the storming stage, members experience significant conflict concerning leadership, power, and control.

Stage 2: Storming or Chaos

Description: A period of frustration and disagreement among the members. There is usually significant conflict around the issues of leadership, power, control, and influence. Members wrestle with the question of how much influence they will exert on the team, as well as who they will allow to influence them. There may be a power struggle between dominant members or different functions.

Key tasks: The team must resolve the issue of how leadership will be distributed. Roles and authorities need to be clarified. The mission of the team needs to be kept at the forefront of all discussions.

Characteristic group behavior: Conflicts are no longer kept below the surface. Long-standing differences erupt into the open, often resulting in intense polarization and fragmentation. Instead of dealing directly with problems, people form cliques or factions; they take sides. Gossip, backstabbing, and scapegoating may occur. Some people try to flee back into the false safety of nominal community (where politeness substitutes for reality); others leave the conflict and retreat into isolation. In this stage, people are intent on defending their own positions or turf. They tend to listen to the opposition only long enough to derive ammunition for the next round of debate. Neither side listens to nor appreciates the viewpoint of the other.

Example: A high school team has formed to explore the potential of moving to a block schedule. Representatives were nominated by their peers and then selected by the principal. The team has successfully organized its strategy for study and has surveyed staff, students, and parents to get their input and ideas. They are now faced with the task of interpreting the data and formulating recommendations. It becomes obvious that, with each potential scenario, at least one program will suffer—enrollment, schedule, number of prep periods, etc. It's also abundantly clear that most teachers will have to change both what and how they teach. Arguments break out; accusations are made and factions begin to form. Some even go back to their departments to rally the troops in preparation for war.

Chaos in some form or other is an essential phase in building community and teamwork. The problem is not the presence of chaos, but rather getting stuck in it. People flounder in the chaos, and their attempts to get out include cutting off debate or discussion. ("Let's just get on with it!" or "Let's just take a vote and be done.") Any *mutual trust* or sense of safety that had started to develop is likely to degenerate into *mistrust,* aggravated by name-calling and personal attacks. There is little you can do except assure people that this stage is normal and that sometimes the only way *out* is *through.*

Stage 3: Norming or Emptying

Description: A period when the team resolves many conflicts, negotiates disagreements, establishes norms of behavior that contribute to team productivity, and develops functional relationships among its members.

Key tasks: Team members openly identify and address their individual issues, agreeing to let go of or empty their personal agendas for the sake of the team's agenda. Review, renewal, or establishment of new ground rules is a key task at this stage.

Characteristic group behavior: People remove their own barriers to communication. They let go of defensive stances (the need to be right, to prevail, or to hold their position); they begin looking for what is best for the system as the whole. They let go of abstractions and speak more personally; they become more willing to share their own experience.

Example: A team of school district administrators, staff and community members has been working on a plan for getting a building referendum developed and publicized. Some dominant members of the team have been taking up huge amounts of time in debates that support their personal agendas (chaos/storming). Finally, after heated arguments about budgets, building locations and boundaries, the team facilitator reminds the group of their common purpose: to get an educationally sound and economically responsible referendum out to the citizens in a timely way. The group then reviews and revises its ground rules and puts new ones in place. They clarify the issues and agree on a decision-making process.

During norming, the team finds a way to channel its chaotic energy into more productive means of communication and problem solving. Emptying, or norming, involves the decision to be a genuine part of the team and a willingness to let go of old patterns, unfinished business, past hurts and resentments, and the need to control the outcome.

In the norming stage, the team resolves many conflicts, negotiates disagreements, establishes norms that contribute to productivity, and develops functional relationships.

In the performing stage, the team can focus on performance and results; all attention is directed toward achievement.

Stage 4: Performing or Fully Functioning Community

Description: The stage where the team can focus on performance and results. Members are realistic in their expectations; the team has resolved even the major conflicts and continued to clarify its behavioral norms. All attention is directed toward *achievement:* productivity and continued team development are now the primary issues.

Key tasks: The team reviews progress on its goals, adjusts strategies and timelines accordingly, and works together to accomplish all aspects of its task.

Characteristic group behavior: Competitiveness gives way to a spirit of cooperation. Individuals respect and honor diversity. Conflicts that arise are addressed *immediately* (not allowed to fester) and resolved according to common ground rules and guidelines.

Example: A team of middle school teachers has been working diligently throughout the year to create a career exploration experience for their eighth graders. After months of planning, surveying, and contacting local businesses, everything begins to fall into place. The team "sings" with productivity. Team members divide up the tasks and complete assignments quickly. Most decisions seem like no-brainers; when disagreements arise, the team knows how to work through them quickly. The team's enthusiasm is permeating the rest of the school. There's already talk about doing this again next year and the improvements that can be made to the process.

A burst of creative energy often appears quite spontaneously as group members discover their sense of community. Barriers that once seemed insurmountable are now manageable. The group becomes clear on both issues and priorities.

Teams become very efficient. They develop a bias for action. They replace self-defeating behaviors with creative and even brilliant solutions. Leadership is spontaneous and comes from anyone on the team, regardless of role or position. Fresh approaches now appear possible and desirable. The team generates great self-confidence through its successes. A bond can develop in such teams, which makes them seem invincible.

Stage 5: Transforming

Description: A period of significant change that may happen in some groups. Types of changes that may occur include losing or adding members, redefining a team's primary mission, or a total break-up of the team. Any of these changes have a major impact on the team and will force members to address their fundamental expectations, goals, norms, and ground rules.

Key tasks: In the case of new membership, the team must revisit its mission, goals, ground rules, and assignments. If the team has accomplished its mission, the transformation is one of closure. Here the team addresses final details, evaluates its process, and celebrates its results.

Characteristic group behavior: In many cases, teams will regress to one of the previous stages and then work their way back to achievement.

Example: Under the direction of a new superintendent, the district is beginning its transition into a site-based decision-making model. Until now, school-based leadership teams consisted of staff members only and the mission of those teams was to oversee planning activities for special events (assemblies, chorus concerts, homecoming, science fairs, etc.). In this new model, the school teams will have the authority to make significant decisions and will manage 80% of the school's budget. Fifty percent of the members of the site teams are required to be parents. In this scenario, both the membership and the fundamental purpose of site-based leadership teams are transforming.

In the transforming stage, teams often regress to a previous stage and then work their way back to achievement; if the team has accomplished its mission, it evaluates the process, celebrates its results, and achieves closure.

Going Through the Stages

All teams generally go through all stages. The speed at which they do this will vary depending on their size, the complexity of the tasks, the personalities of the members, and the circumstances of the situation. They can develop faster if they are given the appropriate training, time to deal with issues, and support as they move through the stages.

Maintaining effectiveness for a team is a dynamic challenge because the stages are neither stagnant nor permanent. Community is a discipline that requires constant practice. Moments of chaos will inevitably arise. But successful teams will recognize the movements they experience, will discuss them, and find ways to return to high performance.

The tools and methods in the rest of this book will help your team be aware of and progress more quickly through the difficult stages of development. Here are some specific things you can do to help a team manage its transitions from one stage to the next:

- Take time periodically to raise the issue of where the team is in its development and to discuss the signs and the strategies that might move it through its current stage.
- In the early stages, build in time for warm-up activities and ice-breakers so that people can begin to become more relaxed and open with one another.
- If you find yourself in chaos, revisit and revise your ground rules to address new or emerging behaviors that may be keeping you in chaos.
- During the stage of fully functioning community, the team should be careful not to become overconfident in its decisions and actions. Always check with people from outside the team to make sure that the team's decisions reflect the reality of those it is meant to serve.

Continuously Improving Your Team's Work

High-performing teams regularly improve themselves and all aspects of their work. They routinely engage in the PDSA cycle: they plan, implement, evaluate, and improve meetings, communication, decision-making, and problem-solving processes. When things go wrong, the group tries to understand the problem at its deepest level, focusing on systemic causes and solutions instead of quick fixes. As a result, the team's effectiveness grows exponentially the longer the team is intact.

Here are some questions that can help you improve how your team is working:

- Is what we're doing the best use of our time right now? (Focus)
- How will doing this help us? Help our students? (Purpose)

- Do we know if what we're doing is having the impact we want? Might there be a better and more efficient way? (Use of data)
- Who else would love to have the chance to do this and would be delighted to help us get it done? (Delegation)
- Are we working together to learn and improve? (Collaboration)
- Do we implement what we learn? (Effectiveness)

Final Check:
Checklist for Effective Teams

Effective collaboration is both skillful and purposeful. As teams develop and learn together, they become more productive in their collaborative efforts, saving valuable time and generating enthusiasm in the process. Teams that consciously and continuously address the people, task, and process issues associated with their collaborative work experience better results because they have accomplished their mission together—and they have enjoyed doing so.

Use this checklist for your team:

✓ Everyone on the team is clear about the purpose, goals, and tasks the team has come together to accomplish.

✓ The expected results are defined, measurable, and achievable.

✓ Work tasks are planned, organized, and coordinated, and priorities are clearly understood.

✓ We are using timelines effectively.

 - Timelines are established and communicated to all who are affected by them.

 - Timelines are realistic and compelling.

✓ The types and scope of the team's tasks are appropriate for this group of people.

✓ We have defined ground rules and check them regularly.

✓ We have defined our decision-making strategies and options.

✓ We follow guidelines for effective meetings.

✓ We manage conflict.

Chapter 4
Group Process and Planning Tools

S MART teams are skilled in an array of tools and methods that allow them to work effectively and work together effectively. Indeed, their ability to incorporate these collaborative tools into their work leads to more efficient use of time and high quality work that is completed within time limits. The task element of the Three Cornerstones of Collaboration (p. 15) is more easily accomplished when everyone on the team is familiar with methods and tools that lead to productive collaboration. With frequent use, teams gain confidence in their ability to tackle even the most difficult and complex tasks.

This chapter addresses three different types of process and planning tools useful in a wide range of situations:

- **Group process tools:** tools that help enrich team members' understanding of a problem, their creative thinking about problems and solutions, and their ability to address issues at deep levels
- **Process mapping tools:** tools that help groups understand and improve work processes and systems
- **Planning tools:** tools that help teams *imagineer*, from start to finish, the tasks that will need to be accomplished in order to complete projects and initiatives

What these tools have in common is their ability to help teams bring *structure* to their work—to both the interactions within the team and the project as a whole.

> Until you are willing to be confused about what you already know, what you know will never become wider, bigger or deeper.
>
> —Milton Erikson, M.D.

Group Process Tools

Group process is a term that refers to the methods and approaches a team uses to accomplish its work as a team. There are six group tools discussed in this section:

- Dialogue (pp. 87–88)
- Brainstorming (p. 89)
- Affinity Diagrams (p. 90–91)
- Multivoting (p. 92)
- Decision Matrices (p. 93)
- Consensus Decision-Making (pp. 94–95)

With the exception of dialogue, each of these tools relies upon the use of visual organization tools such as sticky notes, flipcharts, and white boards. When people can collectively *see* what they are creating together, their ability to think and learn together is enhanced, and time flows more productively.

As a whole, group process tools help team members

- Organize their thinking
- Discuss difficult topics
- Better understand problems at their deepest level
- Think creatively about how to solve problems

Dialogue

What It Is

A true conversation in which talking and listening by all parties creates a flow of meaning among, between, and through a group. Out of dialogue emerges a new and shared understanding. Dialogue is a tool for collective exploration of meaning—not a search for the right, wrong, or best solution.

Use It When

You think adding structure to a team's discussion will lead to a deeper or broader understanding of an issue.

Applications

- To help the team get unstuck from a complex problem
- To help generate a broad range of ideas when creating a values-based shared vision, set of core values, and/or guiding principles for a school
- To discuss with colleagues the quality of student work
- To develop results-oriented goals
- To inquire into the meaning of student results
- To resolve conflicts
- To develop innovative programs

How to Do It

1. Early in your team's development, explain the difference between advocacy and inquiry (use the information and examples on p. 88 as guidance).
2. When the team is discussing difficult or complex issues, request that people be conscious of using both advocacy and inquiry in their statements.

Needed Skills

Dialogue requires two complementary skills: advocacy and inquiry.

- **Advocacy** means seeking to make our thinking and reasoning visible to others as we test our assumptions and conclusions.
- **Inquiry** means asking others to make their thinking visible as we compare our assumptions to theirs.

Tips

- Be as personal as possible. Speak from your personal point of view.
- Replace seeking resolution with living in and working through the question.
- Allow each person the time and space to reflect, to speak with silence.
- Suspend your assumptions and allow others to question them.
- Perceive disagreement as an opportunity to learn and as a sign that this is a place to dig deeper.
- Remain self-aware so that you can consciously use your feelings and perceptions as a resource.
- Respect different points of view as every bit as valid as your own.

Robert Garmston and Bruce Wellman developed a tool (Figure 4.1, p. 88) for conducting dialogue-based conversations.

Advocacy	**Inquiry**
Make your thinking and reasoning visible.	*Ask others to make their thinking visible.*
▪ **State your assumptions:** "Here's what I think, and here's how I got there . . . "	▪ **Gently walk others down the ladder of inference:** "What leads you to that conclusion? What data do you have for that?"
▪ **Describe your reasoning:** "I came to this conclusion because . . . "	▪ **Use unaggressive language and an approachable voice:** "Can you help me understand your thinking here?"
▪ **Distinguish data from interpretation:** "This is the data I have as objectively as I can state it. Now here is what I think the data mean."	▪ **Draw out their reasoning:** "What is the significance of that? How does this relate to your other concerns? Where does your reasoning go next?"
▪ **Explain the context:** "Several groups would be affected by what I propose and here is how . . . "	▪ **Explain your reasons for inquiring:** "I'm asking about your assumptions here because . . . "
▪ **Give examples:** "To get a clear picture, imagine that you are in school X . . . "	▪ **Invite introspection:** "What questions do you have about your thinking?"
Test your assumptions and conclusions.	*Compare your assumptions to theirs.*
▪ **Encourage others to explore your model, assumptions, and data:** "What do you think about what I just said? Do you see any flaws in my reasoning? What can you add?"	▪ **Investigate other assumptions:** "Would we be willing to each list our assumptions, compare them, and explore if there might be other assumptions surrounding this issue?"
▪ **Reveal where you are least clear:** "Here's one area you might help me think through . . . "	▪ **Check your understanding** of what they have said by paraphrasing and probing. "Am I correct that you are saying . . . "
▪ **Stay open:** Encourage others to provide different views: "Do you see it differently?"	▪ **Test what they say by asking for broader contexts or examples:** "How would your proposal affect . . . Is this similar to . . . Can you describe a typical example?"
▪ **Search for distortions, deletions, and generalizations:** "In what I've presented, do you believe I might have over-generalized, left out data, or reported data incorrectly?"	▪ **Reveal your listening processes:** "I have been listening for themes. So far I've heard two. Are there others?"

Figure 4.1   Advocacy and Inquiry: Elements of Dialogue-based Conversations

Note. From *The adaptive school: Developing and facilitating collaborative groups,* by R. Garmston and B. Wellman, 1998, Norwood, MA: Christopher-Gordon Publishers. Copyright © 1998 Christopher-Gordon Publishers. Reprinted with permission.

Brainstorming

What It Is

- A group activity to stimulate creativity and bring out diverse perspectives in a short period of time
- An excellent way to equalize participation and build collective motivation

Use It When

- Having a large quantity of diverse ideas will add value to the team's work
- People need to think out of the box

Applications

- As a first step in developing a shared vision (people post their individual ideas on a flipchart; then the group as a whole discusses the ideas)
- To create a list of solutions when problem-solving
- To identify steps when mapping a process

How to Do It

1. Review brainstorming guidelines.
2. Pose a question to the group.
3. In full view of the group, record all ideas generated (on a flipchart, overhead, sheet of butcher paper, etc.).

Tips

- Brainstorming works best with relatively small groups. If you have a large group (more than 10 to 12 people) break into smaller groups of no more than 5 or 6 people.
- Give the group a clear objective or focus question, otherwise you may end up with answers that are too diverse to be useful.

Guidelines

At the start of a brainstorming session, emphasize the following guidelines to encourage people to contribute freely:

- There's no such thing as a bad idea.
- Quantity of ideas is more important than quality.
- There is no evaluation or criticism of ideas.
- Freewheeling (thinking out of the box) is encouraged.
- Everyone has an opportunity to participate.
- Piggyback or build off of others' ideas.

Modifications

Silent Thinking Time: Begin with a minute for silent reflection before brainstorming.

Self-Stick Notes: Each participant records ideas on self-stick notes (one idea per note) instead of having a scribe write them on a flipchart, whiteboard, etc. Having ideas written on self-stick notes makes sorting and organizing easier and also ensures anonymity.

Popcorn: Individuals call out their ideas in any order. Ideas are recorded on a flipchart.

Round Robin: Individuals say ideas in turn, one at a time, around the group, until all ideas are out and recorded.

Brainwriting: Individuals write one idea on a sheet of paper and then put the paper in the middle of the table and take someone else's paper; they continue to add ideas and build off of what's already written.

Affinity Diagram

....

What It Is

A tool for organizing brainstormed lists into like categories or things that have an affinity for each other (Figure 4.2 on p. 91)

Use It When

You want to involve an entire group in organizing and consolidating many ideas

Applications

- To help articulate elements of a vision
- To organize ideas for problem solving
- To group ideas into categories before multivoting
- To organize statements from interviews or focus groups

How to Do It

1. Use brainstorming (p. 89) to generate a list of ideas. Have people write ideas on self-stick notes. Guidelines:
   - Use short phrases or words—be concise.
   - Write clearly.
   - Write large enough so that someone standing several feet away can read the idea.
2. After the brainstorming, have people post their notes *randomly* on a large sheet of paper.
3. Instruct people to start sorting the notes into groups or categories.
   - This is a silent activity, so there shouldn't be any talking during the categorization process.
   - Anyone can move a note into any category. Notes can be moved from category to category—it's okay to move them around several times until a category that makes sense to the whole group emerges.
   - Place orphans (single notes unlike any others) off to the side.

4. Once there appears to be general agreement among the participants, allow them to start talking.
5. Finalize the categories—discussion may change some of the initial groupings.
6. As a group, write a succinct, concrete phrase that captures the theme or central idea for each cluster of ideas. Write this theme on a header card (a larger self-stick note you place immediately above the cluster).

Tips

- Work in small groups (five or six people).
- Some people are frustrated by not being able to talk. A few gentle reminders to remain silent may be needed.
- The emergence of a group-defined organizational structure is what makes this process powerful. Random placement of the notes on the chart paper, followed by the team working together to group ideas by categories as they emerge, prevents people from assuming they already know the answers.
- Reassure participants that this is an opportunity for people who are not as comfortable talking to really participate on an equal basis with those who are more verbally confident.

Modification

Affinity diagrams can be used to analyze any language data, such as interview or focus group notes. In those cases, the statements used for the affinity exercise do not come from a brainstorm, but must be selected from the notes or transcripts. To do this well, first identify the key question(s) you want answered. Then have team members go through the notes/transcripts and highlight any statements they think relate to the key question. Transcribe these statements onto self-stick notes and begin the affinity process.

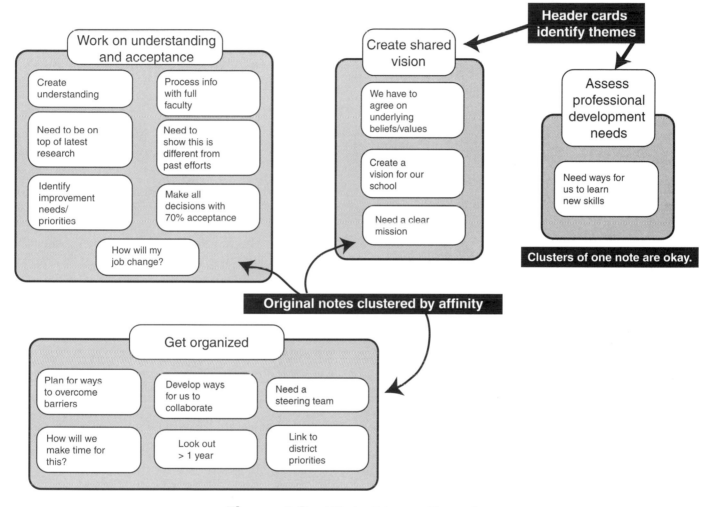

Figure 4.2 Affinity Diagram Example
Note. Copyright © 2001 by QLD, LLC. Reprinted with permission.

Multivoting

....

What It Is

A method for narrowing down and prioritizing lists of ideas

Use It When

There are too many ideas to decide which ones to focus on

Applications

- To prioritize which gaps are most important to focus on when identifying strategic priorities
- To determine which goals are most worthy of pursuit
- To decide which strategies are most worth investing in

How to Do It

1. Complete a brainstorming process or use some other method to generate a list of ideas/options.
2. Determine how many votes each group member will receive.
   - Divide the number of items by three and round up to the nearest whole number. That is how many votes to give each person. For example, if there are 29 items on your list, each member gets 10 votes.

3. Distribute colored sticky dots (one color) to the group. Each person should get as many dots as there are votes.
4. Have people place their dots next to the ideas they favor most.
   - Votes can be distributed one per idea, or, if the group agrees, can be loaded up (that is, any individual can place two or more of their dots on one item).
5. After all the dots are distributed, refine your list by eliminating any items that received no votes at all or only a few votes.
6. If the refined list still has too many items for the group to reasonably handle or address, repeat the process.
   - Count the number of items on the reduced list and divide by three. That's how many votes that people will have in the next round.
   - Distribute colored sticky dots (a different color) and have people revote.
7. Continue multivoting until the final priorities reach a manageable number.

Modification

Instead of using colored sticky dots, record ideas on a flipchart and number them. Individuals vote by writing down the numbers of the ideas they prefer on index cards or separate sheets of paper.

Decision Matrix

What It Is

A table in which alternative decision options are scored against criteria (Figure 4.3)

Use It When

- You want to move from a list of options to a final decision
- You need to simultaneously assess multiple options against multiple criteria
- You want to compare options in a relatively objective and unemotional way

Applications

- To evaluate potential solutions
- To consider alternative data-gathering strategies

How to Do It

1. Use multivoting (p. 92) to identify the top 5 to 10 ideas from a brainstormed list. Write these ideas down the left side of a new flipchart page.
2. Draw a matrix next to the list of ideas.
3. Identify criteria important to the group (numbers of students served, cost, ease of implementation, effectiveness, doable in time allotted, importance to the mission, etc.).
4. Score each idea against each of the criteria (if you have five ideas and four criteria, you will be coming up with 20 scores). Use a scale of zero to five where zero means that particular criterion is not met at all and five means it is fully met.
5. Total the score for each idea by adding the scores for each criteria. Those with the highest scores best meet your stated criteria.
6. Optional: If some criteria are much more important than others, you may want to weight the criteria. This adds extra complexity to the process, so use weighting judiciously. To start, assign each criteria a value from, say, one to five, where five is

very important (for example: if cost is most important, it gets a weight factor of five; perhaps simplicity is less important and gets a factor of two). Then multiply each score against the weight for that criteria. Add up the weighted ratings for one idea to get a total weighted score for that idea.
7. Discuss the highest-ranking items and choose among them or modify them in ways that may capture the best of several items.

Tips

- Agree ahead of time on what the scale (ratings) mean so that there is consistency in scoring the ideas.
- It's easier to work vertically through the table (by criteria) than horizontally (by option). That is, start with one criteria and score *all* options against that criteria. Then move on to the next criteria and again work through all the options (as opposed to picking one option and scoring it against all the criteria, then moving to the next option, etc.).

GOALS	CRITERIA			TOTAL SCORE
	Staff would support	Community would support	Would have great impact on student learning	
Improve safety	1	2	1	**4**
Involve families more	1	1	1	**3**
Improve reading	3	3	3	**9**
Integrate technology	1	2	1	**4**

1 = weak impact   2 = moderate impact   3 = strong impact

Figure 4.3 Decision Matrix Example
Note. Copyright © 2001 by QLD, LLC. Reprinted with permission.

 A template of a decision matrix appears on the CD-ROM.

Consensus Decision-Making

What It Is

Consensus exists when *everyone* on the team feels that she or he can support the decision, even if it is not their preferred option. It is not a majority vote.

Use It When

It is important that everyone in a group supports a decision, both publicly and privately

Applications

- To choose the final option or solution to implement
- To agree on ground rules and team roles
- To determine implementation strategies

How to Do It

1. Make sure everyone is clear about the decision to be made.
   - Example: "We are here to decide which curriculum proposal we will support."
2. Agree on the most important aspects of the decision and set criteria.
   - Example: The option has to be realistically accomplished in 6 months and reach a minimum of 50% of the student body.
3. Discuss and weigh the potential consequences of each option, both positive and negative.
   - Use your dialogue skills (p. 87).
   - Discuss the extent of the impact of the consequences on individuals and the district, school, department, or grade level.
4. Do a Quick Check to see if the group is near consensus.
   - Quick Checks help a group evaluate its progress toward consensus. They can also prevent needless discussion by demonstrating when a team has reached consensus and can therefore move on.
5. If there is no single option that gets broad-level support, continue the discussion, dialogue, and exploration of options.
6. Repeat steps 4 and 5 until the group believes it has reached consensus. Do a Quick Check periodically.
7. When you are fairly sure the team has reached consensus, have a team member write down a statement he or she believes captures the group's decision.
8. Do a final consensus check:
   - Review the decision.
   - Ask team members, "Do you feel you can support this decision both inside and outside the group? Indicate your level of commitment using the Fist-to-Five Quick Check." (See boxed description on p. 95.)
   - If anyone holds up a fist, or only one or two fingers, the group has not reached consensus. You will need more discussion or dialogue.
   - If you get all three, four, or five fingers showing, you can declare consensus.

Tips

- If your team is unfamiliar with consensus, make sure everyone knows what consensus means and agrees that it is the best method to be used in this circumstance.
- Make sure everyone is aware of the timeline for making a decision. Discuss what to do if time runs out and consensus has not been reached.
- People tend to take the word consensus very seriously. They have high expectations for what it means in terms of broad participation in reaching the decision and listening to all viewpoints. Since consensus is *not* the same as a majority vote, don't

Fist-to-Five Quick Check

After you have restated or written down the pending decision, ask group members to indicate their level of support by raising one hand either closed in a fist or with one to five fingers raised (the *fist-to-five*).

5 fingers All for it . . . I can be a leader for this decision.

4 fingers All for it . . . You can count on me to support this no matter what.

3 fingers For the idea . . . I will support it in concept, but may not be out in front of the gang leading its implementation.

2 fingers I'm not sure . . . But I trust the group's opinion and will not sabotage the decision.

1 finger I'm not sure . . . Can we talk some more?

Fist No . . . We need to find an alternative.

call a decision "consensus" if you really mean you just want a majority of support from the group. People will be upset if they believe the group is going to work towards consensus, but then find out that the final option is selected by a majority vote. (This is why it is important for a group to discuss *how* it will make a decision before that decision is made.)

- Develop and use a process for arriving at alternative options for the group to explore.
  - Use a variety of techniques such as brainstorming, affinity work, and discussions.
  - Allocate time for gathering or finding relevant data and research whenever possible.
  - After the decision has been reached, check to make sure that people believe that the integrity of the process that was agreed upon was maintained. Use the outcome of this discussion for future improvements in the group's consensus process.

Modifications

- Use a consensus round robin instead of doing a Fist-to-Five Quick Check.
  - Go around the group one-by-one.
  - Each person states what his or her vote would be at that moment in time. Do not allow any explanation at this point. *This is a quick-moving check where people say things like "Option A," "yes," or "don't know enough to decide."*
  - After you've completed the first round, do a second round where people give one or two reasons behind their thinking. Again, keep this moving.
  - There is *no discussion* during this process. The purpose is to make sure that *each person* gets a chance to state an opinion and reasons with everyone else listening.
  - Have the meeting leader or other team member summarize the results. ("We agree that the two options based on current curriculum are best but aren't close yet in choosing between those two.")

Process Mapping Tools

Process mapping tools help teams *see* processes and systems—the way activities flow in sequence, the way roles and responsibilities interact. Flowcharts are the tool of choice here. Because they are created through a collaborative process using highly visual techniques, all team members have a chance to contribute their ideas. Process mapping tools have many applications, including

- Describing how processes currently work
- Describing how an improved process *will* work
- Clarifying roles and responsibilities
- Planning a project

The following section discusses four main types of flowcharts:

- Basic flowcharts (p. 97)
- Top-down flowcharts (pp. 98–99)
- Deployment flowcharts (pp. 100–101)
- Detailed flowcharts (pp. 102–103)

Basic Flowchart

Figure 4.4 Basic Flowchart of Grant-Funded Research
Note. Copyright © 2001 by QLD, LLC. Reprinted with permission.

What It Is

A visual high-level picture of how work or activities generally flow in sequence in a process or system (Figure 4.4)

Use It When

You want a "high-altitude" picture of a system or process—one without a lot of detail

Applications

- When planning major steps in a process or activity
- When using the Accelerated Improvement Process, to get a quick visual picture of the flow of work (see Chapter 9)
- When conducting a functional analysis of a work unit or department (see Chapter 9)
- When problem-solving
- When creating a plan or developing a new process

How to Do It

1. Decide where the process or system begins and ends.
2. Brainstorm the major steps that occur between that beginning and ending.
3. Sort the steps in time order, and number them in sequence.

Tips

- Agree early on the level of detail (altitude) you want to show at this stage.
- To ensure that you focus on the most important steps, try limiting the number of steps in the process to no more than ten.
- Use self-stick notes to post the steps in order of time.
- Include verbs in the steps rather than just activities or topics. For example, write *acquire funding* instead of simply writing *funds.*

Top-Down Flowchart

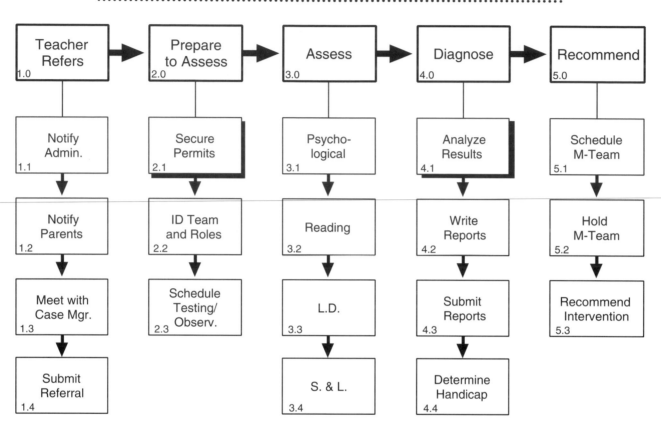

Figure 4.5 Top-Down Flowchart of Special Education Referral Process

Note. Copyright © 2001 by QLD, LLC. Reprinted with permission.

What It Is

A diagram that depicts the major flow (steps) of a process along the top, with detail added vertically below each major step (Figure 4.5)

Use It When

- You want to quickly see the major steps of a process along with some detail

- You want to organize work around major parts of a process

Applications

- To teach someone new to the school or district about the flow of work or information
- With Functional Analysis (p. 204) of a work unit or department to show the flow of work in a core process

How to Do It

1. Develop a basic flowchart that depicts the major steps in a process (usually divided into no more than five to seven steps).
   - Be sure to identify beginning and ending steps in the process before making the basic flowchart
2. Identify substeps needed to complete each major step.
   - Agree on what level of detail will be most useful given the purpose of the flowchart.
3. List the substeps in order below the appropriate major step.

Tips

- Number the steps using an outline form (1.0 is the first major step, 1.1 is the first substep, 1.2 the second substep, etc.).
  - This numbering helps the team be specific when referring to the current process or proposed changes ("What if we changed Step 3.4?").

- This tool does not show time, decisions, or people responsible for the various steps. Use one of the other flowcharts if you need to show that information.

Modification

You can also use a top-down flowchart to summarize a much more complex flowchart. Use a shadowed box to depict any step for which you have more detail. (Some computer graphics software lets you click on the shadowed boxes to get more detail.) Here, too, the numbering comes in handy, because you label the more detailed charts by the outline number. You could, for example, create a separate top-down flowchart for securing permits in the special education referral process. This new flowchart could be identified as the flowchart for Step 2.1 of the Special Education Referral Process.

Deployment Flowchart

What It Is

A flowchart that depicts which individuals or groups play a role in each step of a process (Figure 4.6)

Use It When

You want to visually show which aspects of the work are the responsibility of which individuals or groups.

Applications

- To identify areas of duplication and rework
- To plan a new process
- To assist in delegating and assigning tasks

How to Do It

1. Identify the main functions, groups, or individuals who work on a process. Write these on large cards or self-stick notes and place them across the top of a flipchart page.
2. Decide the boundaries of the process: Where does it start? Where does it end?
3. Brainstorm all the steps in the process (at first, you don't have to pay attention to order). Write these steps on self-stick notes.
4. Place the steps in order on the chart, beginning with the first step and moving down the flowchart in order of time.
   - Place each step under the person/function who has the *primary responsibility* for performing that step.

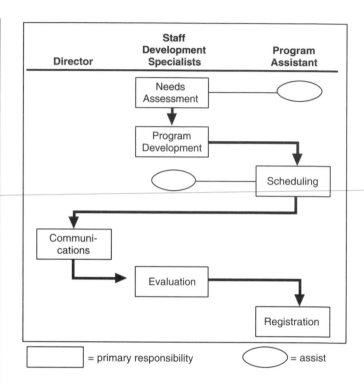

Figure 4.6

Staff Development Deployment Flowchart

Note. Copyright © 2001 by QLD, LLC. Reprinted with permission.

- If other functions/groups/individuals play a role in a step (such as by providing information), use an oval symbol under those columns for that step. Connect the ovals to the primary step with a straight line.
5. Draw arrows connecting the primary flow of the work between the groups represented on the chart.

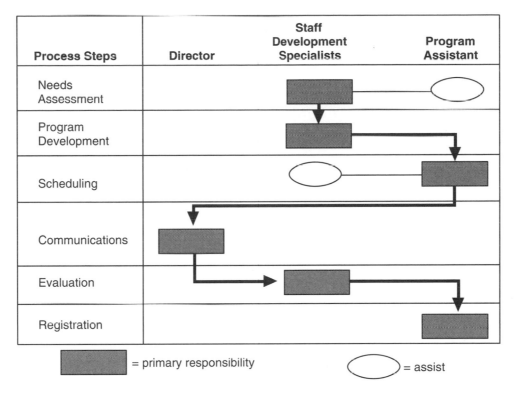

Figure 4.7 Alternative Format for Staff Development Deployment Flowchart
Note. Copyright © 2001 by QLD, LLC. Reprinted with permission.

Tips

- When mapping a current process, a deployment flowchart can become very messy. By writing the steps on self-stick notes, you can easily move them around as you clarify the sequence of work. Take your time and be patient.
- Use different symbols and shapes to indicate different types of involvement.

Modifications

- You can either place text describing a step under the column for the group or person who is responsible for that step (Figure 4.6) or, as depicted in Figure 4.7, you can write the steps down the left side of the diagram. In the latter case, use a symbol (usually a rectangle) in the appropriate column showing who does which steps. Other symbols, such as the oval, can depict people who assist with the step, but are not responsible for carrying out the work.
- Consider using different-colored sticky notes for steps that don't add value to the overall process.

Detailed Flowchart

··

What It Is

A flowchart that shows all the steps in the process and identifies where key decisions are made (Figure 4.8, p. 103)

Use It When

You need to depict all the steps in a process in more detail than is shown in other types of flowcharts

Applications

- To illustrate where there are duplications or rework occurring in the process
- To map an ideal situation and/or the revised situation after the team has made its final recommendations
- As a training and orientation tool

How to Do It

1. Decide as a group where the process begins (first step) and where it ends (last step).
   - What are the *inputs* to this process? What happens before the process begins?
   - What are the *outputs* from this process? What does this process produce?
2. Record the first and last step on sticky notes and post them on a flipchart or large sheet of paper with enough space in between to fill in the remaining steps.
3. Brainstorm other steps you want to include in the diagram. Write these steps on sticky notes and place them on a second sheet of paper.
4. Have a designated facilitator read the notes aloud, with the group telling him or her where to place each note on the main page.
5. When you have finalized the arrangement, draw arrows showing the sequence of action.
   - Use standard flowchart symbols to indicate different types of actions. For example, rectangles or squares indicate an action. A diamond shape is used for decisions.

Tips

- To avoid confusion later on, it's best if a flowchart reads in the same way that text flows on a page: left-to-right and top-to-bottom. That means if there are too many steps to fit in one row, the next sequence of action should start at the left-most position in the second row (that is, do NOT switch directions and have steps flow right-to-left in the second row).
- One challenge in using this flowchart is knowing the right altitude or perspective (level of detail) to use when identifying the steps. If it is too general, it won't tell the team much; if it is too specific, it can be unnecessarily time consuming. Which end of the continuum the team elects will depend on their purpose for doing the flowchart and on the individuals' familiarity with the details of the work.
- Use a large space to construct a detailed flowchart —all the details will undoubtedly take up a lot of room. There may be steps that don't go anywhere (just trail off); some steps may go around and around in an endless cycle. You want to have enough room to capture every variation.

Modifications

- If your purpose is to document the existing process, with all its flaws and problems, have team members brainstorm the steps involved in doing this process *today*, including all the steps of rework (when things aren't done right the first time) and duplication. Don't worry about who does each process step or how much time each takes. Arrange the sticky notes in sequence and draw arrows to connect one step to the next.
- If the purpose is to show how a new process *should* look, include only those steps that will add value. Arrange steps in sequence and draw connection arrows.

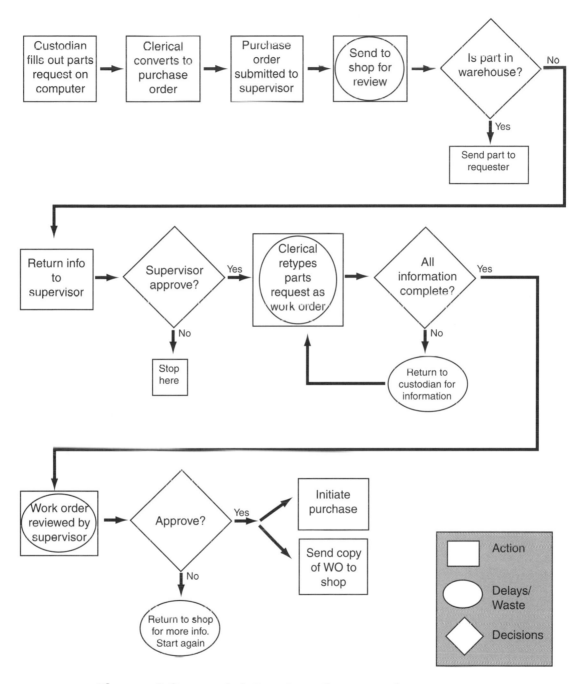

Figure 4.8 Detailed Flowchart of Parts Purchasing Process
Note. Copyright © 2001 by QLD, LLC. Reprinted with permission.

PDSA: The Ultimate Planning Tool

SMART teams apply PDSA (p. 3) to their plans—What did we plan? How did it work out in practice? What worked well? What didn't and why? What did we learn so that we can plan more effectively in the future? Visualizing plans with these tools becomes an important part of that learning process.

Planning Tools

Planning tools assist teams in mapping out future work. Paying attention to *how* plans will work out in practice is an important part of team learning and helps future activities go more smoothly.

Some of the simplest planning tools are flowcharts like those presented earlier in this chapter. They help you plan the basic steps in a project or process. The additional tools in this section add other dimensions to your planning.

- **Tree diagrams** help you *imagineer*—think ahead to what a plan needs to look like, beginning with the end in mind, then working backwards from the end of the project or activity. They can be used to think through the hierarchy from goals to strategies to tactics.
- **Responsibility matrices** help take the guesswork out of processes, identifying who will do what and in what sequence.
- **Gantt charts** can help teams add the details of time and sequence, and get a visual picture of how the work can or could overlap to be done most efficiently.
- **Activity Network Diagrams** (ANDs) help teams think through the parallel sequence of activities and what might go wrong, so that preventative steps can be put in place.

Tree Diagram

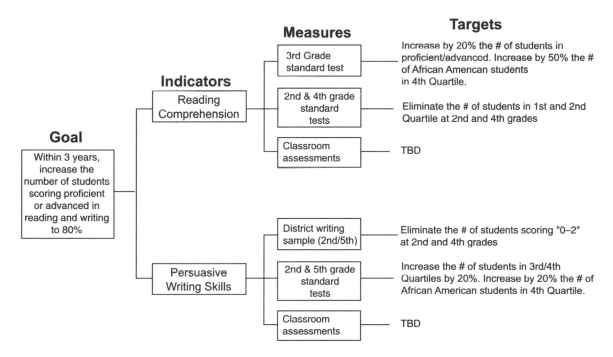

Figure 4.9 Tree Diagram Identifying Components of 3-Year School Goal
Note. Copyright © 2001 by QLD, LLC. Reprinted with permission.

What It Is

A chart used to identify essential components of something (e.g., the targets for goals, the steps in a plan [Figure 4.9])

Use It When

You want to align efforts toward a specific goal

Applications

- When planning SMART goals at the district, school, and/or classroom levels
- When thinking through action plans

How to Do It

Application 1: Developing SMART Goals

1. Determine an area to focus on for improvement. This focus area should be based on a careful analysis of relevant achievement, demographic, and/or climate data. Consider not only this year's data, but also data over time.
2. Write a SMART goal in the left-hand box of the tree diagram (see Figure 4.9).
   - SMART goals are Specific and Strategic, Measurable, Attainable, Results-based, and Time-bound.

- When writing a SMART goal at the school level, consider the most important measure(s) you analyze each year. Chances are these measures are state or national achievement tests and/or key climate measures such as parent, staff, or student satisfaction surveys. See Figure 4.9 on page 105 for an example of an achievement-oriented SMART goal.

3. In the first set of boxes to the right of the goal, identify the indicators that you and the students need to focus on to achieve the SMART goal.
   - Indicators are the standards, benchmarks, objectives, or skill sets that you would look for as evidence of progress on the SMART goal.
   - Ideally, indicators are derived from a careful analysis of test and other assessment data. At the school level, they should be derived from student data over time; at the classroom level, teachers will want to look at *this year's* students. Indicators are the key gap areas that are most in need of improvement. Consider using Pareto thinking (p. 149) to narrow your list down to the vital few indicators.

4. For each indicator, identify measures that will be used to assess progress on that indicator.
   - Measures are tools or assessments (for example, tests, portfolios, performance assessments, surveys, and observational tools).
   - Measures should include standardized and district-, school-, or classroom-developed tools.
   - Measures should be agreed upon by faculty members. They should include summative (end of year) as well as formative (ongoing and/or periodic) tools.
   - Consider using components of tests that focus only on the identified indicators as you monitor student progress during the year.
   - Validity and reliability issues need to be taken into account when designing new measures, as well as when aligning existing measures to the SMART goal: Do the selected tools accurately measure the goal? Are they aligned? Will they yield reliable results?

5. Identify targets for each measure that are attainable within a given timeframe and given your resources and knowledge. These should also be based on a careful analysis of existing data, both snapshot and over time.
   - Careful consideration of targets is important to success and to teachers' and students' motivation to work toward the target. For example, a target of 100% of students proficient on a certain measure when only 25% are currently proficient may demoralize people before they start.
   - Targets should be selected by the teachers who will be working on them; however, the amount of stretch people are willing to commit to should be balanced against the need to achieve school and state expectations. Most importantly, if the target selected is a stretch, resources (time, professional development, etc.) must be made available to support achievement of that target.
   - Criteria for accomplishing or making progress on the targets need to be carefully considered as well. Is a target defining a certain percent or number of students achieving a specific level or is it identifying the desired growth rate for students? Both level and rate should be considered.
   - Targets are what will be monitored throughout the year to evaluate progress on the overall SMART goal.

Failure to Meet Targets

Failure to meet a target should not be cause for punishment or blame, but rather an opportunity for shared dialogue among faculty pursuing that target: Why didn't we achieve this target? What theories do we have about why we didn't achieve this target? What could we do differently to achieve it in the future?

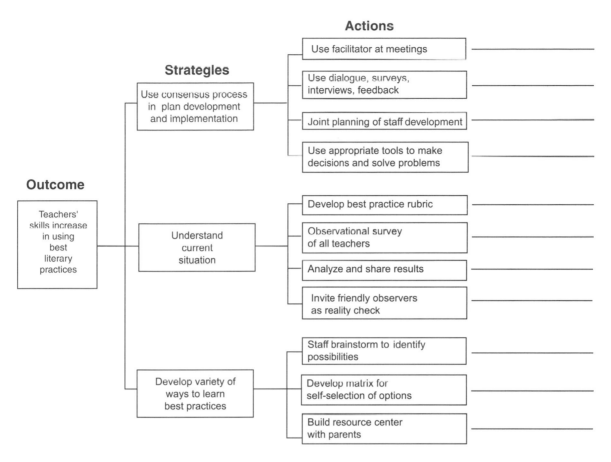

Figure 4.10 Tree Diagram Used to Plan Teacher Development
Note. Copyright © 2001 by QLD, LLC. Reprinted with permission.

Application 2: Developing Action Plans

Tree diagrams also can be used to develop the major activities and tasks needed to accomplish a planning goal (Figure 4.10). The steps in this case are as follows:

1. Write a desired outcome in the left-hand box of the tree diagram.
   - Outcomes are the desired end-result of a planning process. For example: new hiring process, delivery of professional development workshops, or construction of new facilities.
2. In the first set of boxes, record the main activities (strategies) needed to accomplish the desired outcome.

- It may be helpful to first brainstorm these activities on self-stick notes and use the Affinity process to group them into main activities. (See p. 90 for details on the Affinity process.)
- Alternatively, a top-down flowchart can be used to identify main activities. (See p. 98 for details.)
3. In the next set of boxes, record the specific tasks (actions) that comprise each of the main activities. Match tasks with the appropriate strategy boxes.
   - Again, use either the Affinity process or detailed flowcharts to identify detailed tasks.

4. On the lines to the right of each task box, identify who will take lead responsibility for the task and when it will be accomplished.
5. Assign responsibilities for steps, actions, or improvement targets.
   - If using a tree diagram to accomplish a process change, you need to make sure that all of the tasks/steps you've identified are accomplished. This is the only way to achieve the ultimate goal identified on the left side of the tree.
   - When using a tree diagram to identify potential SMART goals related to a strategic schoolwide goal, you will likely come up with more potential goals than you can realistically deal with. In that case, you need to decide which specific goals to pursue.

Tips

- Enlarge the tree diagram and post it on a wall so that everyone can construct the plan together.
- Don't worry that every single box must be filled in for the tool to be done correctly; it is simply a way to organize ideas. Conversely, if there are more ideas than there is space on the diagram, feel free to add more space to the diagram.

 A template of a tree diagram appears on the CD-ROM.

Responsibility Matrix

A template of a responsibility matrix appears on the CD-ROM.

Process	Decision Maker	Process Manager	Back-up	Involved Stakeholders
Word Processing/ computer documentation support	Nick P.	Nick P.	Katie W.	Carl D./ Computer Committee
Coordinate committee meetings (memos, materials, schedule...)	Keisha S.	Phil H.		Giselle S.
Process grant applications	Faculty/ Keisha S.	Phil H.		Giselle S.
Coordinate faculty leave	Faculty/ Keisha S.	Nick P. Phil H.	Marko A. Carl D. Julie C.	Phil H. Susan B. Giselle S.

Figure 4.11 Responsibility Matrix for Faculty and Staff Support Processes

Note. Copyright © 2001 by QLD, LLC. Reprinted with permission.

What It Is

A matrix showing which individuals or groups have what type of responsibility related to core processes in your school (Figure 4.11)

Use It When

You want to clarify roles and responsibilities for carrying out tasks and functions in a department, division, work unit, or other type of organizational unit

How to Do It

1. Determine the core processes for the unit. Record these vertically down the left side of the matrix.
2. For each core process, write in four types of names:
   - The decision maker
   - The process manager
   - People who serve as back-up
   - People involved as stakeholders

Role Definitions

Decision maker: The person who makes the decisions about operating or changing the entire process. The decision maker determines priorities and the scope of responsibilities for the process manager (sometimes they are the same person).

Process manager: The person responsible for doing the task on a regular basis. The process manager answers questions about what to do regarding a specific process or task.

Back-up: the person who operates the process when the process manager is away.

Involved Stakeholders: Includes people who give input to the process, use the service or products, or are otherwise effected by the process and its results. These are the people who should be involved if the process is changed.

Gantt Chart

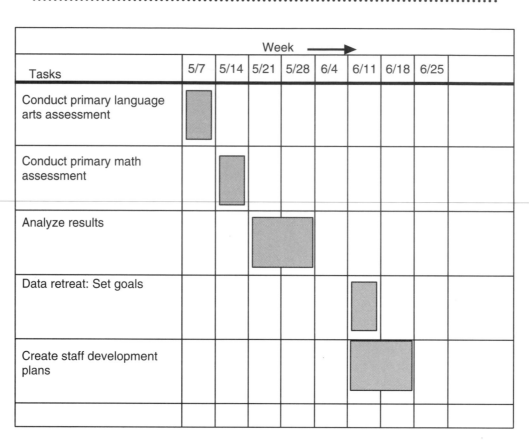

Tasks	Week →								
	5/7	5/14	5/21	5/28	6/4	6/11	6/18	6/25	
Conduct primary language arts assessment	▓								
Conduct primary math assessment		▓							
Analyze results			▓						
Data retreat: Set goals						▓			
Create staff development plans						▓			

Figure 4.12 Gantt Chart for Curriculum Improvement Project
Note. Copyright © 2001 by QLD, LLC. Reprinted with permission.

What It Is

A scheduling tool for action planning that depicts relative timing of process steps (Figure 4.12)

Use It When

You need to be able to judge the timing of action steps

Applications

- To schedule the steps needed to carry out an action plan
- After identifying action steps (such as after you've created a top-down flowchart)

How to Do It

1. Either brainstorm the steps needed to carry out the action plan or use the steps already outlined in a top-down flowchart (p. 98).
2. Arrange the steps (tasks) down the left side of a grid.
3. Across the top, write in appropriate time intervals (days, weeks, or months) over which the plan will be implemented.
4. Estimate how long each step or group of steps will take.
5. Determine starting dates for each step (paying attention to what needs to be completed before you start any given step).
6. For each step, draw in a block that goes from the starting date for that step and extends for the expected duration. Color in these blocks.
7. Review the chart to identify potential conflicts in timing, resource needs, etc. Adjust the schedules as needed.

Modifications

- You can create the simplest form of a Gantt chart easily by hand, but it makes it harder to see timing relationships between steps.
- Project-planning software programs often use Gantt charts, and they let you identify the timing relationship between each pair of steps. (For example, does one step have to finish before another can be completed? Or are the two steps independent—their timing does not depend on each other.) The downside of using software is that setting up the chart can take a lot of time if there are many tasks, many people, or intricate relationships between steps.

Tip

Consider scheduling parallel tasks whenever possible.

 A template of a Gantt chart appears on the CD-ROM.

Activity Network Diagram (AND)

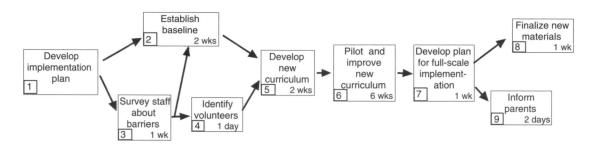

Figure 4.13 Activity Network Diagram of New Curriculum Development

Note. Copyright © 2001 by QLD, LLC. Reprinted with permission.

What It Is

A diagram depicting the flow of work, incorporating dependencies between tasks (Figure 4.13)

Use It When

You want to organize actions into the most efficient path and identify the most realistic schedule for the completion of a project

Applications

Developing a plan to implement a major new initiative (such as developing a new curriculum)

How to Do It

1. Brainstorm all the tasks needed to complete the project. Write them on self-stick notes.
2. Select the first task that must be done and place that self-stick note on the far left side of a large work surface.
3. Ask, "Can any of these other tasks be done at the same time as the first one?"
   - If yes, place the task(s) beneath the first task.
   - If no, go to Step 4.
4. For each simultaneous task identified in Step 3, identify the next task that can occur in *sequence*.

Once again, also identify any tasks that can occur simultaneously with this second round of tasks.
   - For example, in Figure 4.13, the team realized that Tasks 3 and 4 could occur at the same time as Task 2.
5. Repeat Step 4 until all tasks appear in sequence.
   - During the discussions, you may identify tasks that were not included in the original brainstorm. It is okay to write new self-stick notes to incorporate these steps.
6. Number each task.
7. Start with the first task and draw a connecting arrow to the next set of tasks in the sequence.
8. Record an estimated time for that task (number of hours, days, or weeks).
9. Repeat Steps 7 and 8 for each task.
10. To determine the total cumulative time, add up the estimated completion time needed for each path of connected activities.
    - The path with the longest cumulative time is commonly referred to as the project's *critical path*.

Tip

Do not consider wait time as part of the overall critical path. If much time is spent in waiting for a step to be completed, consider using the Accelerated Improvement Process (p. 192) to reduce cycle time.

Final Check: SMART Processes and Planning

My team uses group process tools to make our internal work more productive:

✓ Dialogue

✓ Brainstorming

✓ Affinity diagrams

✓ Multivoting

✓ Decision matrices

✓ Consensus decision-making

My team creates visual pictures of processes and plans using the appropriate tools:

✓ Flowcharts

- basic

- top-down

- deployment

- detailed

✓ Tree diagrams

✓ Responsibility matrices

✓ Gantt charts

✓ Activity Network Diagrams (ANDs)

Chapter 5
Tools for Understanding Perceptions and Opinions

For many of us, our perceptions are our reality. There is a large body of social science research that links perceptions to beliefs, behaviors, and attitudes. Perceptions strongly shape how we interpret information and how we act on that information. Thus, understanding perceptions is key to identifying areas of satisfaction and opportunities for improvement. The data tools in this chapter can be used to better understand how staff, parents, students, and community members perceive their schools and what they are feeling and thinking about their schools. There are three techniques commonly used to gather perceptual data:

1. In-depth interviews
2. Focus groups
3. Surveys

If the information gathered from the perceptual data-gathering tools can be converted into numbers, you can use quantitative tools (such as bar charts and pie charts) to display the results. We'll show examples later in this chapter and provide more in-depth instructions for those quantitative tools.

For many of us, our perceptions are our reality.

Collecting and Analyzing Perceptual Data

Five concepts play an important role in gathering and collecting perceptual data:

- **Sampling:** Gathering data from a selected portion of the total pool of candidates
- **Stratification:** Gathering data from various subgroups
- **Disaggregation:** Separating results from various subgroups so that they can be more easily compared
- **Developing useful questions:** Developing easily understood questions that will be easy to analyze
- **Using scales for evaluation:** Using scales to quantify the extent to which people agree with certain statements

Templates for a data needs chart and a data analysis worksheet appear on the CD-ROM.

Sampling

When you need to collect perceptual data, the pool of candidates (*population*) from which you could collect data is often much larger than can be handled—unless you have unlimited resources and time. Experience has shown that in most cases you can make reliable inferences about a population by sampling a subset of that population (see Figure 5.1)—as long as you think carefully about how to select the sampled subset.

Sampling strategies can vary from the very simple (talk to one language arts teacher in each high school) to very complex (interview five representatives from four different types of schools, two representatives of all key business sectors, etc.). How complex you get is determined by your purpose in collecting the data, the stakes in the outcome (that is, the risk associated with being wrong), and how sure you want to be that the results reflect the population as a whole.

To generalize your findings beyond a particular group, your sampling technique must be random and scientifically valid. So if you're playing a high-stakes game, such as developing a funding referendum or redefining a districtwide curriculum, you will want to be very scientific in your sampling scheme and in interpreting the results. Help from a statistician and/or sampling expert is invaluable in such cases.

Alternatively, if your team is developing an agenda for an upcoming school career day and you don't have time to talk to all staff, speak with a few selected stakeholders.

More details on sampling are provided in the following section.

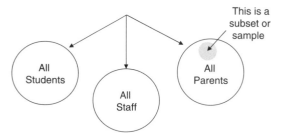

Each of these is a population:

This is a subset or sample

All Students

All Staff

All Parents

Figure 5.1   Sampling

Stratification and Disaggregation

When you are planning an effort to collect perceptual data, another question you have to ask is whether there are different subsets of the population that possess or represent significantly different types of knowledge. If the answer is yes, then you can consider developing separate questions or strategies for approaching those subsets.

Typical types of subgroups include

- Students in certain grades, parents of those students, and staff for those grades
- Teachers of particular disciplines (fine arts), classroom teachers, and paraprofessionals
- Outside stakeholders: business and religious community leaders.
- Various positions with the school/district: teachers, administrators, and staff

Stratification is the process of setting up the subgroups you're interested in finding out more about *before* you gather data from them. For example, if you're doing an overall climate survey involving staff, students, parents, and other community members, you may want to design different questions for each group. Figure 5.2 illustrates the percentages of distinct groups within the community that responded to a community-wide climate survey. Each subgroup was asked different questions. N represents the number of people who received the survey.

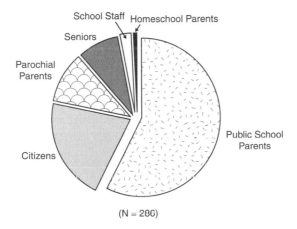

(N = 286)

Figure 5.2 Climate Survey Showing Community Characteristics
Note. Copyright © 2001 by QLD, LLC. Reprinted with permission.

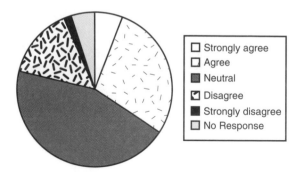

Parent Question: My child is safe at this school (agree/disagree).

- ☐ Strongly agree
- ☐ Agree
- ■ Neutral
- ☑ Disagree
- ■ Strongly disagree
- ☐ No Response

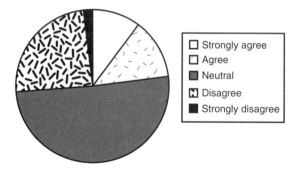

Teacher Question: Teachers are consistent in enforcing the school's code of conduct (agree/disagree).

- ☐ Strongly agree
- ☐ Agree
- ■ Neutral
- ☒ Disagree
- ■ Strongly disagree

Figure 5.3   Climate Survey Showing Results of Survey
Given to Subgroups: Parents and Teachers

Note. Copyright © 2001 by QLD, LLC. Reprinted with permission.

At the analysis stage, you can use **disaggregation** to compare the similarities and differences within the subgroups (for example, by socioeconomic status, race/ethnicity, gender, etc.). Disaggregation means displaying the results in separate charts or graphs, one for each of the subgroups from which you collected data. In Figure 5.3, stratification was used to allow the survey to probe different areas of concern for different subgroups: parents and teachers.

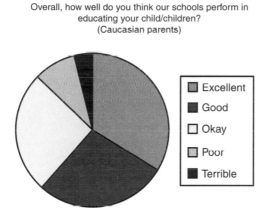

Overall, how well do you think our schools perform in educating your child/children?
(Caucasian parents)

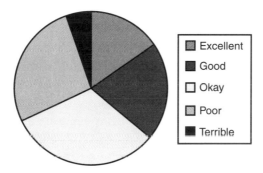

Overall, how well do you think our schools perform in educating your child/children?
(Asian parents)

Figure 5.4 Climate Survey Showing Results from Two Subgroups Within a Gubgroup: Asian and Caucasian Parents

Note. Copyright © 2001 by QLD, LLC. Reprinted with permission.

One way to disaggregate results is to show separate charts for the various subgroups in your sample. The two charts in Figure 5.4 show that, overall, Asian parents are far less satisfied with the district performance than Caucasian parents. (The Okay and Poor segments are much larger for Asian parents.)

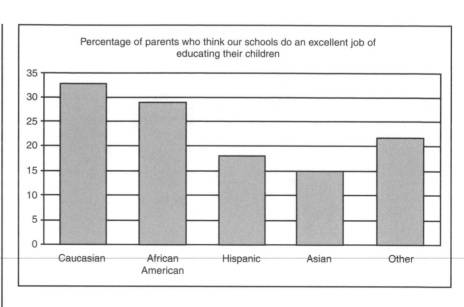

Percentage of parents who think our schools do an excellent job of educating their children

Figure 5.5 Climate Survey Results Showing Most-Favorable
Responses Among Subgroups

Note. Copyright © 2001 by QLD, LLC. Reprinted with permission.

Another way to disaggregate results is to compare particular responses side-by-side. The chart in Figure 5.5 shows the percentage of parents within each group who gave the most-favorable response. In this case the samples were drawn from separate populations, so it would not be appropriate to use a pie chart to compare them.

Instructions for Stratification and Sampling

Stratification and sampling need to be integrated into your data collection plan before you actually begin collecting data. Here's how:

1. Decide what subgroups of the population you are interested in learning more about (how you want to stratify the data collection).

2. Develop *sampling frames* — lists from which the samples will be drawn — for each group.

   - You need to have access to records or databases that can give you a list of potential candidates that fit your stratification criteria. For example, who are all the fourth graders in the district? Or who are the parents of minority students attending our two high schools?

Sampling Tips

- Be wary of *sampling frame bias* where the frame you've defined is different in some significant aspect from the larger population you're trying to find out about. Example: If you want to survey people by e-mail, you will exclude those who do not have e-mail accounts.
- With small samples, it's important to try to get as close to a 100% response rate as possible because results become more and more difficult to generalize from fewer responses.

- Code each entry on the list with a number.
- Determine the total number of candidates in your sampling frames.

3. Refer to the Sample Size Chart (Appendix p. 263) to determine how many people you need to sample from each frame in order to get reliable results.

    - Enter in at any column, any line. If the total number needed in your sample is a 3-digit number, use the last 3 numbers in the random number table to indicate the individual from your list to be selected.

    - For example: If you need 250 in your sample and the random number you've chosen is 3167 (line 1, column 2), then the person who is number 167 is in your sample. The next random number (reading down) is 193. Person 193 is also in your sample. The next number (reading down) is 9249, which is too high. Skip that number and proceed to the next number that is 250 or under.

    - Continue until you have a full sample.

4. Select the samples for each sampling frame using the Random Number Table (Appendix p. 264). Enter in at any column, any line.

    - For example, if you need to select several hundred names for your sample, use the last three digits of each number in the table to identify which number codes to select from your candidate list.

5. Continue until you have a full sample.

Developing Useful Questions

To gather perceptual data, you need to ask people questions. The types of questions you ask depend somewhat on the format you'll use to ask them. For example, you can ask more complicated questions in face-to-face interviews than you can in a telephone survey.

The first thing to decide is whether you will ask *open-ended questions* (those with no predetermined answers) or *closed-ended questions* (where respondents choose from a list of possible answers).

> The real voyage in discovery consists not in seeking new landscapes but in having new eyes.
>
> —Marcel Proust

- Open-ended questions are more likely to lead to new learning. (Examples: What could be done to improve our 9th grade curriculum? In what ways do you feel our school could better serve the community?) However, it is harder to analyze the answers.
- Closed-ended questions are easier to score, but less likely to produce new insights.

Typically, interviews and focus groups focus on open-ended questions, and surveys contain largely closed-ended questions.

No matter what type of questions you'll be using, be sure to develop easily understood questions that will also be easy to analyze. Here are some tips:

- Keep questions simple and clear.
- Avoid jargon, bias, and hypothetical questions.
- Ask only questions respondents would know something about.
- Focus on just one thought per question.
- Include only necessary questions.
- Use rating scales for closed-ended questions.
- Limit potential responses to just four or five items.
- Include at least one open-ended question at the end even if you're doing a survey that is mostly closed-ended questions. Ask, "Is there anything else you'd like to comment on?"

Using Scales to Evaluate Answers

When you add scales to your survey, you can begin to quantify the extent to which people agree or disagree with certain statements. Typically, most scales range from three points to six points. Even young children can be asked to complete surveys. Adults can read questions aloud and have children circle the face that describes how they feel. There are three types of scales commonly used in gathering perceptual data (see Figure 5.6).

Scales	Examples
Rating Scales Respondents are asked to rate the importance of an issue or relevance of an item on a pre-determined scale. Aim for three- to six-point scales. Start with a statement, followed by the scale. Sample scales are shown to the right.	Very Satisfied — Satisfied — Neutral — Dissatisfied — Very Dissatisfied Excellent — Good — Adequate — Below Adequate — Poor Much Better — Better — About the Same — Not as Good — Much Worse Strongly Agree — Agree — No Opinion — Disagree — Strongly Disagree 5 — 4 — 3 — 2 — 1 Usually ☺ — Sometimes 😐 — Hardly Ever ☹
Rank Order Scales Respondents are asked to rank a limited number of options in order of priority or preference. Keep the number small (five or fewer).	How important to you are the following extra-curricular programs? Please rank their importance in order from 1 to 5, with 1 being most important. ___ Drama club ___ Recreational volleyball ___ School newspaper ___ Swim club ___ Computer lab
Gap Analysis Scale Combines ranking with a rating scale to discover both what is important to people and also how well they feel you are doing. This can help you identify the biggest gaps between priorities and performance. (See p. 265 for an example of a gap analysis survey.)	IMPORTANCE — SATISFACTION — GAP Hands-on projects 1 2 3 4 ⑤ 1 ② 3 4 5 -3 Friendly teacher 1 2 3 ④ 5 1 2 ③ 4 5 -1 Interesting homework 1 2 ③ 4 5 1 2 ③ 4 5 0 Importance: 1 = not at all important, 5 = extremely important Satisfaction: 1 = not at all satisfied, 5 = completely satisfied

Figure 5.6 Scales for Gathering Perceptual Data

Note. Copyright © 2001 by QLD, LLC. Reprinted with permission.

The "Heard This Before" Rule

The purpose of conducting interviews and focus groups, in particular, is *learning* about the issues around a particular subject. So, one valid data collecting strategy for interviews and focus groups is to continue gathering data until you stop learning anything new. When you start to think you've heard all this before, it may be time to formally analyze the results and move on.

Surveys are another issue. Usually you want surveys to be statistically valid, which means you need to complete your data collection and sampling plans whether or not the same themes keep arising.

Three Criteria for Perceptual Data

There are three questions that can haunt anyone who collects perceptual data:

1. **Is the research valid?**
    *   Are the questions worded properly?
    *   Do the questions relate to the purpose of the research?

2. **Are the results valid?**
    *   What types of people participated in the research? Do those people represent the diversity of opinions in the community?
    *   Was there a good response rate?
    *   Was the analysis properly done? Are our interpretations of the results accurate? objective?

3. **Can we generalize from the results?**[1]
    *   Do the results accurately reflect the perceptions of the larger group?
    *   Was the sampling procedure random?
    *   To what populations, settings, or variables can the conclusions be generalized?

The concepts covered so far in this chapter—sampling, stratification, disaggregation, developing questions, and scales—are building blocks you can use to help gather useful and valid perceptual data using any of the three methods described in the remainder of this chapter:

*   In-depth interviews
*   Focus groups
*   Surveys

[1] Relates to surveys only. The purpose of interviews and focus groups is to get a deep understanding of targeted issues, not to generalize from those results the opinions of those not included in the study.

In-Depth Interviews

What It Is

One-on-one conversations, either by phone or in person, using open- and/or closed-ended questions

Use It When

- You need to identify and learn about underlying issues and concerns in depth
- A better understanding of the full range of perceptions will clarify questions or needs

Applications

- When designing a new course or program, interview students and parents to get their input about what should be included and how to best engage learning
- To teach students interviewing skills they can use to gather information from each other about what is working and not working well in a particular course or at school
- To perform interviews in order to identify meaningful questions for a broader survey

Advantages Over Other Perceptual Tools

- Can explore complex issues, probe for more information, and clarify questions and answers
- High response rate
- Fast turnaround
- Generates information that can be used to write effective survey questions

Disadvantages Compared to Other Perceptual Tools

- Can be costly if paying school personnel or external consultants to conduct the interviews
- Are time consuming
- Are usually limited in number of interviews due to cost and time

How to Do It

1. Identify what you want to know as a result of the interviews.
2. Develop five to ten open-ended questions that relate to the purpose of the interviews.
3. Create a script for the interviewer to follow. This is particularly important if more than one person will be conducting interviews—you want them all to follow the same protocol.
4. Develop a standard note-taking system for interviewers.
5. Test the questions and script on several representative people before doing the actual interviews. Try out your note-taking system to see if it helps you capture what you want to know.
6. Set up a sampling plan to include representatives from each stakeholder group (see p. 116).
7. Do the interviews, either by phone or in person.
8. Once all the interviews are completed, use an Affinity Diagram (p. 90) to organize the results by theme.
9. Share a summary of the results with the people interviewed, and tell them what the next steps will be. (This will reinforce that you *heard* what they had to say and you're *taking action*. Even if your next action is a survey, you'll be reinforcing the importance of their input.)

Modifications

- Add closed-ended rating scale questions to your open-ended format. For example:
  - On a scale of one to five, with five being strongly agree, do you agree or disagree with the proposal for an open campus at our school?

  Follow up with this question:
  - Why do you feel that way?
- Do in-depth interviews with selected survey participants to clarify and follow up on responses. (Note: Be sure to set up the survey ahead of time to let people know you may be following up with selected individuals; allow them an option to pass and protect their anonymity.)

Tips

- In-depth interviews yield rich information—they allow you to really understand what's important to people. But they aren't statistically reliable—results should not be generalized to larger groups.
- If used as part of a school improvement process, consider inviting members of the school community to conduct the interviews. The process can be a great relationship builder and a real eye-opener for those doing the interviewing.

Focus Groups

···

What It Is

A facilitated conversation with a small group of selected individuals, focused on one specific issue or topic and using structured, open-ended questions

Use It When

- Issues and concerns among stakeholder groups are not immediately apparent to your team
- You need to understand the full range of perceptions of an issue
- You want to compare perceptions between different groups
- You feel that having interviewees together in the same room at the same time will spark greater insights and creativity

Applications

- Before a survey to help design the questions
- As a stand-alone data collection method to help clarify issues with which your team struggles
- To *concept test* early thinking about new strategic directions, curriculum ideas, programs, and policies

Advantages Over Other Perceptual Tools

- Can explore complex issues, probe for more information, and clarify questions and answers
- Triggers new ideas because of group dynamics
- Generates survey ideas

Disadvantages Compared to Other Perceptual Tools

- More costly
- Takes more time
- Sometimes difficult to recruit representative participants
- Complex logistics/coordination
- Need a skilled neutral facilitator

How To Do It

1. Identify subgroups whose ideas are of interest to your project. If you are using more than one focus group, decide whether to mix people from different subgroups together or hold separate focus groups for each subgroup.
2. Develop five to ten open-ended questions and a script for the facilitator. Test the questions and script on a small, representative group. Revise as appropriate.
3. Plan for a 1¹/₂- to 2-hour session per group.
   - Consider going off-site.
   - If at all possible, recruit one or two neutral third-party facilitators. One facilitator can take notes and keep track of time while the other moderates the conversation. If this isn't possible, arrange for recording and transcribing the session (ensure confidentiality, however).
4. Recruit participants according to your sampling/stratification scheme.
5. At the session, seat participants in a circle and perform introductions.

6. Have the facilitator introduce the first question and guide discussion.
   - Allow some free-form responses at first.
   - Make sure every participant gets a chance to respond. Do not allow anyone to dominate the conversation.
   - Have the facilitator direct the conversation to a specific person, one at a time, as a structured way to ensure even participation. ("Maria, what do you think about this? Bill, do you agree with Maria's comments or do you have a different perception?")
7. Watch the time and move on to each subsequent question as appropriate.
8. After the session, collect the notes or transcribe the tapes and identify key statements from the group. Use an Affinity Diagram (p. 90) to organize results into themes. If you conducted more than one focus group, combine results. (If you want, you can code the statements so that you can see if there are differences between the focus groups.)

9. Communicate to group members what you found out and what you will do next.

Tips

- Allow the participants to explore interesting areas in depth. A focus group is a guided—not rigid—conversation.
- Focus groups, like interviews, yield rich information. Their results, however, aren't representative of the whole. Written surveys, implemented with larger numbers of people, are a method for validating interview and focus group results.
- Be sure to probe for more information. Ask participants to provide examples and stories to illustrate their points.
- Allow some silence in the conversation, especially when soliciting input from quieter participants.

Surveys

Statements	Scoring
1. High scores on standardized tests reflect high achievement of students.	1 2 3 4 5 6
2. The schools in our district place high priority on increasing the basic skills of students (reading, writing, and math).	1 2 3 4 5 6
3. In our community, the quality of education in schools is better now than it was 5 years ago.	1 2 3 4 5 6
4. Developing computer skills in early elementary grades is important.	1 2 3 4 5 6
5. Teachers offer challenging assignments and activities for students who are more advanced.	1 2 3 4 5 6
6. Additional assistance is offered to students who need the extra help.	1 2 3 4 5 6
7. Teachers set high standards for student work.	1 2 3 4 5 6
8. Students graduate from our schools well prepared to attend college.	1 2 3 4 5 6
9. Students graduate from our schools well prepared to perform as competent, reliable employees.	1 2 3 4 5 6

1 = don't know; 2 = strongly disagree; 3 = disagree; 4 = neutral; 5 = agree; 6 = strongly agree

Figure 5.7 District Climate Survey Form

Note. From Muskego-Norway Public Schools. Reprinted with permission.

What It Is

A set of questions that ask people about their perceptions or opinions. Usually surveys are written questionnaires, but they can also be conducted by phone (Figure 5.7)

Use It When

- You need to quantify perceptions/concerns identified through interviews and/or focus groups.

- You want to understand the perceptions of large numbers of people.

Applications

- Classroom teachers can survey their students and parents to gauge their satisfaction with a number of issues important to them (for example, interesting curriculum, engaging assignments, teacher availability, classroom climate, communication about student performance, etc.).

- Teachers and administrators can also solicit feedback about their leadership style via surveys because respondents tend to be more honest if they can be anonymous. (See the high school climate survey example in the Appendix on p. 266, which was designed by a principal to get feedback from students.)

Advantages Over Other Perceptual Tools

- Can collect information from large samples more efficiently and with less cost than with other methods
- Less intrusive

Disadvantages Compared to Other Perceptual Tools

- Time consuming to design well
- Less opportunity for follow up (probing and clarification of answers)
- May have a poor response rate
- Those who take the time to respond may be biased (for example, highly dissatisfied, desirous of a new program, active in school events, or less literate in English)

How To Do It

1. Define the population you want to learn about. Think about stratifying this population into subgroups (see p. 117).
2. Make a sampling plan to get a randomly selected subset of the population. Consider sample sizes and response rates when you make the plan. Think about how you will construct the initial sample frame and beware of sampling bias.
3. Develop 15 to 20 focused questions. Decide how to score the answers (rating scale or ranking scale).

4. Design a simple, easy-to-understand survey that people will find easy to complete and return. Use these criteria to evaluate your survey:
   - Does it include a clear statement of purpose?
   - Is it easy to follow?
   - Is it visually pleasing?
   - Are the questions simply stated?
5. Write a cover letter explaining the purpose of the survey, giving instructions for completing the survey, explaining how the data will be used, and ensuring confidentiality.
6. Pilot both the survey and the cover letter with some representative members of the population. Change anything that may reduce the response rate or create confusion. Pay particular attention to educational jargon and readability level.
7. Include a stamped, self-addressed envelope or make the survey easy to return by other means (such as by fax, with a child, or at a convenient drop-off box).
8. Do public relations. Prepare the targeted groups or community. Communicate that this is important.
9. Consider following up to encourage people to respond. Show appreciation for their willingness to take the survey. (Note: In general, a 50% response rate from the population at large is considered quite good.)
10. Share results and action plans with the people you surveyed so that they will want to participate next time. You'll be communicating the importance and value of their input.

Modifications

Conduct the survey by phone instead of or in addition to a written questionnaire. Develop a script for the callers that includes a standard introduction about the survey and its role and importance to your school or district. Develop data collection forms that the callers can complete easily while on the phone.

Tips

- Be clear about the purpose of your survey. Begin with the end in mind, asking, "How will knowing the answers to these questions help us take improvement action?"
- Beware of over-interpreting results. It's important to note the actual numbers of people who answered a question in a particular way because percentages can be misleading if the sample was small. (Fifty percent of respondents sounds like a big number—until you tell people it was two out of the four people in one subset!)

- Consider reviewing surveys from other teachers or other schools doing similar research, and select questions you want to pursue.
- Overcome language barriers in homes of students by translating surveys into the family's language.
- Perceptions can change over time, so you will want to do regular surveys, using the same instrument each time.
- Use pie graphs to show percentages of the whole or total responses in each group.
- Include the total n (number who were sent the survey), along with the response rate, when reporting results.

Final Check: Understanding Perceptions and Opinions

My team cares what various stakeholders think. As appropriate, we use the following tools to gather and interpret perceptual data:

✓ In-depth interviews

✓ Focus groups

✓ Surveys

We apply the following concepts to help create data-gathering methods and results that are useful for our purposes and that lead to valid results:

✓ Sampling

✓ Stratification

✓ Disaggregation

✓ Open- and closed-ended questions

✓ Rating, ranking, and gap analysis scales

Chapter 6
Tools for Understanding Problems and Improving Results

Data collection is important in many stages of problem solving and process improvement. Data help you

- Refine the definition of a problem by quantifying its frequency or impact
- Verify which potential causes of a problem are actual causes
- Monitor whether changes you've made to fix a problem have had the desired impact

The tools in this chapter support each of these uses:

- **The Cause Analysis tools** help you define where to collect data to verify potential causes of a problem.
- **The Numerical Data tools** are versatile charts and graphs that let you use numerical (quantitative) data at almost any stage in problem solving or process improvement.

Use these tools judiciously, avoiding both extremes. Some teams seem to get *data happy*: They can't seem to stop collecting data and end up inundated with much more data than they can possibly analyze. Other teams are so uncomfortable with data that they act almost solely on instinct and gut feelings, rarely using data. Both of these extremes are ill advised. Every team should use data as much as possible to verify (or disprove) what they think is happening, but you don't want to waste time by collecting unnecessary or irrelevant data.

Some teams get data happy: They can't seem to stop collecting data.

> The measure of success is not whether you have a tough problem to deal with, but whether it's the same problem you had last year.
>
> —John Foster Dulles

Cause Analysis Tools

Do you know the secret to finding effective solutions? You have to know specifically what problem it is you're trying to solve—a task that's harder than it sounds! Just think about all the problems in your school that have been solved over and over and over again. Obviously, the solutions that were put in place had little effect on the real cause of the problems.

Do you know the secret to finding solutions that address the real causes of a problem? You have to dig deep beneath the surface *symptoms* of that problem to uncover the root causes. The first three tools in this chapter—*5 Why's Analysis, Cause-and-Effect Diagrams*, and *Relations Diagrams*—provide that critical link that helps you make sure you've isolated the underlying or root causes of a problem. Two important notes about these tools:

- First, they help you think logically about *potential* causes of a problem; you will still need to gather data to verify which are the *real* causes of a problem.
- Second, their effectiveness is directly related to the creativity and depth of the thinking that goes into creating them. That's why these tools are best used with your team as a whole—you want many minds brainstorming ideas so that you have a broad and deep list of potential causes.

5 Why's Analysis

What It Is

A method for uncovering the real reasons underlying a problem—for getting to the root causes

Use It When

- You have tried many solutions that have failed
- You are stuck in a complex problem or issue

How to Do It

1. Develop a problem statement (p. 197).
2. Ask why that problem occurs and identify a potential cause.
3. Ask why that cause occurs, and so on, until you have asked why five times.

Tips

- The number 5 is not sacred. The point is to go down several layers, beyond the obvious symptoms of a problem to the underlying deep causes.
- Stop at a layer where you can still take action. It might be that your team can address an underlying cause identified at your fourth why, but not the deeper cause at the fifth level. For example, an underlying cause of low reading scores might be poverty, but it's unlikely your group will be able to do anything about that cause. However, you might be able to do something to support early childhood development programs or to obtain tutors for children K–2.
- Once you feel you've identified the root cause, consider how you might verify (with data) whether that truly is the cause. If data are unavailable, develop pilot (small-scale) solutions that you think will address the problem. If the solution makes a differ-

ence, your guess at the underlying cause was probably close to the truth; if not, repeat your analysis to identify other potential causes.

Classroom Application

- **Why 1**: Why didn't you do your homework last night?
  I didn't know what to do.

- **Why 2**: Why didn't you know what to do?
  I didn't remember the instructions.

- **Why 3**: Why didn't you remember the instructions?
  I didn't write them down.

Action: Make time to collectively define behavioral expectations.

Schoolwide Application

- **Why 1**: Why do we have so many discipline referrals?
  Because a lot of students act inappropriately.

- **Why 2**: Why do they act inappropriately?
  Because they don't know the rules.

- **Why 3**: Why don't they know the rules?
  Because we haven't explained and enforced them consistently.

- **Why 4**: Why haven't we explained and enforced them consistently?
  Because we haven't agreed on a common set of expectations.

- **Why 5**: Why haven't we agreed on common expectations?
  Because we haven't spent time together defining our philosophy and expectations.

Action: Let's make the time to do that so that we all get on the same page together.

Cause-and-Effect Diagram

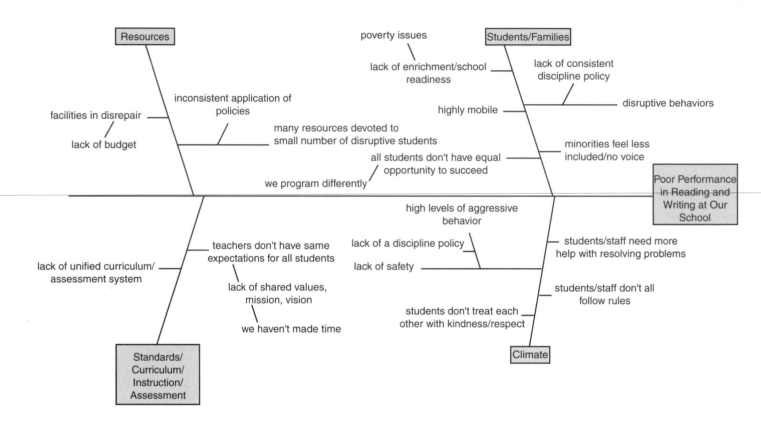

Figure 6.1 Cause-and-Effect Diagram

Note. Copyright © 2001 by QLD, LLC. Reprinted with permission.

What It Is

A structured tool for conducting 5 Why's thinking (Figure 6.1)

Use It When

- You have isolated a problem that has no obvious cause
- You want to expand your thinking before focusing solutions on a particular cause
- There is more than one problem or gap being addressed
- A problem has many branches to its complexity

Applications

- In problem-solving, use it after you have narrowly defined a problem and need to investigate the root causes.
- In designing a school improvement plan, use a cause-and-effect diagram to outline the possible causes of poor student performance. Then research which causes are the biggest contributors in your school.

How to Do It

1. Come up with a succinct problem statement.
2. Identify the major categories that are potential sources of that problem.
3. Select one category and ask "why" until the group feels it has exhausted the possibilities. Capture the ideas on flipchart paper or on self-stick notes (one idea per note).
4. Repeat for the remaining categories.
5. Create the diagram.
   - Write your problem statement at the head of the cause-and-effect diagram.
   - Draw as many major lines, or *bones*, off of the central line as you have categories.
   - Label the bones with the categories.
   - Draw a line off of one major bone and label it with the first level of cause you identified in your analysis.
   - Draw smaller bones from the first cause until all the ideas the team generated for that potential cause are represented on the diagram.
   - Continue adding causes and causes-of-those-causes on the diagram.

The diagram will visually illustrate the most intensely involved categories, and people will be able to see that certain potential causes recur throughout the picture; these are areas for further investigation.

Alternatives

There are several ways of determining what categories are used as the major headings:

- Use standard items such as people, processes, policies, materials, equipment, procedures, facilities, technology, and training.

- Develop your own categories based on the unique aspects of the problem being analyzed. One general rule of thumb, however, is to keep the header categories broad and generic.
- Instead of using categories, label the major bones with surface-level causes. The smaller bones attached to each major bone would then be factors that contribute to that surface-level cause.
  - For example, suppose the problem statement was "students failing to learn material for standardized tests." One major bone might be labeled "out-of-date textbooks." A smaller bone off that cause might be "delays in the purchasing of updated books." The interpretation of this sequence is that delays might cause out-of-date textbooks, which might cause students failing to learn.

Tips

- Consider using brainstorming and the Affinity process to group ideas first, using sticky notes.
- Create the cause-and-effect diagram on a wall or surface large enough for everyone to post their ideas and for 5 Why's Analysis to be conducted.
- Never use people's names or positions on the diagram.

Guideline

Emphasize that the point is not to find a who, but to find systemic and process issues that are causing the problems to occur. Even when a who may look like a likely culprit (e.g., an incompetent teacher), consider how that person might have ended up in that situation (e.g., problematic hiring processes, lack of staff development, lack of mentoring/coaching system, etc.).

Relations Diagram

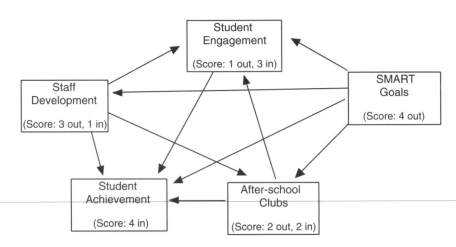

Figure 6.2 Relations Diagram
Note. Copyright © 2001 by QLD, LLC. Reprinted with permission.

What It Is

A systems thinking tool that helps identify the most important causes of a problem (Figure 6.2)

Use It When

A problem is part of a larger system or set of processes that can't be easily analyzed using sequential thinking tools (such as cause-and-effect diagrams)

How to Do It

1. Brainstorm all the issues contributing to the problem. Record these on self-stick notes and arrange the notes in a large circle on a large sheet of paper, whiteboard, etc.
2. Start with any self-stick note and ask whether that issue is *causing* or *contributing to* the impact of each of the other issues or whether it is *being caused* by or is *affected* by the other issues.
   - Each time you decide that the idea/issue on the note you started with contributes to another

issue's impact, draw an arrow *from the original note* to the other note.
   - Each time you decide the idea/issue on the note you started with is affected by the issue stated on another note, draw an arrow from the second note *to the original note.*
3. Move to the next note and repeat the process. Continue working your way around the circle until you have identified the relationships for each self-stick note.
4. Count the number of arrows going *out* of each issue. The issue with the most number of arrows going out is a *key driver,* and possibly a key cause, of the other issues. This issue deserves more investigation into its cause and impact.

Tip

Once you have identified one or two drivers, use 5 Why's Analysis to help you uncover what it is about those issues that causes problems elsewhere. That will help you develop focused solutions that will reduce or eliminate the underlying causes of problems.

Numerical Data Tools

The remaining tools in this chapter provide different ways to understand and present numerical (quantitative) data. There are two approaches for finding meaning in numbers:

> **We need to measure, not count.**
>
> **—Peter F. Drucker**

- **Performing calculations:** Statistics are calculations that describe some property of a set of numbers. An average or a median, for example, is a statistic that tells us about the midpoint of the data values. Such calculations also help us easily compare groups.
- **Creating pictures:** For most people, it is extremely difficult to look at a table of numbers and identify patterns or meaning with any accuracy. Charts and graphs are pictures that make it easier to see patterns and trends (or the lack thereof) in a set of numbers.

This chapter focuses primarily on the second of these strategies—creating pictures of data—because, for many everyday uses, pictures are easier to create and easier to interpret than statistics. Most people have a visceral reaction in response to a *chart* of data—they get a gut feeling about what that data are telling them—that simply doesn't happen when they look at a table of numbers or set of statistics.

However, you will find a few basic statistical calculations here because sometimes statistics help us make sense out of large amounts of data. Some of the most powerful tools in this chapter combine pictures and calculations—you get the intuitive learning that comes from looking at a visual display of the data, plus the rigor of the statistical calculations. When you are plotting data over time, for example, you can use statistics to help you plan and, in certain cases, *predict* how your system will behave in the future. The important thing is to know when it is more appropriate to *compare* and when it is more appropriate to *predict* based on the data you have.

The tools in this chapter fall into two categories[1]:

1. **Snapshot tools**, which give you a picture of what's happening at any given moment in time.
2. **Moving picture tools**, which let you determine patterns and trends over time.

[1]Today it is relatively easy to obtain simple software programs for displaying both snapshot and trend (moving picture) data. Nonetheless, specific how-to directions are included for all the tools in case computers or software are unavailable.

Guidelines for Helping Pictures Tell Their Stories

Use these tips to create useful pictures of data:

- Other people should be able to interpret the graph just by looking at it. All labels and titles should appear on the graph.
- Be careful not to allow over-interpretation. Snapshot graphs do not allow the interpreter to predict what will come next or to know what came before the particular point in time in which the data were collected. Moving picture graphs don't explain *why* something happened, only when.
- Ask, "What conclusions can we draw from this graph? What other questions do we have?"

Snapshot Tools

As their name implies, snapshot data tools capture a picture of what's going on at a given point in time. You would use snapshot tools to understand what is happening in your classroom or school *today*. Snapshot tools are useful for comparing different groups of data (e.g., cohorts of students on the same measure, different classes, or different schools) at one point in time. They should *not* be used to predict what results will be in the future.

This chapter looks at six snapshot tools:

- Bar charts
- Histograms
- Distribution charts
- Pareto diagrams
- Scatterplots
- Disaggregation

 TIP

Watch for subtle, but important differences in bar charts.

Three of the snapshot tools—bar charts, histograms, and Pareto diagrams—are sometimes *all* generically referred to as *bar charts*. When you see examples of these tools, you'll know why: They all use bars of varying heights to indicate the frequency or impact of problems. Their visual similarity hides subtle but significant differences. For example, the bars in a bar chart do not touch because each bar represents a different category. The bars in histograms *do* touch because they represent different segments of a *single* measure. Pay close to attention to the instructions for how to create the various charts; the important differences are captured there. As you become more familiar with these charts, you'll learn how to pick out the different features that convey important messages about the data being displayed.

Bar Chart

Eighth Grade Test of Knowledge and Concepts – Percent of Students in Our School Scoring Proficient or Advanced

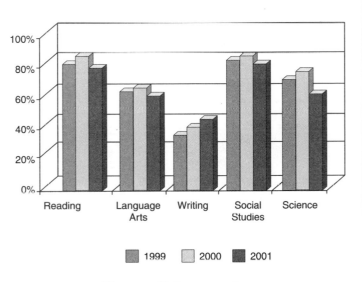

Figure 6.3 Bar Chart

Note. Copyright © 2001 by QLD, LLC. Reprinted with permission.

What It Is

- A snapshot tool that has bars representing how often a given problem or outcome (perhaps a test score) was observed during different times, for different classes, etc. (Figure 6.3)
- Answers how many or how much groups or individuals earned or scored at the time the data were collected
- The data should reflect independent, mutually exclusive categories, and all of it should have been collected at approximately the same time

Use It When

- You have separate, discrete categories of items or information at a single snapshot (or several single snapshots) in time
- You need to see how individuals or groups performed relative to each other on a particular measure
- You are looking at disaggregated data (p. 118)

How to Do It

1. Collect numerical data on the frequency (counts) of problems in various groups, events, etc.
2. Examine your data values and identify the highest value. Round up to the nearest whole number. Divide the vertical axis into equal intervals, with the highest value reflecting the highest data value recorded.
3. Label the individual categories on the horizontal axis. Order does not matter.
4. Create vertical bars to show how that group or individual performed.
5. Title the graph and label each axis.

Tips

- Make sure the categories being compared don't include duplicate counts or overlapping information.
- Each bar should be separated by a visible space to show they are in fact representing separate pieces of information.
- Bars should be visually the same width so as not to imply differences in volume.
- If you have more than 3 or 4 years of data on one measure, a good rule of thumb is to use a line graph to show the data over time. You can begin applying run chart signals for special cause (p. 158) when you have at least 12 data points in time order.

Histogram

What is the distribution of grade point averages for this year's 10th graders?

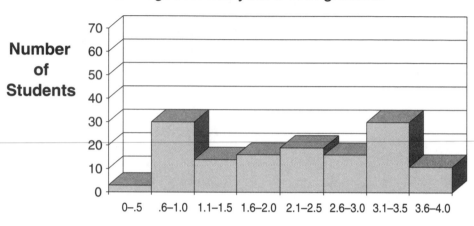

Figure 6.4 Histogram

Note. Copyright © 2001 by QLD, LLC. Reprinted with permission.

What It Is

- A snapshot chart that shows how often different values of a given measure occurred during the data collection period (Figure 6.4)
- An illustration of the full set of continuous data across an entire spectrum or continuum
- A snapshot of items that are related to one another —they are all part of one complete set
- An illustration of the range of variation in the data set

Use It When

- You need to see how a large set of snapshot data is distributed

- You have collected 18 or more data points over time, plotted it on a Run Chart, and you want to see the shape of the variation

How to Do It

1. Collect data on how often different values of a single continuous measure occur.
   - A continuous measure is one where any value within a given range is possible. Examples include test scores, income levels, and heights of students.
2. Determine the range for the entire sample (lowest to highest number in the data set).

3. Decide the number of *class intervals* needed, making sure the intervals are exactly equal in width.
   - For example, if you have test scores that range in value from 15 to 95 points, you wouldn't learn much by labeling *each* data value along the horizontal axes. Instead, cluster the values into eight class intervals of 10 points each (15–24, 25–34, etc.).
   - Make sure your class intervals are mutually exclusive: Every data point should fit into one and only one class interval.
4. Count the number of values within each class interval. (This gives you the frequencies of occurrences for each interval.) Label the vertical axis with equal intervals that reach a value as high or slightly higher than the largest count.
   - If the highest count value is 17, you could label 17 equal intervals of 1 along the vertical axes, nine intervals of 2 (2, 4, 6, . . . 18), or five intervals of 4 (4, 8, . . . 20).

5. Label the class intervals along the horizontal axis.
6. For each class interval, create a bar to a height equal to the count of occurrences within that class.
7. Title the graph and label each axis.

Tips

- Bars should touch each other because all data points can be found somewhere along the continuum represented by the horizontal axis.
- Bars should be the same width visually so as not to imply differences in volume.
- Try to keep the number of class intervals to between five and ten. Too many intervals will create a tight, high pattern, while too few will create a flat picture that doesn't tell you much.

Distribution Chart

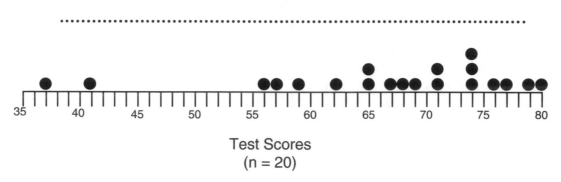

Test Scores
(n = 20)

Figure 6.5 Distribution Chart. This simple distribution chart of test scores conveys a lot of information very quickly. The viewer can tell that in this class test scores ranged from 37 to 80, that all but two students scored above 55, and, in fact, the majority of students scored 65 or higher.

Note. Copyright © 2001 by QLD, LLC. Reprinted with permission.

What It Is

A chart that shows each data value as a dot (or other symbol) along an axis (Figure 6.5)

Use It When

- You want a simple descriptive tool that creates a picture of what is
- You want to see how data values are distributed throughout the range of observed values

Applications

- When you are communicating statistics such as averages and standard deviations (which are highly sensitive to extreme data points) and want to show people how the observed data values were distributed

How to Do It

1. Create an axis labeled with individual data values.
2. Place a dot (or other symbol) above the axis for each time that value was observed.

3. Label the chart with a title; label the horizontal axis.
4. Decide which statistics to include on the graph: total *n* (number of students), mean (average score), mode (most frequent value), standard deviation (variation from the mean), median (number in the middle of the data), range (difference between the highest and lowest values), etc.

Tips

- Distribution charts differ from the various bar diagrams because each individual data value is plotted with a symbol. (Bar charts, histograms, and Pareto diagrams use bars to show *collective* information, such as the percentage or counts of data values falling within various intervals.)
- Distribution charts are different from bar charts because the *categories* are *numerical*.
- Distribution charts are different from histograms because each number on the horizontal axis is discrete. There are no intervals as there are on the histogram axis.

Interpreting Histograms and Distribution Charts

There is not much interpreting that can happen with a simple distribution chart like that on page 144 because it only has 20 data points total. The more data you have, the more likely it is that the data values used to generate a distribution chart or histogram will start to take on a characteristic shape. The charts in Figure 6.6 (p. 146) show three typical shapes.

The shape of distribution charts and histograms reveals important information about the set of data values they represent:

- In a **normal** distribution (Figure 6.6a, also called a bell-shaped curve), the data are distributed symmetrically around a central peak. Normal curves play an important role in evaluating the results of standardized tests, and are discussed in more detail in the next chapter. (See p. 166.)

- **Bimodal** distribution shows two distinct peaks (Figure 6.6b). The interpretation is that there are two distinct processes at work. For instance, if you saw a bimodal distribution in reading scores, it might be that one subset of students is receiving more tutoring or reading practice than another subset of students.

- When the distribution trails off much more in one direction than another, the shape is called **skewed** (Figure 6.6c). The group shown in the example in Figure 6.6 is skewed with a tail to the left: The data values cluster towards higher values and trail off towards lower values. When compared to a group that showed a normal distribution, this group would be said to be higher-performing.

In addition to interpreting distributions based on their overall shape, you can also use several different types of statistics:

1. Measures of distribution of central tendency: mean, median, mode, and midrange. These provide single numbers that tell you something about where the data values cluster. In practice, they are used to represent how a typical student performs (but as you'll see in the following pages, this is not always a valid use for these measures).
2. Measures of *dispersion*: standard deviation and range. Measures of dispersion indicate the spread of the data.

Statistics and Non-Normal Curves

The *interpretation* of some of the statistics described here (such as standard deviation) is based on having data that are distributed normally (that is, they would form a normal curve when plotted out). Obviously, data that form a skewed or bimodal distribution are not normal, and you have to be careful about how you interpret statistics for such data sets.

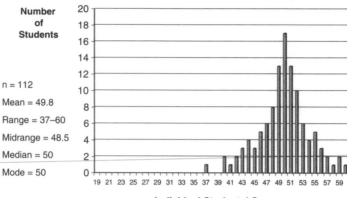

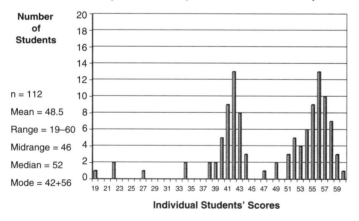

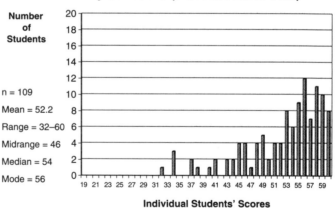

Figure 6.6 (a) Distribution of 3rd grade reading scores for the first elementary school (showing a symmetric *normal* or *bell-shaped* curve); (b) Distribution of 3rd grade reading scores for the second elementary school (showing a distribution with two peaks, called *bimodal*); (c) Distribution of 3rd grade reading scores for the third elementary school (showing an *asymmetric* or *skewed* distribution).

Note. Copyright © 2001 by QLD, LLC. Reprinted with permission.

Raw data: Test scores for 10 sixth graders who took the advanced reading test (listed here in descending order): 98, 93, 87, 85, 85, 75, 71, 69, 68, 50

Measures of Central Tendency

Measure	Example
Arithmetic Mean (average, $\bar{x}$, x-bar) The center point of a group of data. The average of all values is calculated by adding up the values of the data points and dividing the sum by the number of occurrences. The average (mean) might be thought of as a group's typical characteristic, assuming there are no points that fall a great distance from the other points (outliers).	For the data above: Sum of all values = 781 # of occurrences = 10 Mean score = 78.1
Median The mid-point of the data. Half of the data points fall above the median, half fall below. If there is an uneven number of data points, the median is the value of the data that occupies the middle position when the data are ranked in order of size. If there is an even number of data points, the median is the average of the two middle values.	There is an even number of scores, so we add the two middle values, then divide by two. The two middle values are 85 and 75. Median = (85+75)/2 = 80
Midrange The midrange is computed by calculating the figure that lies halfway between the highest and lowest extremes.	Highest score = 98 Lowest score = 50 Midrange = (98 + 50)/2 = 74
Mode The mode is the data value that occurs most frequently in the data set.	85 appears twice, so this number is the mode.

Measures of Dispersion

Measure	Example
Range The simplest measure of dispersion. It is the difference between the highest and lowest data points. It simply tells us the distance between the extremes.	The sixth grade reading scores listed above range from 50 to 98 (a range of 48 points). If a second set of students took the exam, the range would likely be larger or smaller.
Standard Deviation A statistical measure of dispersion that helps you judge the spread of the data. The normal curve spans approximately six standard deviations. Closely grouped data will have relatively small standard deviations and more widely spread-out data will have larger values.	On a test, if the mean is 50 and the standard deviation is 10, a score of 60 falls one standard deviation above the mean.

Note: Measures of central tendency may be similar for data sets, but the picture of the *variation* in each data set might be very different. The three distributions shown on p. 146, for example, all have very similar means, medians, and ranges, but obviously the shapes of the distributions are very different.

Pareto Diagram

. . . .

Pareto of Behavior Referrals

(n = 663)

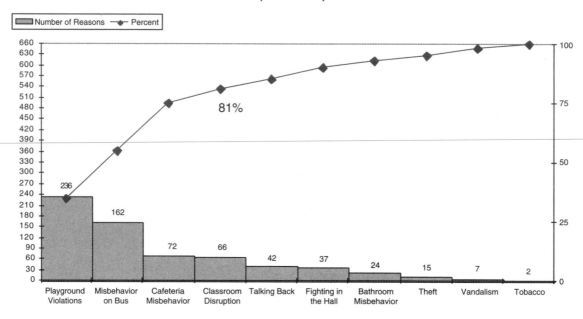

Figure 6.7 Pareto Diagram

Note. Copyright © 2001 by QLD, LLC. Reprinted with permission.

What It Is

- A bar-type chart that shows the frequency or impact of different problems or causes in order from the highest to lowest values. A line shows the cumulative impact of subsequent problems as you move from left to right across the chart (Figure 6.7)
- Shows the relative importance of all the activities, problems, issues, and areas of concern
- Some people find it helpful to think of a Pareto diagram as a hybrid of a bar chart and histogram: It is a bar chart because you are comparing separate, discrete categories of information. It is like a histogram because the categories represent the sum total of the data being analyzed.

Use It When

- You need to focus your actions on high leverage points—the areas that are most likely to yield the greatest results
- You want to choose a place to begin problem solving

How to Do It

1. Use existing data or brainstorm to identify the activities, problems, and issues that you want to compare and rank in order by priority.
2. Select the unit of measurement you're interested in comparing (such as performance on achievement standards, frequency of occurrence, lost instructional time, annual cost, etc.).

3. Gather the necessary data on each problem category either by conducting a new study or by reviewing historical data.
   - Remember to be wary of historical data. You need to make sure that the definitions used at the time are the same as those you are using now. For example, if you are collecting data on different types of behavioral referrals, you must make sure that they were categorized the same way in the past as they are today. Otherwise, the data will be irrelevant to your current situation.
4. List the categories on the horizontal (X) axis and frequencies on the vertical (Y) axis. List the categories in descending order from left to right on the horizontal axis with bars above each category to indicate frequency. The categories containing the fewest items can be combined into an "other" category, which is placed on the extreme right as the last bar.
5. Compare the relative frequency of each category by adding up all observations and determining what percentage of the whole each item represents.
6. Draw the cumulative percentage line showing the portion of the total for each.

Tips

- In most situations, you'll want to create several levels of Pareto diagrams to help you focus as specifically as possible on areas needing attention.
- The most frequent problems are not always the most costly or the most critical. Try to gather data on *impact* or *cost* of various problems, not just counts of their occurrence.
- If frequency is the variable being looked at, it may not be appropriate to ignore some low frequency categories. For example, if there's been only one or two behavioral referrals for carrying a weapon, that doesn't mean that item should be ignored as an area for improvement just because it's not among the vital few in terms of frequency.

Use Pareto *Thinking* Even if You Cannot Create a Pareto Diagram

In many cases, school teams find it difficult to collect data on the issues of greatest interest to them. Try to find some way to rank problems by importance or impact so that you can focus on the most important (vital few).

An Example of Pareto Analysis

In which academic areas are our students struggling the most?

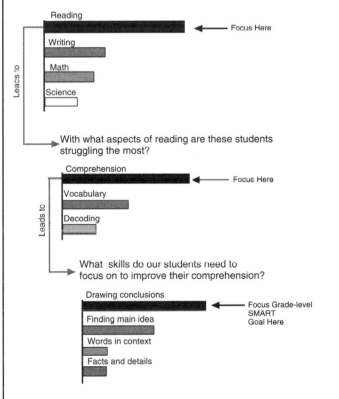

By targeting the most problematic area and progressively breaking it into smaller elements, teachers can focus instruction where the most significant gains can occur.

Scatterplot

....

ACT Scores and GPA

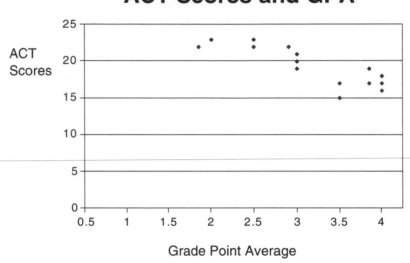

Figure 6.8 Scatterplot showing that there is a negative correlation between GPA and ACT scores. (Many of the highest ACT scores are from students with the lowest GPAs.)

Note. Copyright © 2001 by QLD, LLC. Reprinted with permission.

What It Is

A graph that shows the strength of the relationship between two variables (Figure 6.8)

Use It When

- You want to investigate the relationship between two variables
- You have paired data that *might* have a cause-and-effect relationship
- You have continuous interval (numerical) data for two different variables, both measured on each item/person

Applications

Types of paired data:

- Test scores and attendance
- Class size and student performance
- Dollars invested and student achievement
- Parent involvement and satisfaction with the school
- Class size and reading scores measured for each class
- Behavioral referrals and number of after-school programs offered at each school

How to Do It

1. Record *paired data* (two measures you gather on each item, such as for each student, class, or school).
2. For each pair, determine which of the two you think *might* cause or influence the other. That is the *independent variable*. The other item in the pair is the *dependent variable*. (Caution: Even if the plot reveals a relationship pattern, that does not prove that changes in the independent variable *cause* changes in the dependent variable.)
3. Construct a graphic with a horizontal (X) and vertical (Y) axis.
   - Label the X axis with the intervention (independent variable).
   - Label the Y axis with the effect (dependent variable) you are measuring.
   - Determine appropriate intervals for each type of data and label the axes accordingly.
4. Plot the paired data points.

How to Interpret It

To interpret a scatterplot, you visually determine if there is any pattern in the scatter of data values.

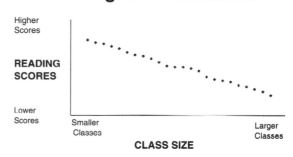

Negative Correlation

Figure 6.9   Negative Correlation: When one variable increases and the other decreases. Example: reading scores and class sizes. (As class size increases, reading scores go down.)

Note. Copyright © 2001 by QLD, LLC. Reprinted with permission.

- There is a negative correlation when one variable increases and the other decreases. In Figure 6.9, as class size increases, reading scores decrease. (Reading scores are higher in smaller classes, and vice versa.)
- There is a positive correlation when the two variables both increase or decrease together.
- There is no correlation if there is no connection between the rise and fall of the two variables.

Correlation Is Not Causation

- Correlation is a measure of the connection or association between two variables. Correlation is a necessary—but not sufficient—condition for establishing a causal relationship between two variables.
- Causality implies correlation; correlation does not imply causality.

- Example: Researchers have found that SAT scores have a relationship to students' grade point average their first year of college. This does not mean that good SAT scores cause students to do well in college. But SAT scores and GPA do seem to be related. There may be a third variable that is causing both SAT scores and GPA to be high.

Disaggregation

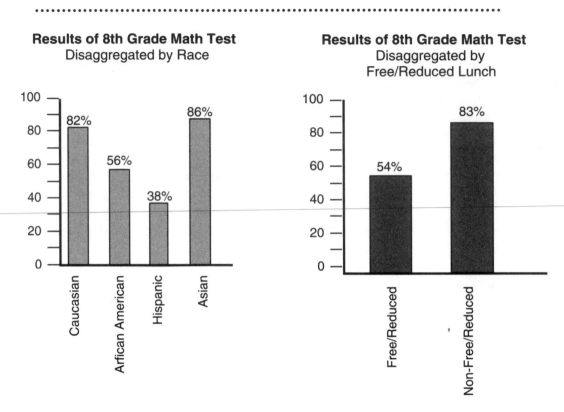

Figure 6.10 Bar Charts Showing Disaggregated Results
Note. Copyright © 2001 by QLD, LLC. Reprinted with permission.

What It Is

The process of separating and then analyzing results achieved by different groups (Figure 6.10)

Use It When

- Identifying differences across subgroups of students in terms of their performance
- Identifying which subgroups, if any, are responding to certain instructional methods differently than others

Applications

- When you are looking at a single measure (test scores, climate surveys, attendance, behavioral referrals, enrollment in special education programs, enrollment in talented and gifted (TAG) programs, climate survey, etc.) and want to better understand the difference between subgroups: Caucasian, African American, Hispanic, Asian, free/reduced lunch, and non-free/reduced lunch, etc.
- When asking are *all* our students able to meet standards and targets?

How to Do It

1. Choose subgroups of interest to your project.
   - Possibilities include general demographic categories: gender, race/ethnicity, income, mobility, etc.
2. Gather the same kind of data within each subgroup.
   - For example, determine how students within those categories are performing on measures of achievement, behavior, etc.
   - Gather data on characteristics of different groups.
3. Display the results by subgroup.
4. Compare subgroups.

Tips

- Make sure the categories being compared are mutually exclusive; that is, they don't duplicate counts and information isn't overlapping.
- Be cautious when drawing conclusions based on differences between groups. Analysis by disaggregation is best done when the measure has been administered in a standardized way and sampling techniques have minimized bias.
- To avoid jumping to conclusions based on demographic characteristics, follow disaggregation analyses with problem solving, using tools and techniques such as 5 Why's analysis, cause-and-effect analysis, and brainstorming.
- If analyzing survey data, be sure to identify demographic variables up front so that you have the information by subgroup when the survey is returned.
- If too few individuals are available to analyze as a subgroup, confidentiality issues can arise.

> **Experience by itself teaches nothing. You must have a theory and you must take action.**
>
> —Dr. W. Edwards Deming

Moving Picture Tools

There are basically two types of moving picture tools: run charts and control charts. They are used to help us understand patterns in the variation over time. Understanding variation allows us to distinguish between important and unimportant changes in process performance (from the standpoint of improvement, that is).

Variation

Variation is how much data values change from one point in time to another. Everything varies: assessment scores, the time it takes to do a task, budget overruns, behavioral referrals, etc. A key to improving results is to reduce variation in the processes that produce those results *and* move the average higher.

Variation comes in two forms: *common cause* and *special cause*.

- **Common cause variation** is created by many small factors present in every process or situation. It is affected by the way the system is designed and managed.

  Examples: teachers who are routinely ill-prepared in their subject areas, students not coming to school ready to learn how to read, or test scores that consistently (and predictably) vary a few points up one year, down another, and so on.

- **Special cause variation** is created by a specific situation, circumstance, or anomaly.

  Examples: test scores dropping several points for 6 years in a row, a school consistently having 20% higher ACT scores than other comparable schools, or a barrage of behavioral referrals after a new behavior policy is put in place.

Processes that have only common cause variation are said to be stable or in control because their behavior is relatively predictable. The *amount* of common cause variation may be more than you'd like, but you can count on a stable process to perform within certain limits, making it relatively easy to predict and plan.

Processes that also have special cause variation are said to be out of control. Their behavior is unpredictable, making it difficult to plan.

Strategies for Reducing Variation

There are different strategies for reducing common cause variation as compared to special cause variation.

- **Common cause strategy:** The only way to reduce common cause variation is to make a fundamental change in the system. You'll need to look at what's happening at *all* times in the process, and use problem-solving strategies to identify process changes (see Chapter 8).

- **Special cause strategy:** Find out what is different in the process when the problem (or desired result) appears. Eliminate the cause, or replicate it if it is a good special cause (for example, an exceptional teaching practice). Note that simply removing special causes usually does not lead to dramatic improvement—it will only return the system to predictability.

An understanding of variation will fundamentally change how you define problems. For one thing, you'll discover that most variation is caused by factors inherent in the system (common causes). The only way to affect that variation is to change the system.

An understanding of variation will also change how you perceive solutions. Once you realize that fundamental system changes are needed to produce fundamentally different results, you begin to realize the futility of actions such as raising standards and simply exhorting everyone to work harder. You'll also begin to see that tinkering with a system is more likely to increase variation than reduce it. These types of changes do not fundamentally affect the system, and therefore cannot lead to improvement.

"Don't Tinker" Does Not Mean "Don't Innovate"

The key message in working with variation is that you have to understand what factors influence variation in order to make any significant improvement. The lesson is that you shouldn't make random changes in a process hoping for better results. But that doesn't mean you should stop changing a process entirely. There is still room for innovation and experimentation, as long as you are prepared to monitor the effects of these actions and make sure they have not made the situation worse.

Run Chart

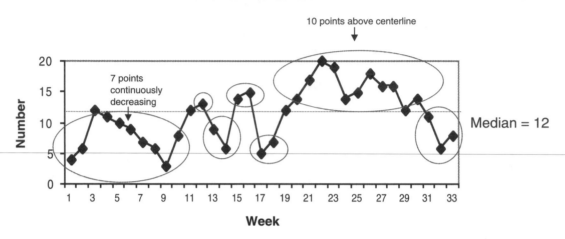

Behavior Referrals

Figure 6.11 Run Chart for Behavior Referrals Showing Special Causes. (Note: This chart depicts simulated data. In the real world, you would look at all your data at the first sign of a special cause and apply your own knowledge to what might be happening.)

Note. Copyright © 2001 by QLD, LLC. Reprinted with permission.

What It Is

A chart of data where points are plotted in time order, and tests are performed to determine whether the variation is due to special or common causes (Figure 6.11)

Use It When

- You want to monitor performance over time
- You want to understand the pattern of variation over time

Applications

- To detect trends, shifts, or cycles
- To decide what type of improvement strategy to use

How to Do It

1. Gather at least seven data points—and preferably more—over time (the same measure, preferably taken at regular intervals, such as weekly, monthly, or quarterly).
2. Construct a horizontal (X) and vertical (Y) axis.
3. Label the time intervals along the X axis. Divide the Y axis into equal-sized intervals that cover a range slightly larger than the range of actual data values.
4. Plot the data in time order.
5. Determine the median (mid-point). Draw a line at this value on the chart. (This becomes the *centerline.*)

6. Perform the tests for special causes (see page 158) and determine whether the variation is due to common or special causes.
   - If any *one* of the criteria is met, then the process is exhibiting special cause variation. You should look for what was different when the problem occurred.
   - If none of the criteria is met, you are dealing with common cause variation. You need to engage in problem solving to identify fundamental changes that will lead to improvement.

Tips

- In many educational circles, three data points going in the same direction is considered a trend. Based on what we know about special and common cause variation, interpreting and acting on results based on just three data points may actually lead to more variation, creating even worse results.
- Because you need many data points to construct and interpret a run chart, this tool lends itself well to measures that are taken quite often in a school's or classroom's cycle (for example, attendance, classroom quizzes, homework assignments turned in, discipline referrals, and medications). Less-frequent measures can also be plotted, however, if you have enough data points (for example, average ACT scores, average graduation rates, college or job placement rates, etc.).
- Changing a measure or assessment will usually change the results. A run chart is a useful tool to use to communicate these changes. A good example of this is when a state increases the standard that students must achieve to pass proficiency levels on a state test (the run chart will show a special cause drop in the overall context of historical variation).

A Run Chart by Any Other Name

Because run charts depict data in time order, they are often called *time plots*. The name run chart derives from one of the tests for special causes (see p. 158).

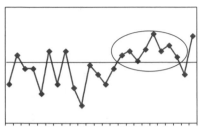

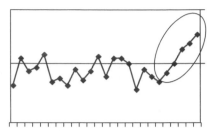

Eight or more points in a run above (or below) the centerline

Six or more points continuously increasing (or decreasing)

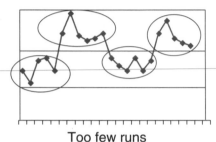

Too few runs

Up-down sawtooth pattern

Figure 6.12   Criteria for Special Causes

Note. Copyright © 2001 by QLD, LLC. Reprinted with permission.

Using the Runs Table

To use the Runs Table, first count the runs in your data. A run is a set of data points that are together on one side of the median. Each time the data cross the median, a new run is created. (Note: You can have a run of just 1 data point.) Then count the total number of data that are not on the median.

Next, go to the Runs Table (p. 267) and locate the number of data that are not on the median. Then, to the right of that number, locate the least number of runs expected, and the most number of runs expected.

If your data set has fewer or more runs than expected, you have a special cause. If not, you are looking at common cause variation.

Interpreting Run Charts: Patterns That Indicate Special Cause Variation

The following rules are standards followed by statisticians to identify special cause variation as illustrated in Figure 6.12:

- Too few or too many runs for the number of data points
  - A **run** is a group of data points below or above the median. Each time the data crosses the median, a new run begins. There can be runs of only one data point if the next data point then crosses the median.
  - Use the Runs Table (see Appendix, p. 267) and the sidebar to help you count runs and take appropriate action.
- Six data points *continuously* increasing or decreasing
- Eight or more data points all together either above or below the median indicating *too few runs*
- Fourteen or more data points in an up-down *sawtooth* pattern

Control Chart

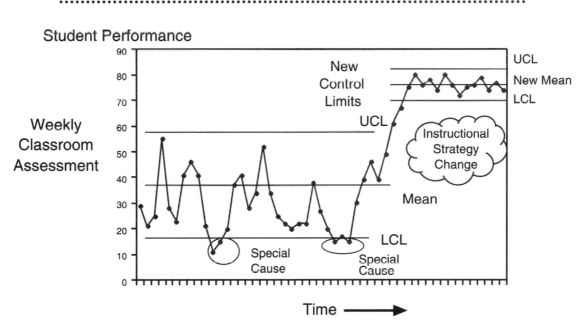

Figure 6.13 Control Chart of demonstrated results of instructional change. Note: These are actual data from a classroom. However, it was not charted at the time it occurred, so the earlier special causes were not detected.

Note. Copyright © 2001 by QLD, LLC. Reprinted with permission.

What It Is

A run chart that also indicates the range of variation built into the system (indicated by *control limits* added to the chart) (Figure 6.13)

Use It When

- You want to find out whether a particular data point is truly outside the normal range of variation for the system
- You want to demonstrate that the action you took resulted in not only improved performance, but less variability around performance (more students doing better)

Applications

- Plot your school's prior and current test results, behavioral data (e.g., attendance, referrals), or classroom assessment results to see if there are significant trends.
- Monitor the impact of an instructional strategy, a specific curriculum, or program intervention on student achievement. Plot results seen *before* the change, and then plot results obtained *after* the change. Apply all the tests for special causes to see if there is a significant change (up or down) in achievement after the change.

How to Do It

1. List all the data points in time order.
2. Calculate the *moving range* (R) between each two adjacent numbers.
   - The moving range is the difference between adjacent numbers. For example:

Data Points	Range Between Adjacent Points (= Moving Range)
12	
10	2
13	3
5	8

3. Calculate the average of the moving ranges ($\bar{R}$).
   - The average is the sum of all moving ranges divided by the number of moving ranges. For example, in the data set shown above, the average of the moving ranges is 4.3 (13 divided by 3).
4. Calculate the average of the data points ($\bar{X}$).
   - The average is the sum of all the data points divided by the number of data points.
   - In the example above, the average is 10 (40 divided by 4).
5. Calculate the upper control limit.
   UCL = $\bar{X}$ + 2.66$\bar{R}$
   UCL = average of the data points +
   (2.66 × average of the ranges)
   In the example above,
   UCL = 10 + (2.66 × 4.3)
   UCL = 21.44
6. Calculate the lower control limit.
   LCL = $\bar{X}$ − 2.66$\bar{R}$
   LCL = average of the data points −
   (2.66 × average of the ranges)
   In the example above,
   LCL = 10 − (2.66 × 4.3)
   LCL = −1.44

7. Plot all the data points in time order.
8. Draw a line on the plot at the mean (average, $\bar{X}$).
9. Draw in the upper and lower control limits.
10. Apply the tests for special causes and interpret the chart.
    - In addition to the tests described for run charts (p. 158), look for any points outside the control limits. Points beyond the limits provide an additional signal of special cause variation.

Tips

- You should have at least 18 data points before performing the calculations that add control limits to a run chart.
- The 2.66 number is a statistical number that roughly corresponds to a standard deviation. The control limit calculations provided here are for a type of control chart called an *individuals chart*. An individuals chart is the right control chart to use when you have relatively slow-cycling data, such as test scores, behavior referrals, attendance figures, etc. There are also *p* (proportion) charts and *c* (count) charts for other situations.

Modifications

- You can use control charts with data that are not time-ordered, but in that case the ONLY special cause test that applies is whether a point is outside the control limits. For example, you could plot the test results from many schools and determine the range of variation to see if any of those schools were outside the limits (truly under- or over-achieving). Other special cause tests, shown on page 155, all deal with data that are time-ordered.

 A worksheet for computing control limits appears on the CD-ROM.

Summary

Instead of feeling drowned in data and starved for information, we can move toward making meaning of data by asking ourselves, "What do we need to know? How can we best find out?" Then we can select the appropriate data tool for gathering, analyzing, and interpreting the data. With data in hand, we need to once again ask, "What more do we need to know? How can we best find out?" In this way, we become better informed as decision-makers, more knowledgeable about our systems and our practices, and better able to make improvements on behalf of our students.

Final Check: Understanding Problems and Improving Results

My team probes for the underlying causes of problems through

✓ 5 Why's analysis

✓ Cause-and-effect diagrams

✓ Relations diagrams

My team uses a variety of tools for analyzing numerical data, getting both a snapshot of the current situation and a moving picture that shows the history of performance by using

✓ Bar charts

✓ Histograms

✓ Distribution charts

✓ Pareto diagrams

✓ Scatterplots

✓ Disaggregation

✓ Run charts

✓ Control charts

My team realizes how important it is to understand *variation* when choosing appropriate reactions to problems in the workplace.

Chapter 7
Tools for Measuring Student Performance

Measuring student performance is not just about collecting data. Measurement—or assessment—should make a difference. Assessments that make a difference are used for the purposes for which they were designed, and their results are focused at the appropriate level for improvement action. The overall assessment program should be balanced, providing well-designed, multiple assessment strategies and ongoing staff development to ensure a high probability that results will increase educational effectiveness.

In this chapter, we'll look at the two main types of assessments in use in schools today:

- Standardized assessments (norm- and criterion-referenced)
- Curriculum-embedded assessments (performance assessments, portfolios, and student self-assessments)

Standardized Assessments

Standardized assessment tests are mass-produced and mass-administered. Developed to measure student progress on national or state standards, they broadly sample a student's knowledge in a subject and/or skill area, and are used to provide data for comparisons between students, schools, and districts. The goal of standardization is to ensure that all students are assessed under uniform conditions so that interpretation of their performance is comparable and not influenced by differing conditions.

When used for the purposes for which they were designed, standardized test results can be a useful way to start the conversation about improvement:

- The results can provide a broad picture of how groups of students are performing compared to other districts, or within the student population, and how disaggregated subgroups of students are doing relative to other subgroups.

> Everything that can be counted isn't worth counting, and everything that is worth counting isn't always countable.
>
> —Albert Einstein

Communicating With Reporters, Parents, and the Community About Standardized Testing

1. Include an opening paragraph that provides highlights about the district's complete assessment program and where standardized testing fits into the overall system. Emphasize the importance of having multiple measures of student learning in order to get a complete picture. Clarify the purposes of standardized testing in general.

2. When communicating about a specific test, answer the following questions:
   - What is it called and who created it?
   - What are its uses and purposes?
   - What are the stated objectives?
   - When is it administered in the district?
     - At what grade levels, on what dates, how much time it takes to administer and complete, who is excluded from taking the test, and support for those who need extra assistance
   - When do results come back?
   - How are data reported?
     - Percentile ranks, stanines, standard scores, and proficiency categories (provide definitions and examples of each)

(Sidebar continued on page 165)

- When tracked over time, results can be used to analyze patterns, generate hypotheses, and create strategic plans.
- The results also provide feedback on a district's curriculum; results can point out areas of weakness, which can then be improved.

Standardized tests are *not* the best method of improving instruction; identifying at-risk, gray area, or underachieving students; or giving feedback on individual student learning to parents, students, and teachers. However, when used in combination with other forms of assessment, they do provide one more piece of the overall puzzle.

There are two types of standardized tests: norm-referenced and criterion-referenced.

Norm-Referenced Tests

When we want to compare how our students are performing *relative to another group*, we say that the data are *norm-referenced*. That means that the test data have been converted to the *normal curve* so that scores can be compared to a larger population of test takers. In principle, the sample size of the test takers is large enough and the sampling procedures have been pure enough that results approximate the general population—and so fall into a normal (bell-shaped) curve. Any subsample taken from that larger pool of data can be understood and compared using standard scores and positions. Norm-referenced tests allow schools to compare their students' scores with national and/or state scores from pre-selected same-age groups. Results are reported in raw numbers, percentiles, and standard scores.

To understand norm-referenced tests, you need to first understand the *normal curve* (p. 166) and four types of measures used to describe a set of data values:

1. Measures of *central tendency*: including mean, median, and mode (see p. 147)
2. Measures of *dispersion*: standard deviation and range (described on p. 147)
3. Measures of *distribution*: tools that condense data into a manageable form showing how data values are distributed throughout the range (histograms/distribution charts) (described in Chapter 6)
4. Measures of *position*: measures that reflect the position of a given result relative to its position along the normal curve (quartiles, stanines, etc.). See p. 167.

Note that three of these measures have already been discussed in Chapter 6. The focus here will be on the normal curve and the measures of position.

 Tips

- Some measures of central tendency are sensitive to extreme data points (points that fall far outside of the majority). Always include some indication of the dispersion/variability of the data.
- Much is lost when you group data into a single data point like a mean and then try to generalize from it. Do so with caution!

(Sidebar continued from page 164)

- What is important about the test scores?
- What is a significant change or difference?
- Are there particular scores to which we should pay attention? Are there particular groups of students or certain types of curriculum we're targeting for improvement?
- How are the test data used?
  - How will the district/school use it?
  - How will the teachers use it?
  - How will parents use it?
  - How will students use it?

Source: Wisconsin Assessment Consortium, 1997. Adapted with permission.

Norm- and Criterion-Referenced Tests

Norm- and criterion-referenced tests are two entirely different ways of judging performance, and they don't easily translate to each other. However, sometimes norm-referenced scores are used to establish criterion for the purpose of accountability cut-offs.

Both criterion- and norm-referenced tests should be administered in a standardized manner.

The Normal Curve

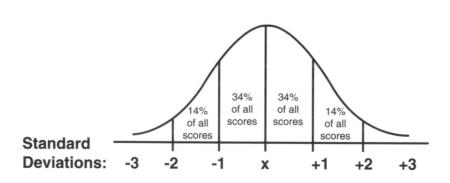

Figure 7.1 The Normal Curve
Note. Copyright © 2001 by QLD, LLC. Reprinted with permission.

What It Is

A bell-shaped graph (Figure 7.1) that shows the symmetrical dispersion of data around a central peak

Special Properties

- It is representative of the general population.
- It is *symmetrical.* The area to the left of the mean (x) equals the area to the right of the mean.
- The tails never quite touch the baseline, but continue to approach it as the curve moves away from the mean.
- All the *measures of central tendency* (mode, median, and mean) are the same value. (See p. 147.)
- The height of the curve at any given point denotes the frequency of scores at that point.

Application

Norm-referenced data are reported using standard scores such as stanines and positional measures such as quartiles and percentiles (p. 167). Typically, reports include national, state, and local norms. (See Figure 7.2.)

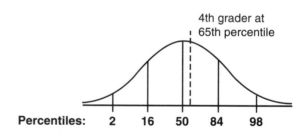

Figure 7.2 This 4th grader did better than 65% of the 4th-grade test takers.
Note. Copyright © 2001 by QLD, LLC. Reprinted with permission.

Tips

- Once people understand the theory behind the normal curve, they can understand sampling theory, percentiles, stanines, and standard scores on norm-referenced measures.
- Local norms would be presented as a normal curve, so half of the students in the district are above the midpoint, the other half are below, even if—compared to the national norms—the majority of students fall above or below the 50th percentile.

Measures of Position for Norm-Referenced Tests

Results of norm-referenced tests can be reported in a variety of ways depending on which measure of position is used as the reference point. The following table shows some of the common reference points related to norm-referenced tests:

Measure of Position	Example
Standard Scores A standard score is simply any raw score that has been redefined in terms of a standard, constant mean and a standard, constant standard deviation (p. 147).	• SAT scores are standard scores with a mean of 500 and a standard deviation of 100. ACT scores have a mean of 20 and a standard deviation of 5.
Stanines A standard score widely used on standardized tests. Stanines slice the normal curve into nine categories, with a mean of 5 and a standard deviation of 1.96.	• A stanine score of 7, 8, or 9 falls into the top 30% of the normal curve, representing above average performance.
Quartiles Numbers that divide the ranked data into quarters; each set of data has three quartiles. The upper limit of the *first quartile* is the number at which 1/4 of all the scores fall below that value. At the upper limit of the *second quartile,* half of the data points fall below that number (the value of the second quartile is also the median value). The *third quartile* is the number for which 3/4 of the population earned a lower score.	• Twenty-five percent of the population will fall into each quartile. When reading your local results, you will use the national scores at each quartile to determine the percent of your students in each.
Percentiles Percentiles are numbers that divide a set of ranked data into 100 parts; each set of data has 99 percentiles. The logic is the same as for quartiles. At the 90th percentile, 90 percent of the population earned a lower score.	• If a student's score places him or her at the 98th percentile, he or she scored better than 98% of the test takers in the population.

Criterion-Referenced Tests

Criterion-referenced tests are designed to identify what a student knows in relation to specific objectives. Standards-based, criterion-referenced assessments allow schools to compare how students do against a predetermined, specified standard of performance.

Criterion-referenced standards can be expressed as

- **Numbers:** percent of students meeting or exceeding a particular score
- **Categorical descriptors:** percent of students demonstrating minimal, basic, proficient, or advanced levels of performance
- **Rubric:** numbers of students scoring at each level on a performance test

Figure 7.3 shows results from three different types of criterion-referenced tests.

Note: Curriculum-embedded criterion-referenced comparisons, also called *rubrics*, are used to evaluate student work and inform the teaching-learning process. You can find more information on developing rubrics on page 175.

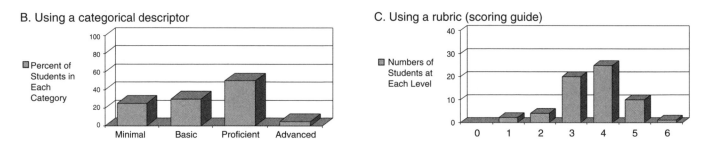

Figure 7.3 Criterion-Referenced Comparisons
Note. Copyright © 2001 by QLD, LLC. Reprinted with permission.

Criterion-Referenced Test

What It Is

A test designed to identify what a student knows in relation to specific objectives

Use It When

- Valid and reliable cut-off points have been identified that clearly and accurately describe levels of performance
  - For example: advanced, proficient, basic, and minimal; above standard, at standard, and below standard; level I, II, III, IV; and so on
- You want to diagnose students' strengths and weaknesses with regard to specific content areas
- You want to identify areas of the curriculum that may need improvement

How to Do It

Constructing a criterion-referenced standards-based test is time-consuming, exacting, and complex. Each of the steps described require extensive collaboration:

1. Identify the purpose for which the scores will be used (to diagnose students' strengths and weaknesses, to monitor student achievement on standards, to certify whether or not students have met academic standards, etc.).
2. Define the content or performance that will be measured on the test.
3. Choose the formats of the test (multiple choice, short answer, essay, etc.), and decide what proportion of the test to devote to each.
4. Write initial test questions. Review them with experts and a sample of students. Revise the test.
5. Pilot the test with a sample of students to check for clarity and understanding of the questions. (This is a trial run of the test's validity.) Statistically analyze the responses to assess which questions do the best job of distinguishing levels of proficiency.
6. Conduct reliability and validity studies of the test. (See an assessment expert for assistance.)
7. Develop directions for administration of the test and interpretation of results.

Advantages Over Norm-Referenced Tests

- Do not need a large population of test takers (to build a reference base)
- Can more easily differentiate levels of performance (compared to norm referenced) for individual students, so follow-up actions are more targeted

Disadvantages Compared to Norm-Referenced Tests

The scoring process is more complex than with norm-referenced tests because scoring standards are more subjective.

> We should be doing assessment *of* learning and *for* learning.
>
> —Rick Stiggens

Curriculum-Embedded Assessments

Teachers know that many student accomplishments can't be measured using typical tests. Yet still they need some means to assess, track, and communicate evidence of student progress toward standards, benchmarks, and SMART goals.

Curriculum-embedded assessments are measurement tools that assess the complete range of thinking and learning. Often the assessments are so embedded in ongoing instruction, it would be difficult for an outside observer to tell that assessment is occurring. These types of assessment tools provide students with information to make adjustments to their learning strategies. They also provide teachers with the kind of in-process feedback they need in order to make ongoing adjustments to their instructional strategies. Waiting until the end of the school year to see a student's standardized test results is just too late: Teachers, students, and parents need feedback throughout the year.

There are three types of curriculum-embedded assessment tools:

- **Performance assessment** where students are asked to demonstrate their skills and knowledge (p. 171)
- **Portfolio assessment** where a student's work is gathered in one place (p. 173)
- **Student self-assessment** where students are asked to assess their own performance against selected criteria (p. 174)

Characteristics of Curriculum-Embedded Assessments

- The assessment is authentic in that it mirrors real-world use or involves a real problem-solving situation.
- It reflects the student's interests and experiences, and is interesting enough that students want to demonstrate their highest levels of performance.
- It is a positive learning experience and is seen by the participants as worthwhile.
- It includes a rubric and scoring guide (p. 175) that is known and understood by everyone—especially the learner—before the assessment is given.
- It includes student reflection on their thinking processes.
- It includes hands-on, manipulative materials, and information that the students collect, interpret, analyze, and apply to the problem.

Performance Assessment

What It Is

An assessment that asks students to demonstrate their skills and knowledge.

Use It When

- You want to deepen a student's knowledge of a subject area
- You want to understand whether a student has mastered a skill, set of skills, or knowledge base

Application

After learning how to make estimates and graph results, students in a 5th-grade class created paper airplanes for which they estimated flight time and distance, then graphed results. See the Airplane Rubric on page 268 of the Appendix.

How to Do It

1. Define what you want students to know and be able to do as a result of the teaching process. Identify learning outcomes in one or more categories:
   - Declarative knowledge—facts, concepts, principles, and generalizations
   - Procedural knowledge—skills, processes, and strategies
   - Attitudes, values, habits of mind—how students need to act toward others, toward their own learning, etc.
2. Identify the purpose and audience for the assessment:
   - Why are we assessing? for what purpose? (e.g., diagnosis of student skills, to know the impact of instruction, or to get data for SMART goals)
   - Who will use the assessment information?
   - How will the assessment information be used? (e.g., on a student report card, for student reflection, in a teacher's SMART goals portfolio, or in a school improvement plan)
3. Select a performance assessment method that matches the learning outcome (i.e., don't use multiple choice for assessing ability to write a persuasive essay).
   - Constructed response: Assessment requires fill in the blank, short answer, the labeling of a diagram, showing work, and visual representation (e.g., graph, illustration, flowchart)
   - Products: Students produce tangible indicators of the application of their knowledge and skills (e.g., essay, research paper, log/journal, lab report, story/play, poem, portfolio, art exhibit, science project, model, video/audiotape, spreadsheet)

An assessment that asks students to demonstrate their skills and knowledge...

- Performances: Teachers observe students demonstrating their skills and knowledge through performances that mirror actual performances in the outside world (e.g., oral presentation, dance/movement, science lab demonstration, athletic competition, dramatic reading, debate, musical recital)
- Process focused: Teachers interact with students to assess students' learning strategies and thinking processes (through interviewing, observation, conference, learning log)

4. Develop rubrics to score performance assessments. (See p. 175.)

Advantages Over Other Assessment Tools

- Provides immediate information about a student's progress
- Helps identify underachieving students early on
- Provides detailed information to parents
- Provides invaluable information to students so learning can be adjusted/refocused
- Provides immediately useful information to teachers so that instruction can be adjusted

Disadvantages Compared to Other Assessment Tools

- Time intensive to design, assess, and score
- Can be difficult to score consistently, across all students' performances

Tip

Alternative assessments can also be standardized when consistent procedures are used for constructing, administering, and scoring. When they are standardized, summary data from students' progress across the district can be compared and analyzed.

> Good assessment tools should demonstrate item by item and objective by objective correspondance to district standards, expectations, and curriculum.
>
> —Linda Darling-Hammond

Portfolio Assessment

What It Is

A purposeful collection of student work in one place that demonstrates student progress over time

Use It When

- You want to help students reflect on their development as thinkers, learners, and creators of quality work
- You want to visually communicate student progress over time to students and parents

How to Do It

- First, clarify the purpose of the assessment and the criteria for selection.
- Using portfolios as part of an integrated assessment system is more a process of experimentation than a lock-step recipe. Ideally, teachers should collaboratively decide what student work to sample as benchmarks: what kinds of work, which assignments, and when they will be collected. Involving students in the process of selection after careful discussion of criteria encourages self-reflection in students as well as a sense of pride of ownership and quality.
- Two types of work samples are usually included in portfolios: **core** and **individualized** items. Core items show growth of the quality of student work over time. Individualized items are more personal, showing unique characteristics of the student and the classroom activities engaged in over the year. Core items might include essays, mathematical problem solving, and science labs; individual items might include journal reflections on how the student felt about the work.
- Consider using developmental guidelines and checklists that are based on national standards and knowledge of child development. Tie these in with carefully defined rubrics (p. 175), and work with students to help them select the best pieces to include in their portfolio.
- Both teachers and students grow in the process of portfolio development. Questions become more sophisticated as skills and knowledge develop. For example, at the beginning of a year a teacher might ask a student, "What piece of writing did you like best?" By the end of the year, a teacher could ask, "Which piece of writing is most persuasive?" or "Which piece flows in the most organized and logical way?"

Tips

- Don't use portfolios to compare one student to another.
- Establishing clear criteria (using rubrics) for selection of pieces to include is key.
- Keep portfolios separate from daily or weekly work folders.
- Consider storage needs because video, audio, drawings, and other modes of expression may need to be stored (but also consider using CD-ROMs to store portfolio information).

Student Self-Assessment

What It Is

Evaluations where students judge their own learning and/or performance

Use It When

- You are looking for ways to grow students' lifelong learning skills so that they will become more independent learners
- You want to engage and involve students at any grade level (even kindergarten) in assessing their own learning
- You want to increase student learning in areas where they must demonstrate particular skills (such as writing assignments, music, art, physical performances, lab experiments, etc.)

How to Do It

1. Develop rubrics (p. 175) that will help students know what the targets are. Establish proficiency levels with clear examples to demonstrate what each level looks like.
2. Educate students in the proficiency levels.
3. Have students regularly assess their performance against the established rubrics.
4. Hold conferences with each student as part of the ongoing classroom instruction so that they get into a habit of assessing their own work and getting feedback on their perceptions.

Tips

- Students need clear criteria against which to evaluate themselves.
- Teacher conferences and feedback are critical for accurate self-assessment.
- When students have clear criteria and coaching, and are able to be part of the selection process, their ability to critically self-reflect increases.

R u b r i c

	Novice	Apprentice	Proficient	Distinguished
awareness of audience/ purpose	(face)	(face)	(face)	(face)
idea development	huh?	O.K. I see but I need more.	Very clear message	Beautiful message
organization	loose pieces	Some ideas fit together. Need more pieces.	Ideas fit together.	Special fit
sentences wording	And the dog.	I like my dog. I love my dog.	My favorite thing about Snoopy is his friendly bark.	Snoopy, with his friendly bark, wiggles all over when he's happy to see me.
surface features	(uses)	(uses) . ?	(uses) . ? ! " "	(uses) . ? ! " " ..

Figure 7.4 Elementary Writing Rubric, Designed by the Classroom Teacher
Note: Provided by American Learning Systems. Author unknown.

What It Is

A set of agreed-on definitions or representations of different levels of student achievement or skill (Figure 7.4)

Use It When

- Proficiency at a given skill is difficult to assess through regular or standardized testing practices
- Students could benefit from having clear expectations about what will be assessed and the standards needing to be met *before* their performance is assessed
- You want to increase scoring consistency with multiple assessors

Application

Students were taught how to use a six-trait writing rubric to improve their written work. This tool was used at every student-teacher writing conference and also used to help the students build writing portfolios.

How to Do It

1. Collaborate with other teachers to examine student work together. Focus on a particular assignment that all the students have done.
2. Identify how the particular discipline associated with the student assignment (language arts, math, science, art, music, etc.) defines quality performance for a particular age group(s). Review the standards (content and performance) in that discipline's area, and involve teachers highly skilled in that area and experienced with that age group.
   - If possible, gather samples of criteria (from standards-based tests and curriculum-embedded rubrics) from other schools, districts, etc. Review these as models that can be adapted.
3. Select different examples from the students' work that reflect a range of performance levels.
4. Use the examples to help you decide how you want to describe levels of performance: qualitative descriptions, rating scores, proficiencies, etc.
   - Talk together about the characteristics of the work samples you chose: What distinguishes a good from a poor sample?
   - Decide how many levels of performance you will use and what criteria you will use to describe each level.

5. Capture the descriptions in writing by level.
6. Develop examples of the various levels (adapt the selected examples of students' work as needed for each level).
7. Test and improve the criteria.
   - Gather another sample of students' work and score these as a group to see if the criteria help make accurate judgments. This is a check on the rubric's reliability—can multiple evaluators make the same decision about the work?
   - Make improvements in the descriptions.
   - Test again until you get reliable results from different evaluators.
8. If you will be having students use the rubrics for self-evaluations, test them on selected students as well. Revise as necessary. If using anchor papers to show what is meant by the criteria on the rubric, be sure the anchor students' confidentiality and anonymity are protected.

Tips

- Examples of performance can be captured with anchor papers that serve as a standard against which other papers or performances can be judged. For example, in a math problem-solving performance assessment, anchor papers are selected from students' actual work, each exemplifying different levels of quality (1, 2, 3, etc.).
- Holistic scoring uses a scoring rubric and/or anchor papers to assign a single, overall score to a performance.
- Analytical scoring breaks skills/performances into discrete units and assigns a score to each.

Final Check: Measuring Student Performance

✓ My team understands the appropriate uses for standardized assessments and curriculum-embedded assessments.

✓ We have reviewed the properties of the normal curve and understand the various measures used to describe a set of data or individual data points (such as the measures of central tendency, distribution, dispersion, and position).

✓ We use norm-referenced tests to compare our students' performance against other groups.

✓ We use criterion-referenced tests to compare individual student performance against pre-determined criteria or objectives.

✓ We use performance assessments, portfolios, and student self-assessments to evaluate skill proficiency.

✓ We know how to develop rubrics.

Chapter 8
The Benefits of Thinking Like a System

Each year the farmer entered his corn in the state fair where it won a blue ribbon. One year a newspaper reporter interviewed him and learned something interesting about how he grew it. The reporter discovered that the farmer shared his seed corn with his neighbors. "How can you afford to share your best seed corn with your neighbors when they are entering corn in competition with yours each year?" the reporter asked. "Why sir," said the farmer, "didn't you know? The wind picks up pollen from the ripening corn and swirls it from field to field. If my neighbors grow inferior corn, cross-pollination will steadily degrade the quality of my corn. If I am to grow good corn, I must help my neighbors grow good corn." He is very much aware of the connectedness of life. His corn cannot improve unless his neighbor's corn also improves. So it is in other dimensions.

—James Bender, author of How to Talk Well[1]

"If I am to grow good corn, I must help my neighbors grow good corn."

The farmer in Bender's anecdote illustrates a principle that's known as *systems thinking*, a focus on optimizing performance for the system as a whole, often by working across traditional boundaries. We know from research that higher quality learning and teaching result when schools operate like a system rather than a "heap of pieces." They achieve more when teams—not just individuals—are learning together, when the school as a whole is focused on a common mission and vision, and when professional development is aligned and congruent with that focus. We know that for most schools the ability to be effective is directly related to the larger district's effectiveness and efficiency. In short, we know the power of thinking and acting like a system.

The principles, tools, and methods described in this chapter and throughout this book lay the groundwork to help your school start thinking like a system.

[1]Bender, J. (1963). *How to talk well.* New York: McGraw-Hill.

> Upon this gifted age, in its dark hour, falls from the sky a meteoric shower of facts . . . they lie unquestioned, uncombined. Wisdom enough to leech us of our ill is daily spun, but there exists no loom to weave it into fabric.
>
> —Edna St. Vincent Millay

What Is a System?

A *system* is a collection of parts that interact to function as a whole. One truism concerning a system is that it cannot be divided to get identical separate parts; a heap of parts can. For example, a pile of sand can be divided and you will have two piles of sand. A horse, however, will not be two separate horses if divided!

Another truism about a system is that each part continually affects the others over time. For example, what happens with your registration process today could affect learning tomorrow. If a student couldn't get into a course that lays the foundation for getting into AP classes (which would likely lead to higher SAT and ACT scores), this could, in turn, affect whether a student goes on to college.

Thinking Like a System

Systems thinking is a way of thinking and talking about the forces and interrelationships that shape the behavior of systems. Someone who is a systems thinker can see four levels operating at the same time:

1. Events
2. Patterns of behavior
3. Systemic structures
4. Mental models

Events and Patterns of Behavior

We are all accustomed to perceiving *events* in isolation: we would not necessarily see a connection between a disruptive third-grade class one day and a rambunctious kindergarten a week later. Each teacher would deal with the problems in their own classes separately.

A systems thinker, however, would look for trends and patterns across traditional boundaries. For example, a principal who is a systems thinker might ask the following questions: What is the cause of this behavior in the two classrooms? What do the classrooms have in common? Do other classrooms have this same characteristic? Am I seeing disengaged learning, a lack of consistent behavior expectations, or new teachers struggling for classroom management? Am I seeing this in other parts of our school? What policies, procedures, practices, and processes might be leading to this behavior?

Doing so can expose deeply rooted problems that can surface in a variety of guises. Being able to see the underlying problem lets a systems thinker identify improvements that have far-reaching impact. Variation tools, such as run and control charts (pp. 156–160), are designed to help us see those patterns and trends when our intuition and perceptions cannot. The Historygram process (p. 218) is a way to identify patterns in human relationships.

Another tool for understanding patterns and cycles is a **feedback loop**. Feedback loops drive everything that changes through time. Most people think in linear, non-feedback terms—they see a problem, decide on an action, expect a result, and think that's the end of the problem (Figure 8.1).

Figure 8.1   Linear Thinking
Note. Copyright © 2001 by QLD, LLC. Reprinted with permission.

A systems thinker understands that in reality an action produces a result that in turn creates future problems and actions—with no beginning or end, only a constant dynamic interaction (Figure 8.2).

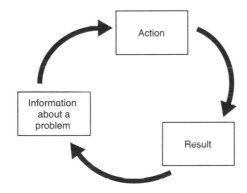

Figure 8.2   Systems Thinking
Note. Copyright © 2001 by QLD, LLC. Reprinted with permission.

Every action and change in the world occurs within a network of feedback loops. Understanding feedback loops is essential to understanding and managing change. Among other things, thinking in terms of feedback loops helps you anticipate unintended consequences to a proposed change. For example, suppose a school considered a simple change in its lunchroom policy. They would have to think carefully to make sure that the change wouldn't cause students to opt out of the hot lunch program, because having fewer students participating could lead to budget problems, recess problems, and perhaps even health issues for the students.

To understand feedback systems, what you need to know is that every system is made up of two variables—**levels** and **rates**:

- *Level* is how much (accumulation)
- *Rate* is how fast (the flow)

In filling a bathtub, the water is the level, while the *flow of the water* is the rate that changes the level. In other examples: a group's degree of frustration is a level that changes in response to the changing surrounding pressures; a school's budget is a level that changes in response to changing state funding policies; a school's average test scores are at a level that changes with the focus on results-oriented school improvement and staff development. Feedback loops can be developed in multiple layers to describe a system's interactions, and thereby better understand a pattern of events.

Consider this real-life example of level and rate interactions in a school district: A district has been under-investing in staff for years (a *rate* of investment). Teacher salaries are low; there is little staff development once teachers are on the job; teachers and schools have been left to their own devices (producing a lower than desired *level* of performance). In short, there has been no system for improving the quality of the teaching-learning process. Over the course of many years, student achievement has continued to decline (a low performance *level*). Over those same years, as parents have talked to other parents, families have begun moving out of the district and/or choose to send their children elsewhere (an increasing *rate* of abandonment). The district has lost over 60% of its students over 10 years (*level*). Scores have continued to decline (*level*). With the loss of students comes the loss of resources, resulting in the district cutting staff development even more (a decreasing *rate* of investment in staff development). The district is now officially in a state of crisis (a low *level* of performance).

Here's another example: A school team convened to look at programming options for the following year. As the team explored the possibilities for introducing new strategies such as multi-age structures, multiple grade teams, and reductions in class size, their enthusiasm heightened (a *level*) as did their desire to make the changes quickly (*rate*). What the team forgot is that they exist within a powerful system where changes of this magnitude (*level*) cannot be implemented swiftly (*rate*) because so many other parts of the system must also change. The introduction of new structures and smaller class sizes have an impact on scheduling, facilities, philosophies of teaching and learning, communication with parents, and the like. Fortunately in this case, the principal was aware of the entire system and could help the team understand the impact that such changes would have both in the near term and long term. The team then came up with a *series* of strategies for addressing these systemic issues, including working with their colleagues to develop the same level of enthusiasm they had for the change.

The links between *level* and *rate* are sometimes obvious, sometimes not. To uncover and understand your school's or district's own level and rate stories, do the following:

- Gather together a group of people representing different perspectives and describe various stories of crisis and control in your school or district.
- Sketch out these stories by drawing feedback loops to show cause-effect and reinforcement loops.
- Conduct a dialogue together to talk about "how things got to be this way" and what is keeping the problem or issue from being resolved. Use relations diagrams and/or cause-and-effect diagrams to get at the underlying root cause(s) of the problem.
- Decide together what actions you will take to put in place a longer-term, more systemic solution that addresses underlying causes and dynamics.

Three Principles of Social Systems

A *social system* is any group of people who share common space, whose actions affect and influence each other (even slightly), and/or who have a shared purpose. For example, a school is a social system, a department team is a social system, a community is a social system. Three principles of social systems are relevant to the ideas in this chapter:

- The source of most difficulties is internal to the system—although the tendency is to blame outside forces or "them."
- Often people take actions they believe are solving the problem, when in fact the actions themselves are the cause of the problem in the first place.
- The nature of the dynamic feedback structure of a social system tends to mislead people into taking ineffective, even counterproductive, action.

> The discipline of working with mental models starts with turning the mirror inward; learning to unearth our internal pictures of the world, to bring them to the surface and hold them rigorously to scrutiny.
>
> —Peter Senge

Systemic Structures

A systems thinker also understands how *structures* in a system relate to a system's performance. Structures include, among many things, how people work together, policies and procedures, school calendars and schedules, contracts, job descriptions, and how decisions get made.

For example, in the low achievement district caught in the negative feedback loop in the previous section, it may be that the school day and contract agreements are also contributing to the lack of time for teacher professional development. And perhaps the district's policy of giving teachers a small amount of dollars to spend on their own professional development each year, with no alignment to improving student achievement, is contributing to the situation. A systems thinker examines all such possibilities.

Mental Models

A systems thinker is aware of *mental models:* the underlying assumptions that act as filters for all we perceive. These filters can cause problems when we leap to conclusions without data. The systems thinker listens for these mental models in him or herself and others, and brings those assumptions to the surface through reflection, inquiry and dialogue.

Example

Here is a real-life example of how different mental models affected a team's dynamics. This particular team had one member, Pat, who always left the team meetings early. Four people on the team each had a different interpretation of why she left (see Table 8.1 on p. 185).

Because each person viewed the same event—Pat leaving a meeting—from a different mental model, each reached a very different conclusion from the others. The problem is that we are seldom aware of our own mental models, let alone being able to talk about them articulately. That's why people so often jump (erroneously) to conclusions.

Table 8.1 Example of a Mental Model

	Person A	Person B	Person C	Person D
Infer Meaning/ Interpret the Observation	Pat has a lot of important things to do.	Pat has too much to do.	Pat always seems to leave when I'm talking.	Pat leaves after the items she's in charge of are discussed.
Evaluate and Impose a Value	Pat is very valuable to us.	Pat is unorganized and can't prioritize.	Pat doesn't respect me.	Pat doesn't value anything she's not in charge of.
Assumption	Pat has everything under control.	Pat is out of control.	Pat is heartless and manipulative.	Pat is not a team player.
Conclusion	Pat should be rewarded.	Pat should be trained.	Pat can't be trusted.	Pat should be reprimanded.

Fact: Pat regularly leaves the team meeting early. Why? Each of four teammates would give a different answer based on his or her mental model.

The best strategy for this team (which they eventually followed) was simply to ask Pat why she left meetings early. It turned out that Pat had a disabled child who had a regular therapy appointment scheduled at the precise time this team had been meeting. Once that fact was known, the team made a simple change that solved the problem (the team meetings were rescheduled).

Jumping to conclusions leads us to put certain fixes in place that aren't fixes at all, but simply add to the problem or create problems. Had Pat's supervisor been on the team and had the same perception as one of her teammates, Pat could have ended up in training or with a reprimand in her file.

The way out of this trap is to become aware of our mental models and be willing to discuss them as a team before we jump to conclusions individually.

Blame the System, Not the Person

There is a rule of thumb associated with systems that has a profound impact on how you approach improvement. It's the **85/15 Rule**:

- 85% of the problems in a system are due to inherent problems with that system. They can be changed only through the intervention of the people who shape the system (principals, superintendents, etc.).
- Only 15% of problems are under control of the individuals working within the system.

What does this mean in practical terms? For a simple example, think about the staff who have to enter registration data into a computer. They can determine when they start and begin their work, but they must use hardware and software purchased under administrative and budget policies set at the school or district level. Similarly, it is administration that determines whether and how these staff are trained in the software. Staff also have no control over the *input* for this system: how the registration forms are designed, who completes the forms, etc.

The first consequence of the 85/15 Rule is that whenever you encounter a problem, you look for causes that lie within the system before trying to blame an individual. Suppose, for example, that you encounter registration data that was entered incorrectly into the computer. The first reaction of a nonsystems thinker might be to blame the person for being incompetent. By contrast, a systems thinker would wonder what made it likely that the person either did not know how to do it correctly or did know but was prevented from doing so. For example, was he or she trained properly? Is the software particularly difficult to use?

The 85/15 Rule teaches us that fundamental, systemic improvement requires action not only from the individuals closest to the issues, but support and involvement from the decision makers who designed the system in the first place. A systems thinker understands the futility and danger of blaming individuals for problems when most of the variation in performance is due to how the systems are designed.

Another consequence of the 85/15 Rule and systems thinking in general is that you begin to appreciate why a collaborative approach to improvement is needed: Each person within a system will be uniquely affected by whatever the broader system does (or does not do). Each will have insight into different parts of the puzzle. And you need to bring all the pieces together to see the whole puzzle.

Other Lessons

- When things go wrong—someone makes a mistake or isn't performing well—first ask what *system structures* might be contributing. For example, in the case of a struggling teacher, what is it about our recruitment, selection, hiring, and development policies and processes that might be contributing to his or her difficulties? (In his later years, Dr. Deming suspected the percent of problems outside the control of individual employees was even higher—96/4!)
- Keep in mind that nearly all employees come to work wanting to do a good job, wanting to feel and *be* competent. Look for barriers in the system that are preventing that from happening (and treat the other folks as "special causes" to be addressed individually—not with blanket policies).

Sub-Optimization and System Thinking

There is one aspect of systems thinking that many people have a hard time grasping: You can't optimize the performance of the system as a whole by optimizing the performance of its individual pieces.

Think of it this way: An orchestra plays at its best when each individual section—the strings, horns, woodwinds, percussionists, etc.—adjusts its performance to that of all the other sections. What may work best for the second violinists may make it harder for the violas or cellos to play well. They must listen to one another carefully so they can come in at the right moment, playing at just the right pace, strength, tone, pitch, and key. The net result is a beautiful, harmonic symphony.

Other Examples of the 85/15 Rule

- A state test assesses student knowledge of earth science but the curriculum does not include earth science. Subsequently, students do poorly on this section of the state test. Who can make a change in the curriculum? Can the students alone? The teachers alone? Who has responsibility and authority for the 85%?

- Students come to school without needed supplies such as paper, pencils, calculators, etc. Each school has a limited operating budget and cannot request more than its allotted amount. As a result, students either go without needed materials or teachers buy materials with their own money. Who can change the budget priorities?

- In many districts, teachers are regularly surplused, or let go, based on third week counts and individual teacher seniority. If a school needs a reading specialist but that teacher is surplused, the school loses the teacher, with the result that students needing extra assistance receive none. Who has responsibility and authority over changing the labor-management contract/policy?

In most schools (and, in fact, most businesses), each part is focused on optimizing its own performance. Each classroom, department, unit, etc., is dedicated to achieving its own aims and purposes regardless of what happens in the other units. Some examples include:

- Students are given two hours of homework a night—by *each* academic teacher.
- The payroll office is closed over the lunch hour to give its staff time off—precisely the time when teachers are free to complete business-related tasks.
- Afternoon classes are cancelled to give the PTO time and space to prepare for a fundraiser.
- Individual teachers are singled out for teacher of the year—without acknowledging the tremendous support and assistance from colleagues who helped these teachers be so successful.

What's the alternative? We have to begin to accept that some **suboptimization** of the parts is necessary to optimize the whole.

Acting on Systems Thinking

The next two chapters of this book provide practical methods and approaches that apply systems thinking to the everyday work of SMART teams and shape how an entire school or district can approach systemwide improvement.

Final Check: Thinking Like a System

✓ Our school looks for patterns and underlying trends, not just isolated events.

✓ My team is aware of feedback loops that interact with the process/system we are studying. We know what effects our process/system has on other parts of the system and how changes outside our process/system affect it.

✓ My team is comfortable talking about the mental models that influence our perceptions of events.

✓ When presented with problems, we blame the process, not the person.

✓ We are working to pace the performance of our process/system to optimize the system as a whole.

Chapter 9
Improving Processes and Systems

T he principles, tools, and methods described in previous chapters provide a basic *toolkit* teams can use in a variety of ways to improve student learning. This chapter brings together different concepts and methods that teams can use to improve processes and systems. Results can be improved by working on—and improving—the underlying processes and systems that create them.

The first thing that teams learn about improvement is that it is as much a mindset as it is a set of tools or methods. There's a saying in the continuous quality improvement world: "When Murphy speaks— listen!" Someone truly interested in continuous improvement knows that mistakes and errors are opportunities to learn from a process, to understand what's gone wrong so it can be fixed. For example, if a school district typically has errors in its fall registration process— with the result that students are double-registered, enrolled without their free/reduced lunch support, or not registered at all—that's a perfect opportunity to dig deeper into the causes of these problems and fix them so they won't happen the next time around.

This chapter describes a practical mindset to improvement that is known as **Levels of Fix**. It also presents different methods teams can use to make improvements depending on the scope and difficulty of the problem.

Levels of Fix: A Practical Approach to Improvement

Real teams live in the real world where things go wrong every day. Yet sometimes all the talk about improvement teams, problem-solving, long-term solutions, and even "focusing on the vital few" can give the impression that improvement can be accomplished only by involving

> If you keep doing what you've always done, you'll keep getting what you've always got.
>
> — Anonymous

Levels of Fix

✓ **Level 1:** Fix the problem

✓ **Level 2:** Improve the process

✓ **Level 3:** Improve (or redesign) the system

lots of people in an extensive effort. In fact, every problem can potentially be addressed at three different levels of effort:

Level 1 Fix: Solve the immediate problem.

Level 2 Fix: Improve the process that created the problem.

Level 3 Fix: Improve or redesign the system that created the process that led to the problem.

Level 1 fixes are a necessity. If you and your team encounter an obvious error or problem, you have to take immediate action to prevent further damage—especially because our work directly impacts the welfare of children and because we operate so often in the public eye.

Level 2 fixes should be the minimal goal of most teams—to improve the process so that the problems or gaps identified by the team will not happen again.

Level 3 fixes are ideal because improving a system usually has far-reaching impact. But they also require extensive effort and input, not to mention authority, so they may be impractical in many cases.

Consider the example from Chapter 8 about school registration problems.

- A **Level 1 fix** might be to automatically issue temporary meal tickets to students who encountered registration problems and didn't receive their free/reduced lunch tickets. That way, no student goes hungry.
- In the meantime, an improvement team could step back and ask, "Why are we having these registration problems?" They could create a flowchart and look for places where responsibilities were unclear or unnecessary steps were included. Their investigation (including the use of data) could lead to permanent improvements in the registration process: a **Level 2 fix**.
- Ideally, a team with a broader mission could look across several processes—not just registration—and ask, "Do the problems identified with the registration process occur elsewhere in the organization?" The answer might uncover policies, procedures, and norms causing widespread problems, errors, or inefficiencies. Fixing those underlying problems could lead to improvements across many

processes, such as registration, enrollment, scheduling of classes, and assignment of advisors. That would be a true **Level 3 fix**.

The rest of this chapter describes various methods your team can use to identify and make improvements in your school's processes, which will mostly fall within the realm of Level 2 fixes. However, keep in mind that if you encounter obvious problems, you should also implement Level 1 fixes so the problems do not continue or worsen. Similarly, keep your eyes open for deeper, system-level improvements (Level 3 fixes) that can have a broad impact on your school.

Processes and Improvement

The key to making improvements is to begin thinking about your school as a dynamic organism comprised of many interrelated processes. A **process** is simply a series of sequential steps leading to an **outcome**. Every process has **inputs**, which are transformed through the process steps (that should add value to those inputs) to create a desired **output** used by those who depend on the process to do their work.

Every person associated with the school and district—students, families, teachers, support staff, administrators, and board and community members—is engaged at one time or another in a process. For example:

- Students who flow through the K–12 system encounter processes during registration and enrollment and when scheduling classes, attending classes, engaging in extra-curricular activities, taking tests, eating lunch, getting locker assignments, and graduating.
- Teachers involved in the K–12 system work with processes such as recruitment, selection, and hiring; orientation and professional development; teaching and assessing; researching best practices; developing curriculum; and school improvement.

How well these and other processes work has a lot to do with how people perceive the quality of the school and district.

Level 1 Fix: Take immediate action to prevent the problem (use a muzzle on an aggressive dog). Level 2 Fix: Improve the process so problems or gaps don't happen again (build the dog a large fenced-in area to keep him away from people). Level 3 Fix: Improve or redesign the system that led to the problem (learn how to train the dog to curb his aggression).

A Customer by Any Other Name . . .

Dr. W. Edwards Deming once said, "Use your horse sense. There are no customers in education!" His words were a reminder that education is a human system, not a manufacturing system: Our students are not a raw product. Point well taken. However, the concept of a customer does seem relevant if you

- View educational systems as providing services to students and families (the ultimate aim being to educate children well).
- Believe that in these times of school choice, students and parents are evaluating and choosing schools based on the quality they provide—much as consumers choose between products.
- See that there are many internal processes in educational systems, and each of these processes have customers, the people who depend on the quality of what that process produces in order to do *their* work well. For example, the customers of the hiring process are the school communities that benefit from the teachers and administrators that are hired; the customers of the staff development processes are the employees engaged in building their knowledge and skills.

However, many people in education are uncomfortable with the term customers. If that's the case, look for alternative terms that convey the same intent as customer, such as client, beneficiary, or users.

When you're working on a SMART team, your mission may require that you make process or system improvements. There are many alternative approaches available; this chapter focuses on five:

- **Accelerated Improvement Process (AIP):** An intensive, rapid-fire improvement method that leads to concrete results within a short timeframe by blending minimal meeting time with individual or small-group work by team members.
- **Problem-Solving:** A more in-depth improvement method for complex problems that must be studied thoroughly before you can identify potential solutions.
- **Functional Analysis:** A method for (re)aligning a division, department, or work unit's work around a clearly defined purpose that supports the district/school vision and mission, and serves people well. The analysis helps you refine and redefine roles and responsibilities and opportunities for job training, and expose areas in need of process improvements.
- **Breaking Through Gridlock:** A method for identifying deep (Level 3) fixes for intractable problems.
- **System Metaphors:** A method for sorting through which elements of a system will benefit from further attention and which can be phased out.

Accelerated Improvement Process

The Accelerated Improvement Process (AIP)[1] is a concentrated improvement method in which teams make time to meet in intensive improvement marathons and commit to doing improvement follow-up work between meetings.

The AIP starts by identifying a particular problem or goal and ends with the development of an implementation plan. (Implementation is handled separately.) Development of the plan is typically completed within 6 weeks of the project's starting date.

---

[1]Developed by the University of Wisconsin—Madison's Office of Quality Improvement, 1999.

The process is built around three meetings, with the majority of work being performed by team members between meetings.

Meeting 1: The team, with input from the project sponsor (positional leader or leaders), defines the scope and purpose of the project (pre-work).

Between meetings: Team members gather information or data on problems related to the purpose, and understand the process through flowcharting.

Meeting 2: Members share what they have learned, and the team focuses on possible solutions and the analysis of those solutions, including data that needs to be collected from customers of the process. The outcome is a list of prioritized solutions.

Between meetings: Team members collect and analyze data/information on potential solutions.

Meeting 3: The team reviews the solutions again in light of the data they have collected. The team then finalizes their recommended solutions, incorporating concerns and suggestions raised in the data-gathering phase, and develops a plan for implementation. (At this meeting the project sponsor learns about the recommendations and agrees to support the implementation plan.)

See the following page for a summary of an AIP project.

Principles of AIP

The Accelerated Improvement Process (AIP) works well within a school environment because it produces practical implementation plans very quickly. This is accomplished by applying five principles:

1. Recommended ideas must be actionable; all ideas will be prioritized.
2. A majority of the work (data collection, flowcharting, planning, etc.) is done outside the formal meeting time.
3. Meeting time is spent on generating solutions, prioritizing solutions, and developing implementation/action plans.
4. Multiple tasks are done simultaneously.
5. Team meeting time is concentrated into three very structured meetings.

 Templates for the Accelerated Improvement Process appear on the CD-ROM.

Summary of an AIP Project

Purchasing/Work Orders

Process: Accounting services approves all requisitions for building services, sites, central stores, and all invoices. This creates a backlog of goods delivered, delays in making efficient purchases, and frustration on the part of site personnel.

Mission: To reduce cycle time of all purchasing systems and to explore standardization of processes in order to better serve our customers.

Team: Madge Klais, Tom Pierce, Doug Pearson, Lois Nachreiner, Marilyn Blackley-Braun, and Belinda Lukas.

Current Situation and Need for Improvement: Currently all requisitions for purchases, regardless of amount, must go from purchasing, to accounting services, back to purchasing, and finally back to accounting again for payment. Also, because purchase requests for fall have to wait until July 1, there is a major delay in delivery to schools for fall opening.

Performance Measures:

- Reduced number of sign-offs thus saving cycle time.
- Less delay in accounting services.
- A system easier to understand at all levels.
- More timely delivery of goods.
- Free up time for accounting services personnel.

Anticipated Organizational Impact:

- Empowerment of purchasers to buy goods and pay on time.
- Lower margin of error due to less handling of invoices.
- Less paperwork flowing back and forth.
- Direct users are more knowledgeable of system.
- Vendors are paid more quickly.
- Better service to end-users (custodians, principals, etc.).

Possible Unanticipated Impacts:

Use monitoring methods (accounting practices and satisfaction surveys, for example) to capture and solve possible negative effects.

Source: Madison Metropolitan School District. Reprinted with permission.

Problem-Solving

When a problem has been around for a long time, and previous efforts to resolve it haven't resulted in sustained improvement, it may be worth the time to dig deeply into its causes in order to develop a more systemic long-lasting solution. In these cases, a group of people who understand the problem(s) and the process (because they work with it everyday) is convened to address and resolve the problem at a deep level (Level 2 or Level 3 fixes).

The challenge of solving problems in groups is that most of the people in the group are there because they already have a solution in mind. They come to the group with preconceived notions about the problem—what it is, how bad it is, and how to fix it. What typically happens is that the group jumps right into arguing about which solution is best before it has taken the time to really define and understand the problem from all the angles. This approach is ripe for conflict and disengagement.

An effective team will talk about the process it intends to use to attack the problem. A methodical, easy-to-understand process unfolds naturally and moves the group through a logical progression of thinking. The process engages all participants and helps the group investigate the full spectrum of the problem. The 7-Step Problem-Solving Method (Figure 9.1) is just such a process. Note that

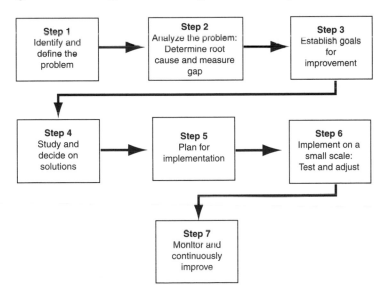

Figure 9.1 The 7-Step Problem-Solving Method
Note. Copyright © 2001 by QLD, LLC. Reprinted with permission.

throughout this process, data should be collected, analyzed, and interpreted to be sure that the right problem is being solved with the right solution.

7-Step Problem-Solving Method

✓ 1. **Identify and define the problem**
2. Analyze the problem
3. Establish goals for improvement
4. Study and decide on solutions
5. Plan for implementation
6. Implement on a small scale
7. Monitor and continuously improve

Step 1. Identify and Define the Problem

Step 1 is to develop a collective understanding of the problem. Problems often manifest themselves in different ways throughout a school. Each person who works in the school may experience the problem in a unique way. When problem-solving in groups, it is important for each person to have the opportunity to describe the problem from his or her perspective. This will assure that the group understands the whole problem, not just one or two pieces of it.

If you are facilitating or leading your team, first have the group discuss what they think the problem is, where the problem occurs, who sees it as a problem, how often it occurs, and what aspects of quality are in jeopardy as a result of the problem. *Use data as much as possible* to confirm (or disprove!) what people *think* is happening. Once you start using data regularly, you'll be surprised at how often everyone's perceptions (including your own) can be inaccurate.

The following questions and guidelines can help define the current state of the situation:

- What is the problem we're attempting to solve?
- In what areas does the problem occur most often? (Collect data.)
- For whom is this a problem and how bad is it? (Collect data.)
- How often or how much does the problem interfere with student learning?
- What's at stake if we don't solve this problem? What's at stake if we do solve this problem? (Collect data.)
- How did we come to have this problem? What is the history? (Consider using the Historygram process, page 218, when examining these questions.)
- Once the current state is well understood, take time to ask and answer the following questions: What do we want to be different after we solve this problem? What is the desired state we would like to achieve?

In addition to listening to each other, the group may want to ask their colleagues in the school or community to verify or extend their thinking about the problem.

The process of identifying and defining a problem can be lengthy and challenging, especially if the group is diverse and each person experiences the problem quite differently. Too often when teams set out to solve a problem, they end up with a Band-Aid approach because the real, whole, and underlying problem is not detected.

 TIP

Beware of solutions in disguise! Sometimes problems are stated as the opposite of some desired solution. For example, the statement "We don't have enough computers" is a problem-statement that poorly disguises the speaker's preferred solution ("Buy more computers!"). If you hear solution-oriented statements, ask the speaker what benefit would come from implementing the (disguised) solution: "How would having more computers help us?" Once you've identified the underlying problems, you may find other solutions that may work just as well, be less expensive, or be better for more people.

Be patient with learning as much about the problem as you can before attempting to define the problem too narrowly. The time you spend up front in the definition and identification phase could save you huge amounts of time later on in the process.

Writing a Problem Statement

Once your group has learned about the ways in which the problem manifests itself, write a simple, concise statement that captures the essential elements of the problem being addressed. A problem statement should

- Be objective and factual—not imply a solution
- Identify key characteristics of the problem such as:
  - Where and when it is and is not observed
  - Extent or impact it is having on student learning
  - Observable evidence of its existence
- Be relatively short
- Identify the problem at its deepest level of manifestation
- Identify for whom this is a problem and when

Example: *This is the third year in which more than 60% of our sixth graders and 40% of our seventh graders have received warning reports for potential failures due to incomplete homework after the first 6-week grading period (current state). We want our junior high school students to be able to successfully complete their homework assignments and turn them in on time (desired state).*

When everyone is clear about what problem the group is solving, you can then begin to analyze why you think the problem is occurring (Step 2).

Step 2. Analyze the Problem

It is important at this stage that all individuals have the same information concerning the problem and understand it in the same way. Analyzing the problem for root causes and gathering additional data about the problem provides a deeper understanding. There are four key questions your team should answer:

- *Why* is the problem occurring?
- *Where* is the problem occurring?
- *How big* is the problem?
- What are the *biggest drivers* of the problem?

Why Is the Problem Occurring?

The first level of analysis is to determine why this is a problem and why the problem exists. Use 5 Why's Analysis (p. 135) and/or cause-and-effect diagrams to dig deeper and deeper into root causes of the problem. Be careful: These tools identify *potential* root causes. You will need to verify them with data or experimentation (see sidebar "Verifying Potential Causes"). You will be using the "logic-data chain" (see p. 63) throughout the problem-solving process, as you theorize about what is going on, gather data to verify your theories, and then theorize again about what may be causing the problem, gather data again, and so on.

7-Step Problem-Solving Method

1. Identify and define the problem
✓ **2. Analyze the problem**
3. Establish goals for improvement
4. Study and decide on solutions
5. Plan for implementation
6. Implement on a small scale
7. Monitor and continuously improve

Resist the Solution Temptation!

The more people get involved in discussing likely causes of a problem, the more they start thinking about potential solutions. The purpose of using the 7-Step Method, however, is to avoid the rush to solutions before causes have been verified with data. You can, however, document solution ideas that team members suggest at this stage, and revisit them later in Step 4.

Example: *The problem statement shown on page 198 identifies a problem with middle school students not completing and handing in their homework. The group already knew how many and which students were having the problem but they didn't know what was causing the problem or what impact the problem was having on student learning. After conducting a cause-and-effect analysis, they might suspect that the way in which these students organize their materials and the many different ways in which their teachers give homework assignments were two areas that should be studied further.*

Where Is the Problem Occurring?

Flowcharting the processes in which the problem is evident will help the group pinpoint where in the system to look for potential solutions. As described in Chapter 4, flowcharts are pictures of how work flows over time. Regardless of what type of flowchart you choose, the first step is to determine the scope of the process you will be depicting. Where does it start? Where does it end? Once you've determined those boundaries you can begin to identify the steps and their sequence.

Example: *The group studying the middle school students with homework problems has several alternatives. They could work with the students to create a detailed flowchart of all the steps in their process from the time assignments were given until the homework was turned in. Or the group could also use a flowchart to chart how each teacher assigns homework (and identify ways to standardize the process to make it easier for students to successfully organize and complete their assignments). A third alternative is to create a flowchart that depicts the process used by students who don't have trouble getting their homework in on time. Such a chart could show steps that other students could use.*

How Big Is the Problem?

The team needs to gather data to show how big the problem is—how often it occurs, what impact it has, etc. The important thing is that the team decide what the most important "gap" or need is and then gather data to measure the extent of the problem in relation to that need. Many of the snapshot data tools (pp. 140 to 153) can help answer this question.

Verifying Potential Causes

There are two ways to verify whether potential causes actually contribute to a problem. The first is to **gather data** that links the presence of the cause with the occurrence of the problem. If it is not easy to gather data on a potential cause, you can also **experiment** by making changes in a process, procedure, or policy to remove the suspected cause. Be sure to treat the changes as actual experiments: Try them on a small scale and define specific procedures for measuring performance before and after the change is made.

A subset of this question is whether the frequency or impact of the problem is changing over time. Here, run charts or control charts (the moving picture tools from p. 154) are essential.

> **Example:** *The team already knew that 60% of the sixth graders and 40% of the seventh graders have demonstrated the homework problem for each of 3 years. The team might also want to know if those percentages change during the year; if there is a correlation between homework assignment completion and test results, the type of assignment, the level of support at home, etc.; or if there are common demographic profiles of students who struggle with homework, such as attendance, enrollment in special services, behavioral factors, after-school employment, etc.*

What Are the Biggest Drivers of the Problem?

Sometimes a problem can't be addressed by a straightforward cause-and-effect approach because the potential causes are intricately linked. In these cases, asking about the big drivers can help identify the root causes. A relations diagram (p. 138) is useful for answering this type of question.

Step 3. Establish Specific Goals for Improvement

As mentioned in earlier chapters, problem-solving goals should meet SMART criteria. The team's definition of its goals will relate directly to its purpose and to the problem it is attempting to solve. If the group is working on more than one problem, it will have more than one goal. There may also be multiple goals for one problem, especially if the analysis step has unearthed more than one potential root cause and/or more than one major area of gap or need.

Table 9.1 illustrates a sequence that shows how to link problem statements with verified causes and improvement goals.

Step 4. Study and Decide on Solutions

Throughout the course of its problem-solving, your team will have begun the process of identifying possible solutions. This is the point where the ideas that have bubbled up from the process are pulled together and enhanced. First, go back through your meeting records and find the ideas that you've already generated. Then brainstorm

---

7-Step Problem-Solving Method

1. Identify and define the problem
2. Analyze the problem
✓ 3. **Establish goals for improvement**
✓ 4. **Study and decide on solutions**
5. Plan for implementation
6. Implement on a small scale
7. Monitor and continuously improve

Table 9.1   Linking Problem Statements With Verified Causes

Team Type	Problem (as it was understood at the start of the project)	Cause(s) (verified with data)	Improvement Goals
School climate team	Poor attendance at Family Fun night (only 10% of parents attended the past 2 years).	50% of parents who did not come reported they never heard of the event and did not recall seeing any announcements.	Increase attendance at family fun night by 30% over the course of the next 2 years.
School climate team	Too many behavioral referrals.	Most referrals were related to hallway incidents; an increase happened when hallway supervisors were reassigned.	Reduce the number of behavior referrals related to hallway incidents by 20% each year over the next 3 years.
School improvement team	Less than 25% or one fourth of students in grades 4 and 5 scored at or above "proficient" in nonfiction writing.	Students found the assignments confusing. Students felt they had little opportunity to practice prerequisite skills.	50% or more of students will demonstrate proficiency in student performance in nonfiction writing as measured by the district writing rubric.
School improvement team	Too many students receive failure notices 6 weeks into the semester.	The biggest problems were in the sixth and seventh grades. Records showed many students in those grades had missing or incomplete homework.	Reduce by half the number of sixth- and seventh-grade students who receive failure notices after the first 6 weeks due to missing or incomplete homework.
Ongoing department team	Nobody comes to team meetings. (Average attendance was at 50% for the past 12 months.)	Policies on attendance were not clear. A shift in classroom schedules interfered with the standard time set for the meeting.	Increase attendance and participation at team meetings to an average of 80% for the entire school year.

and discuss additional ideas. That way, you can be sure to start with a list that both respects people's original ideas *and* what the team has learned through its efforts up to this point.

From Options to Solutions

Typically, a team will generate many potential solutions to the problem(s) being studied. Narrowing the ideas down to a manageable few can be a real challenge for some groups because it is the part of the problem-solving process that often has the most emotion attached to

Approval for Solutions and Plans

Sometimes teams will need to get approval from their positional leader before they begin implementing a chosen solution. Check with your positional leader to determine when she or he wants to see your ideas. Some will want to check the proposed solution *before* the team develops a plan; others will want to see the plan accompanying the proposed solution.

it. The challenge is less for teams that have diligently included all members along the way and have done a good job of collecting and analyzing information about the problem. For such teams, deciding on the solution is seen as just another step, not a point of conflict.

One way to narrow the ideas is to look for research to identify promising practices in the area of concern. Another option is to develop a set of criteria relevant to the decision you face. Some criteria the group may want to consider are

- No or limited lost instructional time
- Extent to which a wide variety of students will benefit
- Doable in terms of time, energy, and financial resources required
- Equitable
- History of positive results

The group should decide on the criteria together and then match each idea to each criteria to find the best fit. A decision matrix (p. 93) can help you keep track of the criteria your team is using and how each potential solution matches those criteria.

Documenting Your Proposed Solution

Once your team has decided on what solution it will propose for the problem being studied, you need to document both what the solution is and why that option was chosen (that is, how well it fits your criteria).

Step 5. Plan for Implementation

Planning tools and templates can help the team reach conclusions in ways that will ultimately facilitate implementation and garner collective support for the team's recommendations. There are a variety of tools described in Chapter 4 that can help you with this step.

Before you finalize the implementation plan, your group should ask itself the following questions:

- Who will be affected if this decision is implemented?
- Who will be responsible for seeing that it is implemented?

7-Step Problem-Solving Method

1. Identify and define the problem
2. Analyze the problem
3. Establish goals for improvement
4. Study and decide on solutions
✓ 5. **Plan for implementation**
6. Implement on a small scale
7. Monitor and continuously improve

- What are the important tasks or actions that must be taken to assure successful implementation?
- Who should do each task and when?
- What skills will these actions require? Do the people who will need to implement the decision or solution have those skills?
- Do the people who must implement the change believe change is needed?
- How will we know if we have been successful? How will we measure our progress? When should we measure our progress?
- What resources will be needed to do this well?

An implementation plan should address each of the questions raised above, providing ways to involve and communicate with everyone affected by the change. The plan should also reiterate the team's mission. Clearly stated tasks, doable time frames, reasonable costs, and lots of involvement on the part of those who must ultimately accept and perform the change will all help to facilitate effective implementation.

Step 6. Implement on a Small Scale

This is the step that most teams miss. If at all possible, test your solution(s) and implementation plan on a small scale and get feedback from those who are implementing it to see if it's manageable and productive. This is the essence of the PDSA cycle. The plan doesn't have to be implemented for a long time (such as a year-long test), but should be tried for a sufficient period to gather enough data to see whether it works. If it does seem to be manageable and working, implement the solution broadly. If it isn't working, find out why and either make adjustments or try a different strategy.

Step 7. Monitor and Continuously Improve

Continuous improvement is driven by repeated application of the PDSA cycle, each time working with larger scales or longer time periods. Initial improvements are sometimes the result of a halo effect: improvements appear to be working simply because people are paying attention to the problem. Therefore, build in a long-term mechanism for monitoring results to assure that improvements are both real and sustained. Then, as the solution becomes the new way of operating, it can be incrementally improved again and again.

7-Step Problem-Solving Method

1. Identify and define the problem
2. Analyze the problem
3. Establish goals for improvement
4. Study and decide on solutions
5. Plan for implementation
✓ 6. **Implement on a small scale**
✓ 7. **Monitor and continuously improve**

What Is a Small-Scale Test?

A small-scale test should have one or more of the following characteristics:

- **Short time frame:** We'll try it out for 2 weeks (or 4 months, as appropriate).
- **Geographical limits:** We'll try it out at Ozawa Elementary before taking it to other elementary schools.
- **Just a few people:** We'll work with 3 of the 10 art teachers.
- **No more than 25% of the total budget**

A small-scale test could also include observing how well solutions similar to yours have worked in other settings. For example, if you are experimenting with student self-assessments or a new technology, find other schools that have used procedures or equipment close to those your team wants to use and arrange an on-site visit.

Functional Analysis: Aligning Processes

The late Dr. W. Edwards Deming explained that, "A system is a network of interdependent components that work together to accomplish the aim of the system." Being clear about the *aim* of a system is key to improving how the system functions overall. A school or district's work units, departments, divisions, and other ongoing organizational units can make significant improvements in their performance by first working through a functional analysis.

Here is one 8-step functional analysis process[2]:

Step 1: Clarify mission, values, and customers of our service.

Step 2: Create system flowchart.

Step 3: Identify core processes.

Step 4: Identify responsibilities for core processes.

Step 5: Learn customer needs.

Step 6: Prioritize and flowchart processes.

Step 7: Make improvements to processes.

Step 8: Check results and hold gains.

You will want to have all the members of the work unit or department work through this process together so that all will share a common vision of the purpose of what they do, how they do it, and how they personally fit into the bigger picture.

> **Example:** *In a large university, the history department chairperson convened all the administrative support staff to work through this process.*

Step 1. Clarify Mission, Values, and Customers of Our Service

Members should brainstorm their answers to each of the following questions on sticky notes and group them using the Affinity Diagram process. Use the multivoting process as needed to narrow down the list. Be sure to talk about each piece in enough depth that there is shared understanding and consensus.

---

[2]From *Administering a department: A guide for identifying and improving support processes in an academic department,* by M. Cotter, J. Simmons, and K. Paris, 1997, Maryville, MO: Prescott. Copyright 1997 by the University of Wisconsin—Madison Office of Quality Improvement. Used with permission.

8-Step Functional Analysis Process

✓1. **Clarify mission, values, and customers of our service**
2. Create system flowchart
3. Identify core processes
4. Identify responsibilities for core processes
5. Learn customer needs
6. Prioritize and flowchart processes
7. Make improvements to processes
8. Check results and hold gains

? **KEY QUESTION: What is our purpose/mission?**

Another way to think about this question is to ask, "Why do we exist?" There is a particular purpose, or set of purposes, the department or work unit plays in the larger organization, and this needs to be articulated clearly and succinctly.

> **Example:** *The history department's mission is education, research, and service.*

? **KEY QUESTIONS: Whom do we serve? Who is affected by our work?**

Another way to ask this is, "Who receives the services we provide and products we create? For whom are we doing this work?" In the process of answering these questions, the group will probably find that there are primary and secondary *customers* (or if you prefer other terms, use *clients*, *users*, or *colleagues*).

- Primary customers are those without whom the department or work unit would not exist. They really need you and you need them!
- Secondary customers are those people you serve who count on you to get their work done — but their work is happening on behalf of your primary customers as well.

> **Example:** *In the history department, faculty and students are primary customers. Secondary customers are people in their own college of history, other departments/colleges, research funding agencies, the legislature, the general public, and the university's administrative offices.*

? **KEY QUESTION: What are our values?**

Our beliefs drive our values—we value what we believe in. This question gets to the heart of how we want to be known by others: What do we believe about the work we do, how should we conduct ourselves, and how should we treat each other and those we serve? And even more importantly, how do we practice those beliefs now and what more do we need to do to actually live those beliefs? The answer might be a statement of core values or a list of guiding principles—or both.

✸ **OUTCOMES for Step 1**

A shared perspective of how our work supports the broader purpose of our school district and how we want to operate as a department or work unit, and a prioritized list of customers.

Focus on Primary Customers, Not Secondary Customers

In education, we sometimes confuse our primary and secondary customers, which can cause us to sacrifice primary customers' needs for secondary needs. For example, if our mission is to serve all students and families, but we act as if a special interest group is our primary customer, we may make decisions or use our time in ways that actually harm students and families.

8-Step Functional Analysis Process

1. Clarify mission, values, and customers of our service
✓ 2. **Create system flowchart**
3. Identify core processes
4. Identify responsibilities for core processes
5. Learn customer needs
6. Prioritize and flowchart processes
7. Make improvements to processes
8. Check results and hold gains

Step 2. Create a System Flowchart

This step focuses on clarifying, at a high level, how your work unit or department provides its main services or products. The key is to agree not to go into too much detail—yet. Have members talk about the core processes used to carry out the mission (you may want to break into smaller groups around these functions). Using sticky notes to flowchart the core process, decide on the first step (first major activity) and the last step, then fill in the intermediate steps. Use these top-level flowcharts (like Figure 9.2) to talk about how the core processes connect or interact with one another.

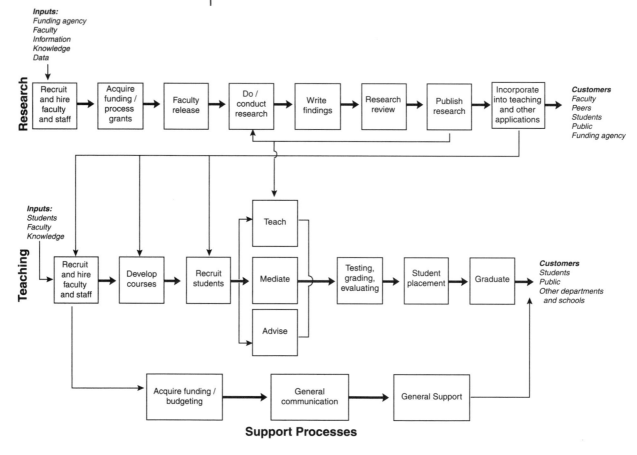

Figure 9.2   History Department System Flowchart

Note. From the Office of Quality Improvement, University of Wisconsin—Madison. Reprinted with permission.

? KEY QUESTION: What do we do to carry out our purpose/mission?

🔍 KEY TASKS: Identify the major activities we engage in to serve our customers, and describe how these activities relate to each other.

✹ OUTCOME: A clear picture of what the department does to accomplish its mission.

Step 3. Identify Core Processes

The purpose of this step is to be very specific about the tasks and activities each individual staff member engages in on a day-to-day basis. The guiding framework all along continues to be the unit or department mission and those served by it.

Each staff member should brainstorm on sticky notes their tasks and activities, and then sort these under the system flow steps. You may want to use color coding or another system to identify different participants.

? KEY QUESTION: What are the primary staff functions?

🔍 KEY TASK: Sort tasks and processes under system flow steps.

✹ OUTCOME: A clear picture of how every member's job activities support the mission of the department across the many processes.

> **Example:** *In the history department, every staff member wrote down onto self-stick notes all the steps, activities, and processes they individually managed using the broad steps identified in the system flowchart as the starting point. The whole group then organized these self-stick notes using the Affinity Process. Header cards identified the department's core processes.*

8-Step Functional Analysis Process

1. Clarify mission, values, and customers of our service
2. Create system flowchart
✓ 3. **Identify core processes**
4. Identify responsibilities for core processes
5. Learn customer needs
6. Prioritize and flowchart processes
7. Make improvements to processes
8. Check results and hold gains

8-Step Functional Analysis Process

1. Clarify mission, values, and customers of our service
2. Create system flowchart
3. Identify core processes
✓ **4. Identify responsibilities for core processes**
✓ **5. Learn customer needs**
6. Prioritize and flowchart processes
7. Make improvements to processes
8. Check results and hold gains

Watch Out for Complexity

Complexity is a general term for unnecessary work—anything that makes a process more complicated without adding value to the service or product it produces. Complexity comes about when people continue trying to fix problems in a process without a systematic plan for doing so. They may try to solve one piece of the process, or rearrange or add a step, not realizing the solution negatively impacts every other part of the process. As problems accumulate, more and more steps are added to compensate or work around them. Each of these extra steps adds another opportunity for mistakes and errors and adds to the overall time the process takes. The real work—where value is really added to the process—becomes buried by the amount of time fixing and reworking. The solution is to step back and engage in a Level 2 Fix to change the process in fundamental ways that eliminate the need for the complexity.

Step 4. Identify Responsibilities for Core Processes

This step helps you begin to identify specific responsibilities for managing the core processes, essentially building into your department or unit a mechanism for ongoing, continuous improvement.

? **KEY QUESTIONS: Who is responsible for the primary functions? Who are the decision makers, process managers, backups, involved people?**

KEY TASK: Complete a Responsibility Matrix (p. 109) and share it with everyone so that people can go to the right person with their questions.

OUTCOME: Identification of gaps or overlaps of roles, responsibilities and functions; clear decision-making structure.

> **Example:** *History department staff members worked individually using the Responsibilities Matrix format to identify their roles (decision maker, process manager, etc.) in different core and subprocesses. They summarized the individual matrices on a large chart and discussed where overlaps, gaps, and discrepancies occurred. The group as a whole decided what needed to be changed and updated, and agreed on a final version.*

Step 5. Learn Customer Needs

This step helps you understand how to add more value to your work unit or department. By talking with customers, either directly through interviews or indirectly through written surveys, you will get a rich amount of information about what to improve about your area. You might even discover that certain activities you thought were essential to delivering your service are not really necessary, thereby freeing up resources to focus on higher priority activities.

? **KEY QUESTIONS: What are you getting that you need? What are you getting that you don't need? What do you wish you were getting?**

🔍 **KEY TASK: Find out what customers of these core processes want and need.**

Example: *The department staff conducted a series of focus groups with selected groups of customers to find out how they experienced the quality of the department's services. They then designed a simple survey they administered to a larger sample of customers to find out which areas of their service were in most need of improvement.*

Step 6. Prioritize and Flowchart Processes

❓ **KEY QUESTIONS: Which processes are most important to our clients? How do these work now, step by step?**

Example: *Based on an analysis of their core work, the history group zeroed in on processes that were used every day that could be upgraded, documented, and standardized relatively easily. For example, they used basic flowcharts to describe the steps that should be used for photocopying, responding to inquiries, and issuing parking permits.*

Step 7. Make Improvements to Processes

🔍 **KEY TASK: Use the Accelerated Improvement Process (AIP) to eliminate rework, duplication, and nonessential steps.**

Example: *The history staff also knew from their own (frustrating) experiences that some processes were in need of major overhaul. Customer feedback confirmed these opportunities. Accelerated Improvement Process teams were charged with completely redesigning these processes to reduce cycle time (eliminate redundancy, rework, and wait time) and to improve quality. For example, the teams used the AIP to improve the student registration process, creating ways to manage the rush of students at registration time and thereby improving the quality of that service.*

8-Step Functional Analysis Process

1. Clarify mission, values, and customers of our service
2. Create system flowchart
3. Identify core processes
4. Identify responsibilities for core processes
5. Learn customer needs
✓ **6. Prioritize and flowchart processes**
✓ **7. Make improvements to processes**
8. Check results and hold gains

8-Step Functional Analysis Process

1. Clarify mission, values, and customers of our service
2. Create system flowchart
3. Identify core processes
4. Identify responsibilities for core processes
5. Learn customer needs
6. Prioritize and flowchart processes
7. Make improvements to processes
✓ 8. **Check results and hold gains**

Step 8. Check Results and Hold Gains

KEY TASKS: Check how the improved processes are working. Standardize them to hold the gains. Identify how improvements can be continued.

Example: *Having made improvements to their daily work processes (Step 6) as well as to problem-ridden processes (Step 7), the staff conducted more focus groups and surveyed their customers again to find out whether the improvements were being noticed and to identify even more ways to improve those processes. The staff documented the standardized processes, shared their documentation with all customers and stakeholders, and incorporated it into their new employee training process.*

Breaking Through Gridlock

Sometimes groups get stuck in problems that seem so complex and overwhelming that it's difficult to see through to a Level 3 fix that will truly resolve difficulties. Here's a 4-step process for breaking through the gridlock of a complex problem:

1. Identify the Original Problem Symptom

- Hold a forum or series of focus groups and/or interviews to get more data from a large group of stakeholders.

    Questions might include: "How are you experiencing the problem now? How does it impact your work? How does it impact students and families? How does it impact others? What is your desired state?"

- Try not to focus just on a single event.

    Look back over time and identify a class of symptoms that have been recurring. Use the Historygram process (p. 218) to identify key events in the progress of the problem, with general time frames when each event occurred. Looking at the events over time can expose patterns and trends, leading to greater understanding.

- Whose interests are being served by the way things are?

    This is a very difficult question for people to answer when *their* interests are the ones being served! It might be useful to invite in **friendly observers** (p. 239) who are knowledgeable about the system and problem so that they can give their objective feedback.

- What information do you have or need to have that has importance to the problem? What do you need to know? How can you find this out?

  Don't overload yourself with irrelevant data. Prioritize your need to know, always asking, "How will knowing this help us solve the problem? What will we do with the information we get?"

2. Map Out all the Quick Fixes (Level 1 Actions Taken in the Past)

Use feedback loops (p. 181) to map out all the fixes that have been used in the past to address the identified problem. You are looking for the balancing loops that preserve the problems by keeping them in control. (Perhaps if the problems were out of control, there would be more impetus for finding permanent solutions.)

3. Identify the Impact

Look for ways that past solutions affected the organization—especially unanticipated effects that locked people into patterned responses. Examine the side effects of quick fixes from the perspective of all the players in the system.

4. Identify Fundamental Solutions

By now, you have defined the problem clearly, carefully and fully, and it's time to decide whether you have enough information to identify and select potential solutions or to go deeper into root cause analysis (pp. 191–193). If you decide you know enough to develop solutions, be sure the selected options address the problem from everyone's perspective.

An Example of Breaking Through

A registration and enrollment team found themselves lost in the complexity of the problems they encountered. The net effect of all the problems was that students were getting lost in the system.

The team reviewed the problem more holistically and discovered that a multitude of mini-processes had sprung up at each school to address the very diverse registration needs of different populations of students (English as a second language, special education, homelessness, etc.). The process was further complicated by the fact that there was no electronic data entry at the school sites where students were registering, causing the whole system to operate manually, slowly, and with errors and duplication.

After looking carefully at all the fixes that had been put in place (the group flowcharted the myriad ways students register), the group decided that a central registration site was the best solution. They surmised that the resulting standardization would make all the processes run more smoothly, and the one-stop-shop location would make it easier on families.

The team is currently piloting the system in one section of their district, gathering feedback from the families and other stakeholders, and monitoring cycle time and errors. They will base their final implementation plan on the results of the pilot.

System Metaphors

Suzanne Bailey of Bailey Associates has developed a specialized exercise for improving systems called **system metaphors**.[3] Using this exercise helps teams sort through priorities and decide which programs and activities can be ceased, which need more focus, and which are simply in a maintenance mode. It can be used as part of an ongoing process of assessing, renewing, and celebrating initiatives.

The exercise is based on the metaphor of a gardener and will help participants focus on how programs and activities move through a cycle from buds to blooms to full flower to withering flower to compost (which feeds the next cycle of innovation).

---

[3]From *Making Progress Visible: Implementing standards and other large scale change initiatives* (p. 40–41), by S. Bailey, 2000, Vicaville, CA: Bailey Alliance. Copyright 2000 by Suzanne Bailey. Reprinted with permission.

Metaphor Exercise

1. **Identify the functions of your school system:** Have your team brainstorm what functions, programs, ideas, etc., are present in your school system. Include everything from fully functional systems to ideas they have heard from rumors. Categorize these ideas as follows:

   Seeds: Ideas or mandates on the horizon blowing in from the outside; they haven't landed yet but they're coming.

   Buds: New programs just starting this year that need lots of attention, training, focus, and funds.

   Blooms: Programs that have been in place, adopted by some staff, but still need attention.

   Full flower: Programs in full implementation by almost all staff with results beginning to show; support is still needed for modifications.

   Withering flower: Programs that may no longer serve the school's priority needs but are continued simply because they are automatic. They have become second nature to all staff and will continue happening with no special attention or funding. They can fall off the tree to make room for new programs.

   Compost pile: Previous programs no longer being implemented — but they built the skill foundation needed for new ideas. All but forgotten, they nourish the roots of the tree.

   Garbage can: Programs that have not produced results or are no longer funded.

   Pests: Things that eat away at the roots of the tree (distracters and detractors, for example, political infighting, lack of resources, etc.).

   Energy: Things that keep the tree energized and growing (resources, trust, communication, skills, capabilities, etc.).

2. **Post the sticky notes on the tree:** Some parts of the tree will be fuller than others, some will be emptier—there will almost always be patterns.

3. **Talk about the patterns:** What causes them? What are our beliefs and values that serve as the roots of the tree?

Materials for Metaphor Exercise

Needed: Large sheet of butcher paper, large sticky notes and markers, large picture of a tree

Time: 4 hours

4. **Clarify the group's vision:** What does the preferred future look like? Record that vision in the skies above the tree.

5. **Determine goals for reaching that vision:** Record these in the trunk of the tree.

6. **Revise the tree:** Go through the sticky notes in the branches and evaluate each based on the program's ability to help reach the vision and goals. Some programs will need to be cycled off the tree (these are no longer relevant or will not produce results toward the vision), while others will need to be added.

Final Check: Selecting Robust Improvement Strategies

Whether improvement strategies are being used schoolwide, by a team of teachers, or within an individual classroom, it is important to step back and make sure we're not simply paving the donkey path—that is, making an ineffective or inefficient practice just go more smoothly. The following checklist can be used to assess whether truly robust—significant and sustainable—strategies are being designed.

Our improvement strategy does the following:

✓ Links directly to goals focused on student learning.
  • The litmus test for all improvement strategies should be, "How will this improve student learning?"

✓ Provides methods for going beyond what we have already done; encourages creativity.

✓ Has some basis in research or best practice.
  • We know far more about effective teaching, learning, leadership, and improvement than we did even 10 years ago. Don't ignore a broad and deep body of knowledge that can help you avoid reinventing the wheel or inventing the wrong wheel.

✓ Incorporates staff and student development.
  • Improvement strategies should always increase learning on the part of both students and adults. They should expand knowledge and skills, as well as attitudes and experiences.

> Assume that any significant innovation, if it is to result in change, requires individual implementers to work out their meaning.
>
> —Michael Fullan

✓ Helps us develop plans that are reasonable in terms of time and resources.
  • If there isn't enough time, money, staff, or space to implement the improvement strategy, the planning will have been a waste of time. Although lack of time and resources shouldn't put a complete stop on moving forward with an exciting idea, time-lines for implementation may have to be moved and other funding sources sought.

✓ Helps us increase our efficiency in both teaching and learning— less is often more.
  • Sometimes we need to step back and ask whether we're focusing too much on quantity while ignoring quality. Integrating curriculum, instruction and services, and reducing rework and redundancy may result in higher quality solutions.

✓ Provides tools to help us identify the "vital few" activities most likely to have the greatest impact.

Chapter 10
Becoming a SMART School

Teams of any kind—SMART or otherwise—operate within the context of the school environment. Their chances of success are directly related to how much work the school has put into creating an environment that encourages a focus on priorities, supports the use of data for reflecting on past and current practices, and promotes collaboration among teachers, staff, students, parents, and the community. These are SMART schools.

This chapter looks at improvement and learning through a broader lens, focusing on the school as a whole instead of individual teams and providing processes and methods for becoming a SMART school.

Preparing Your School for Change

Improvement requires change. So before beginning any schoolwide effort, you need to prepare your school for change.

The first step might be to acknowledge that there will be resistance to change. There may be good reason for the resistance. Depending on how the change is introduced (sent from on high versus created on site), it could appear to be yet another fad or political demand that people view as an unnecessary distraction. It is important to put the change into a context that is meaningful—a context that acknowledges *and* honors past contributions and successes.

The Historygram process is a way to build a bridge between the past and the future, a way to honor the past while moving forward. It allows those who have been around the longest to talk about past parades they joined or led. The school community as a whole takes time to reflect together in an effort to understand the patterns, cycles, and trends of their collective history.

> When you start on your journey to Ithaca, Then pray the road is long, full of adventure, full of knowledge . . .
>
> —from *Journey to Ithaca*, by Cavafy, the Poet of Alexandria

Materials for Historygram

- markers, tape or self-stick paper
- large pieces of shelf or butcher paper or tag board or foam cardboard
- magazines (optional)
- scissors (optional)
- large (5 × 7) header cards

The Historygram Process

- Bring together a diverse group representing many parts of the school community. Include people who have been around a long time as well as those who have just joined the schools, just moved to the community, etc.

- Group people according to when they came into the school or district.

- Have each group develop storyboards showing the following information from their era:
  - Major initiatives and their goals
  - Major crises or turning points
  - Symbols, ceremonies, and traditions
  - What was happening in the world
  - What was happening in the community
  - A name or title for the era
  - Values that we want to take into the future

- Have each group share its story.

- Capture the values separately on a collective poster to be developed into a vision of the school's future at a later time.

- Have the group as a whole summarize the learning by identifying themes, patterns, and cycles that have made up the school's history and identify patterns they want to continue or stop.

This process gives the entire school community an opportunity to view the number and types of changes that have occurred and gives people a chance to take the best parts of the past with them as they move into a new, uncertain future. In doing so, people feel honored and can view the tremendous accomplishments they have been a part of achieving throughout their time in the organization. People literally see their contributions and their successes. But they also see that they have experienced a lot of change, reinforcing the value of resiliency and continuous improvement.

Core Questions for SMART Schools

There are any number of improvement approaches and models used to support schoolwide improvement. Each tends to have the same essential elements: the use of data, collaboration in teams, a results orientation, and a process for learning and ongoing improvement.

Regardless of the formal approach or model, a well-designed and well-implemented schoolwide improvement process should help you answer five key questions. Here is a brief description; further details are provided in the sections that follow:

1. **Where do we want to be?**

   This question helps the school community *focus* on their beliefs, core values, vision, mission, and function. It is also the question that invites people to dream about their preferred future, to imagine what is possible by moving beyond their daily concerns and challenges.

2. **Where are we now?**

   This question helps the school community *reflect* on the current situation to get a data-based view of what their school really looks like. In answering this question, school members gather baseline data to identify both strengths and weaknesses. The resulting picture helps point the way toward improvement priorities.

3. **How will we get there?**

   This question engages the school community in identifying and prioritizing goals with supporting rationale and improvement activities. This is where the school community reaches out to educational literature and best practice research to identify instructional strategies, curriculum, programs, and structures that they want to try out in their school. Benchmarking against successful schools with similar demographics and resources is another practice that can help focus improvement ideas. And, of course, staff development that develops teachers' skills and knowledge in the targeted improvement area is key to building the school's capacity to achieve its goals.

School Improvement Is Not a Dirty Word

For many schools, the term "school improvement" is pejorative: It means the school has been identified by the state and/or district as underperforming and therefore in need of improvement. Although low-performing schools have the most to gain from adoption of a formal school improvement process, schools that may be performing adequately or even well are missing a wonderful opportunity for re-energization and renewal when they ignore school improvement. In this book, school improvement refers to processes for building strong, vibrant professional learning communities—SMART schools—that are committed to continuous, never-ending improvement because it's the best way to *do school*. It's always the best way, not just when we're in trouble, not just when we have new staff coming on board, not just when we have a new strategic plan, but now, always, and long into the foreseeable future.

4. **What are we learning?**
   To answer this question, teaching teams and the school community as a whole use collaborative processes and data tools to periodically monitor the results of their implementation strategies, sharing what they're learning along the way and adjusting their approaches as needed.

5. **Where should we focus next?**
   This question is asked at the completion of each learning cycle: When an approach or strategy is found to work well, it becomes incorporated into the ongoing functioning of the school so that all students, teachers, and families can benefit. Then new priorities and goals are established based on new data gathered from results.

As usual, *asking* these five questions is the easy part. It's finding the answers that takes work.

Question 1: Where Do We Want to Be?

The answer to this question gives a school a sense that it knows where it's going, knows what it stands for, and knows what's important. This question deserves to be answered carefully and thoughtfully, with the voices of everyone involved in the school's enterprise —teachers, paraprofessionals, support staff, administrators, parents, students, and community members. (Review and renew the answers to this question periodically, as part of an ongoing process of building collective will—shared motivation—for continuous improvement of student results.)

There are three elements to answering this question:

- **Mission:** What the school exists to do.
- **Values:** What people associated with the school believe and hold dear.
- **Vision:** What the school and its community would like to achieve.

Core Questions for SMART Schools

→1. **Where do we want to be?**
 2. Where are we now?
 3. How will we get there?
 4. What are we learning?
 5. Where should we focus next?

The quality of education for children depends more on basic human and social resources in school, especially on the commitment and competence (*the will and skill*) of educators, and on students' efforts to learn.

—Center on Organization and Restructuring of Schools, 1995 research results based on studies of over 1,400 schools over 5 years (*emphasis ours*)

Mission

A school's mission answers the question, "What is our purpose?" or, "Why do we exist?" That may seem like an obvious question with an obvious answer, but when you get right down to it, there are many possible missions that any single school might pursue. If you polled individuals from inside and outside your school and asked, "Why does this school exist?" you may be surprised by the many different responses:

- To prepare students for the world of work
- To instill the joy of learning
- To develop basic skills in the areas of reading, writing, and arithmetic
- To meet the academic, social, and emotional needs of students
- To prepare students for college
- To have as many students graduate as possible
- To assure that all our students know and can pursue their personal dreams

None of these purposes are either right or wrong. But depending on which one (or any number of other possible missions) your school chooses, your course of action and choice of curricula and instructional practices will differ.

A clear statement of purpose, when developed collaboratively by those who must carry it out, will create cohesiveness, commitment, and understanding. The mission gives meaning to our work. When we know why we exist, we can be better at choosing how we will work and what work we choose to do. That is the essential value of a mission.

Creating a Mission Statement

The mission statement should communicate the essential aim of the school in a concise and memorable way. Once a written statement is created, the dialogue about what the statement means and how it will be used must be ongoing.

Question 1: Where Do We Want to Be?

→ Mission

Values

Vision

Mission Discussion

Rick DuFour and Bob Eaker (1998) aptly point out that most educational mission statements look and sound very much alike on the surface. When a school community begins to probe the underlying meaning, assumptions, and beliefs that exist in the minds of those who interpret the mission statement, they discover that the real mission might be quite different from what appears written in the plan or on the wall.

The only way to truly know the mission of your school is to talk about it and decide what best defines the purpose you want for your school. The mission of a school evolves out of community discourse and consensus building. It's much more than just a compelling statement. A mission statement becomes a mission when it lives in the hearts and minds of the teachers, staff, parents, administrators, and students. It is the reason we choose to work and learn at *this* particular school.

Copying From Others

Some schools have found mission statements from other schools that they like and would like to copy or modify for themselves. If your school adopts this strategy, that's fine—the *conversations* about what the statement means are more important than the words on a page. Just be sure to discuss the statement with stakeholder groups.

Creating a statement from scratch can be done in a variety of ways. If possible, include all staff and faculty and a representative group of parents in drafting a statement. If the size of your staff or timeline limitations prohibit everyone from being included in every step, appoint a small group to take the lead in creating a draft statement and then use various methods for involving others in reacting to, making suggestions, or revising the draft statement.

Brainwriting a Mission Statement

1. Divide your group into three smaller groups of no more than eight people (if you have a very large group, break them into six or nine smaller groups), all seated around tables.
2. Label three sheets of flipchart paper (or large pieces of butcher paper) with the following titles (one per page):

   AIM: What are we here to do?
   ACTION: How will we accomplish our aim?
   AUDIENCE: Whom do we exist to serve?

3. Review the rules of brainstorming (p. 89).
4. Give each table one of the three papers and a colored marker (a different color for each group). Tell them they have 2 minutes to generate responses to the question on their page. They should write brief phrases or words and number them as they go.
5. At the end of 2 minutes say "switch." The groups pass their paper (not their markers) to another table. Be sure that once the rotation starts, all papers go in the same direction each time. Give the groups 1 minute to review what the previous group wrote and 2 minutes to add more ideas.
6. The process of switching and timing continues until each group ends up with their original paper. (That is, each group has worked on all three sheets.)
7. Have the groups review the final lists together. People may ask questions for clarification wherever they do not understand what another group meant (or can't read their writing). Here's where the different colors are useful—if there is a question about something written in blue, the group knows where to find the answer. If you are working with more than three small groups, those groups with the same question (all papers labeled AIM, for example) should work together to reduce duplications and come up with one list that includes all ideas. Once the lists are cleaned up, the papers are posted on the wall for everyone to see.

Materials for Brainwriting a Mission Statement

- markers of 3 different colors
- flipchart paper
- tape
- colored dots

---

8. Narrow the number of ideas that the group will agree to use in its statement using a multivoting process (see p. 92). The goal is to develop a targeted list of words and phrases that most closely match the group's sense of what the school's mission ought to be. This, then, is the pool of ideas that will be used to create the mission statement.
9. Develop draft mission statements. Because group writing can be time-consuming, and, for some people, downright painful, divide the whole group into two or more smaller groups. Have each group write a statement, using the words and phrases from the list.
10. Share and compare statements as a whole group. Frequently, one or two will emerge as clear favorites or there are parts of one or two that everyone will like.

When schools are unable to coordinate teachers' diverse aims for students into a curricular mission focused on high-quality student learning, it is difficult for even the most gifted teachers to make a positive difference for students.

—F. M. Newmann and G. Wehlage

Sometimes it's useful to provide a structure or a framework for people to complete during this exercise. Not only does having a framework assure that essential parts of the statement are included, it's also a way of gaining consensus among the groups so that the different statements can be compared and merged. Here's one example:

Mission Statement Format

Our mission as a school community is _____ .
AIM and/or AUDIENCE

We do this by _____ .
ACTIONS

We do this so that

_____ .

REASON/PURPOSE

From this format, the school developed the following statement:

Our mission as a school community is to challenge our students to reach their academic potential. We do this by teaching them new knowledge and skills and respecting them for who they are. We do this so that they are prepared to meet future challenges with confidence and expertise and so that they experience the absolute joy of learning throughout the rest of their lives.

Checklist for Evaluating Your Mission Statement

Our mission statement

_____ Is clear and understandable

_____ Is brief enough for most people to remember and say in one breath

_____ Clearly specifies the school's fundamental purpose

_____ Has a primary focus on a single strategic thrust (such as learning)

_____ Reflects the distinctive competence and culture of this particular school

_____ Is broad enough to allow flexibility in implementation, but not so broad as to create a lack of focus

_____ Will help school personnel, parents, and community members make decisions

_____ Is energizing and compelling

Compare this sample mission statement to the format shown right above it. The mission or aim in this statement is to challenge students to reach their academic potential. The audience is the students. The actions are teaching and respecting. The *so that* portion of this statement gives future direction and definition to the outcomes that are desired when the mission is accomplished. People usually find the last part of this type of mission statement (the *so that*) most compelling.

The sample statement shown on p. 223 describes a noble and worthy purpose. However, it is likely to have different meanings to different audiences. For example, reaching academic potential is an often-used and equally often-debated phrase. That's why it is important to start with a draft statement and then have everyone in the school discuss what it means to them. Share the mission with parents, try it out on students, and get their reactions.

Using the Mission to Maintain Focus

A mission statement is most worthwhile when used daily. Many schools print their mission statement on their walls, stationery, business cards, refrigerator magnets, and the like. That's a good way to keep people aware of it, but these strategies alone won't guarantee its proper use. Here are some ideas for using your mission statement to help your school stay focused on its true purpose:

- Begin faculty meetings by reviewing the agenda against the mission: "How will this decision or discussion help us fulfill our mission? How is this consistent with our mission?"
- When a new program or initiative is introduced, create some time to have people discuss its relation to the mission.
- When deciding about new curricula or determining what not to teach, use the mission as your guide.
- Have people reflect on what they are currently doing or would do differently in light of the mission statement.
- Budget decisions are a good test for a mission. Are your resources being allocated in support of your mission?
- Staff development should support the mission as directly as possible.

Core Values

Core values are deeply held commitments that drive the conduct of the people within the school. When we live and work according to our core values, they become the driving force behind our actions. Anyone visiting our school will see them at work; they are anchored in behaviors and observable to even an untrained eye.

Core values are different than beliefs, although the two words are often used interchangeably. There is a practical difference: *Beliefs* are an expression of what we believe to be true. *Core values* are absolute commitments that translate directly into behaviors.

The two are closely related, however. Beliefs frequently reflect our core values and vice versa. For example, if I am deeply committed to meeting the needs of every individual child, it's probably because I believe that all children have the capacity to learn and that children learn in different ways. That belief serves to strengthen my commitment (core value/behavior) to differentiating instruction.

Why Is It Important to Identify Core Values and Beliefs?

The ultimate success of our collective efforts will rest on the degree to which we can agree upon and act in accordance with shared values and beliefs. Therefore, if we want to build shared responsibility in our schools, we need to make our values and beliefs explicit. Both core values and beliefs guide decision-making and actions. If a plan, decision, or set of actions is contrary to or inconsistent with either the values or beliefs of the people within the school, frustration, conflict, and uncertainty prevail. Conversely, when our plans, decisions, and actions align with our values and beliefs, there is energy, commitment, and focus.

Our beliefs are based on our underlying assumptions. By their very nature, underlying assumptions are subconscious. They shape how we think about and interpret what we hear, see, and feel. Most people are not even aware of the assumptions they are using when they make a statement or act in certain ways. That's because our assumptions are derived from our lifetime of experiences and are deeply embedded in who we are as individuals.

> ## Question 1: Where Do We Want to Be?
>
> Mission
> → **Values**
> Vision

> The collective power of a school faculty united behind a few important, commonly prized outcomes for students is virtually unlimited.
>
> —John Saphier and John D'Auria

Surfacing assumptions is an important part of developing shared values and beliefs. It requires honesty, open communication, and trust. It's a good idea to approach this kind of conversation as a facilitated process with ground rules and clear guidelines for how the process will unfold. (Guidelines for meetings and dialogue are given on pp. 64–75 and 87.)

For example, in discussing SMART goals, people might begin surfacing their concerns and fears about being able to help students reach their targets. Some may express frustration that a target such as "*all* students are proficient in *all* academic areas by the time they graduate" puts too much of a burden on students and teachers. In digging deeper into the reasons behind these concerns and fears, you might discover that teachers don't feel competent to move all students forward, or they may have assumptions about students' abilities (based on poverty, race, family situations, etc.). Conversations about the targets and assumptions, conducted in an atmosphere where it's okay to say what you really think and feel (without fear of blame or shame), can open new possibilities for growth and learning. (A useful consensus-building process for having honest conversations appears on p. 227.)

Three Types of Value Statements

During your work to identify core values and their assumptions, you may see what Jon Saphier and John D'Auria (1993) describe as three different types of value statements:

1. Core values as outcomes for students
2. Core values as commitments to each other
3. Core values as beliefs about conditions for learning

Together these three sets of values define what the school stands for.

Consensus Building on Profound Issues

The following Consensus Building process, developed by Bob Chadwick and further refined by Anne Rodgers Rhyme, is a way to get people talking about the things that matter to them in real and honest dialogue. It is a method for uncovering basic beliefs, sharing feelings (as important as thoughts), and working through conflict.

Process for Consensus Building on Profound Issues

Guidelines:
- Establish verbal territory (speak in turn for as long as each person needs)
- Listen with respect (make eye contact, do not interrupt, and remember what the speaker has said)
- Use your whole brain to listen and problem solve (the thinking *and* the feeling brain)

Time: 4 to 16 hours

Process:
1. Set up: Sit in chairs facing each other in a circle; No tables or paper and pencils for distractions or as "guards"
2. Grounding ("get your voice in the room"):
    - Introduce yourself and your relationship to _____ (issue/problem).
    - What are your expectations for the session?
    - How do you feel about being here?
3. Frame the issue; Develop details of the issue/problem:
    - What is the issue from your point of view? How do you feel about it?
4. Possibility thinking:
    - What are the worst possible outcomes of not resolving the issue/problem?
    - What are the best possible outcomes of resolving the issue/problem?
5. Generate solutions:
    - What new beliefs/behaviors will foster the best outcomes?
    - What new strategies/actions within your circle of control or influence will foster the best outcomes?
6. Talk about issues and solutions (steps 3–5) one by one in the circle, speaking in turn. Balance participation: If a woman spoke the first time, start next time with a man. If you went around the group clockwise the first time, go around the group counter-clockwise the next time. Continue the discussion until areas of consensus start to naturally arise.
7. Closing:
    - How did you feel about the session?
    - What did you learn that would help us resolve the issue/problem?

Source: Adapted from Consensus Associates, Terrebonne, Oregon. Used with permission.

Core Values as Outcomes for Students

The core values that define what we want our students to know and be like get to the heart of what makes a school community proud. These core values are stated as measurable outcomes to strive for and monitor over time. They help to determine *what* is taught.

> **Examples:** *Our students will leave here*
> - *Knowing how to solve everyday problems and will have the skills and knowledge to do so*
> - *With the confidence that each is worthwhile, has something to offer to their community, and takes responsibility for making positive contributions*
> - *With respect for human differences of all kinds*

Core Values as Commitments to Each Other

Here the focus is on the adult behaviors that will support the outcomes the school community desires for its students. These core commitments are strongly linked to our underlying beliefs about educators' roles and responsibilities in the system.

For example, if we believe that everyone shares responsibility for improving the learning environment for students, our promises (core commitments) will reflect a *collective set* of actions and policies about safety, respect, discipline, and managing the teachable moment even if we're dealing with somebody else's students. Those promises would be quite different if we believed that individual teachers are solely responsible for the success of the students in their classrooms. This second belief would foster actions and policies designed to protect individual teachers' rights, academic freedoms, responsibilities, and accountability.

Core Values as Beliefs About Conditions for Learning

This set of core values pertains to what people in the school believe about learning. These beliefs provide the strongest rationale for determining how we choose to teach. For example, if we believe that learning involves making mistakes, we will view and deal with mistakes differently than if we believe that mistakes are a sign that learning has not occurred. Similarly, if we believe that consistent effort is the main determinant of success, then we will set high standards and encourage all children to work hard to meet them. If, however, we believe that innate intelligence is the main determinant of success, then we will set high standards and encourage only those children we perceive to be highly intelligent to meet them.

How to Identify Core Values

Core values and beliefs, like underlying assumptions, are not always readily apparent. People need time to reflect individually about what they personally value and believe. They also need a collaborative process for examining and articulating their shared values and beliefs.

1. Explain the difference between a core value and a belief to staff.

2. Give people time to reflect on Saphier and D'Auria's (1993) three questions:

    *   When your students leave you, how do you want them to be different, as people, as a result of being with you all year long?

    *   What promises are you willing to make to your colleagues that will support your school's success in achieving its mission?

    *   What are your fundamental, bedrock beliefs about how children learn and your role in making that happen?

3. Choose one of the three questions (it doesn't matter which one) and have staff write their responses on self-stick notes (one idea per note). Post them randomly on a large chart or butcher paper on the wall.

    *   If the group is very large, divide into smaller groups and create several charts for each question.

4. Repeat step 3 for the other two questions.

5. After all three questions have been answered and the charts are full, conduct an Affinity Process (see p. 90) to categorize the ideas into like groups.

If there are several Affinity Charts being constructed simultaneously by smaller groups, ask the groups to report only on what they wrote for the main headings. Identify the commonalities and discuss the differences. Then rearrange the participants into small groups around the three questions and have them write four to five value or belief statements that capture the common ideas generated by the group at large.

Vision

A *vision* is a compelling picture of a preferred future that motivates us to act. Some refer to vision as a hope or a dream. But vision is more than that. It might start as a hope or a dream, but it doesn't become a vision until there is some specificity about what that dream will look like in reality. What distinguishes a dream from a vision is the detail of the vision in action, something people can see or envision themselves doing. That is what makes a vision compelling. That is why vision motivates us to act—sometimes in ways that are very different than we ever would have imagined.

Vision is the manifestation of our stated values, the actualization of our common mission. When groups create their visions, it helps them to start with their mission and value statements. The vision is the best possible future that can be created by successfully accomplishing the mission in a way that is consistent with one's values and beliefs.

Shared vision answers the questions, Where do we want to be in the future? How great can we become? and What do we want to create together? Shared vision captures the collective imagination of everyone in the school. It is a vivid picture of a place that could potentially be very different because the school community has collectively committed to creating it together.

Developing Shared Vision

Too often, groups begin the visioning process by trying to write a vision statement. Though this is not an impossible task, it is a more difficult way to begin because people have not had the time to think, interact, and dream together. What typically happens in these situations is that groups become mired in the words and ultimately lose sight of the purpose . . . to develop shared vision.

Question 1: Where Do We Want to Be?

Mission

Values

→Vision

We make our future dreams come true by acting on our own values today.

—Marvin Weisbord

The vision statement is a communication device that is best created *after* a group has engaged in the *process* of visioning. It is the visioning process that causes people to think differently, to be creative and to design a future that is consistent with their mission and values.

In setting the stage for visioning, it is important for people to think about the future as something potentially quite different from today. The key is to create opportunities and to provide time and structures for people to talk about their hopes and dreams.

There are a number of processes for creating shared vision. The best ones

- Keep people focused on a key question about the future
- Involve a diverse mix of stakeholders
- Build in time for both large- and small-group discussions

Although there are no hard and fast rules for how many people to involve in developing a vision, it is important to involve those who will be in a position to lead or influence others, those who will bring fresh perspectives, and those who are highly regarded by their peers. We suggest involving individuals from the following stakeholder groups:

- Parents
- Community members
- Board members
- Principals
- Central office administrators
- Teachers
- Other school staff
- Students or graduates where appropriate

The key to effective visioning is helping people get out of their current way of thinking and acting. This is not to suggest that the current way is bad or wrong, but if we are to create a new vision, we need to be able to see a different picture. Sometimes the existing structures,

Why Shared Vision Is Important

When individual visions come together into shared vision, there is a collective power unlike anything else a group or school could experience. Simply by virtue of the energy it creates, shared vision becomes a resource or an asset that propels the organization toward a better future. Shared vision provides long-term direction and excitement about the future. It provides motivation for change and fuel for the challenge. Shared vision is a key factor in creating both alignment and commitment to the journey of continuous improvement.

Without shared vision, when times get tough—enrollment falls, a safety crisis occurs, contract talks stall, test scores decline—conflicts are more frequent, intense, and enduring; communication breaks down; and factions and isolationism become the norm. Creating shared vision is a proactive way to help the school community remain cohesive and focused in times of crisis.

systems, and even facilities are so limiting that people can't see a different future. That is why we suggest using processes that are not typically how a group/staff/community works together. For the same reason, it's also a good idea to conduct the visioning activities in locations other than your existing school if at all possible.

The following examples show different processes you can use to generate vision in groups:

Blue Sky Scenarios: An entrepreneurial approach—ignore all that was or is and create something totally new from scratch. Imagine that there is no school building and that there are no existing rules, contracts, or policies. There are no limitations of resources nor mandates from the district, state, or federal government. Now, review your mission and values. If you could create the school of your dreams, what would it look like?

Forecasting Scenarios: This is what some refer to as reality-based visioning—attempting to predict the future by analyzing trends and then designing around those predictions. What are the big trends in education? What impact will technology have? standards-based reforms? the accountability movement? What will be happening with our financial resources in the future? our human resources? our demographics? Have groups use the same facts to develop separate scenarios and share them with each other. Take the best and most likely elements from each to craft your vision.

Time Warp: Take an imaginary trip through time, ending up somewhere in the future (5 to 10 years out). Turn on the evening news. What are the stories they're telling about your school? Begin the dialogue with, "What will you be proud to hear them saying about us?" Or, "Imagine it is 5 years from now. Our school has just received the Blue Ribbon Schools of Excellence Award. This award is given to only a select few schools in the nation. Recently visitors from all over the United States have been visiting to learn what is going on to make this such an outstanding school." Describe this award-winning, ideal school. What kinds of things do you see? What does the school look like? What is happening with students? staff? parents? community?

Mapping: Map out the assets of your community and how each relates to the others. What are your human assets? your technology assets? your financial assets? your geographic assets? Which emerge as natural connections? Which needed connections are missing?

Role Play: Have people return to their core values and beliefs and then create a way to communicate those values to the rest of the group. One rule: There are no rules. They can use any form of expression they like—a skit, dance, poem, rap, newscast, song, or picture. Then allow 5 minutes for each group to perform or share their vision of the future.

Pictogram: A visual representation of the future. Give each small group a large piece of chart paper, poster board, or butcher paper, plus boxes of markers, some sticky dots, construction paper, glue, stickers, or even small toys or light objects that they can attach to the picture. Their task as a group is to create a visual image of the future. There are two rules for creating a pictogram: (1) Everyone must be involved in the actual creation. (2) The group may not use words—only symbols—to express their ideas. Share the individual pictograms with the large group and identify common themes and patterns.

These processes are designed to get people thinking creatively about their future and to actively involve all the participants in the creative process. The most important part of this is the conversations that go into creating the vision itself, not the document, skit, or picture. You may need to reassure people that artistic talent is not the point. It's the shared dream that really matters.

Once a group has had the opportunity to create a vision together, writing the statement becomes an exercise in capturing the ideas and energy that the vision(s) generated. This may take anywhere from a couple of hours to a day or two, depending on the process selected and the number of people involved.

> To have a vision within a domain in which one can take no action is hypocrisy.
>
> —Peter Senge

Examples of Vision Statements

- We are committed to successful learning, child by child.
- Every child is a promise—we will be a community of learners and leaders, united in our goal to enrich the lives of all our children through learning.
- We will be a safe place to learn and work, where all of our collective energy and resources are directed toward the unique and diverse learning needs of every child.

Keep the Conversation Going

It's important to keep the vision conversation going and to return to it often. Why?

- As new people (staff, students, and families) enter the school community, they will need to become acquainted with and committed to the vision.
- By its very nature, a vision is not physically present; it is in the hearts and minds of those who created it. Therefore, it must continually be shared if it is to become reality.
- The vision will reform and reshape itself as it evolves into reality. That reformation should be guided by desire, not by default.

Characteristics of Vision Statements

The vision statement, like the mission statement, should be concise and compelling. The words are very important because they must convey meaning beyond simple understanding. They must be inspirational, communicate promise, and create an image of something that cannot be seen today, but is possible tomorrow. Vision statements

- Are concrete—have observable, detectable qualities
- Focus on ends not means—communicate what, not how
- Are achievable and compelling—believable, but beyond what *is*
- Manifest the mission and values—as the school community lives its values and accomplishes its mission well, this is what you will see as a result

 Tips for Writing Vision Statements

- Have a larger group (an entire staff or a mix of staff and parents) generate some sample statements. You may want to divide the group into small mixed subgroups (each smaller group represents the diversity of the entire group as much as possible).
- Designate a team to write an initial draft of a vision statement.
- Before sending the team off to draft the statement, use a *walkabout* process in the larger group to help people see the breadth of statements generated and clarify any confusion. To do this, post each group's statement on the wall. Have everyone walk around and *silently* read the statements. They can make comments by leaving sticky notes on the chart page, such as suggestions, compliments, requests for clarification, etc. The small groups then return to their statements, read through the comments, and incorporate any changes they would like to make. The statements and comments are given to the team that will draft the full vision statement.
- Afterward, the team writes a draft statement that incorporates the ideas from all the others and circulates their draft to *all* staff for comment (not just those who were included in the initial work).

Keeping the Vision Alive

Writing a vision statement is not what creates successful districts and schools. The visioning process is a journey, one kept alive by the way that everyone in the school community frames each and every conversation and in the way actions are supported in pursuit of the vision.

Through modeling, reinforcement, and recognition, a vision is kept alive and will begin to gain momentum as people play with it a little. They need time to imagine what it would be like for them to be in this future and how their personal lives will be different. It is especially important for leaders to share what the vision means to them, revealing their personal thoughts about the vision and how they see it unfolding. It is important that leaders write and talk about how they see the vision connecting to the mission and values of the school.

To keep the vision alive, ask people what they think:

- "Do you think the vision is feasible?"
- "Is it something you are willing to commit to?"
- "Does it reflect what you want?"

Listen respectfully to their answers, exploring what they have to say through dialogue. Invite comments and incorporate those comments into the emerging vision statement. This will help to create a sense that this vision truly is shared.

You can reinforce a vision by

- Continually encouraging people to dream and hope beyond the day
- Using planning and goal-setting sessions that include visioning
- Providing time to pursue the vision and goals

When people are doing things that will lead to or enhance the vision, bring those actions to the awareness of the individual and group to help everyone see how they contribute to the development of shared vision. These *visioning by grass fire* practices ultimately help people internalize the vision into their daily behavioral repertoire.

What If We're Not Ready to Create a Vision?

Sometimes a school has been through so many changes, so much strife, that it really isn't ready as a community to start dreaming about the future. In these cases, it may be helpful to conduct an oral history storytelling process that we call the *Historygram* (p. 218). In these situations, make sure each storyboard includes a list of values from the past that participants want to carry into the future. These values are then used as a springboard for visioning and creating shared values for the future of the school.

For more information about the Historygram process, see "Capturing an Organization's Oral History" by Jan O'Neill in *Educational Leadership*, April 2000. Also see *Building Shared Responsibility* by Anne Conzemius and Jan O'Neill, published by ASCD, 2001.

Core Questions for SMART Schools

1. Where do we want to be?
→2. **Where are we now?**
3. How will we get there?
4. What are we learning?
5. Where should we focus next?

Question 2: Where Are We Now?

Gathering and analyzing data on which to base a school's improvement plan and evaluate results may require a wide variety of qualitative and quantitative tools, balanced with a good share of intuition and common sense about what all the data mean. Previous chapters described various types of tools you can use to collect and analyze diverse information (see Chapters 5, 6, and 7).

In addition to the tools presented in previous chapters, there are two specific strategies that are particularly helpful in answering the question, "Where are we now?": **needs assessment** and **friendly observers**. When used together, these strategies generate high-quality, in-depth information your school can use to understand where it is today.

Needs Assessment

When we think about improving student learning, we tend to focus only on student academic or behavioral indicators. Research has shown, however, that many other factors affect student learning, such as parent and community involvement and support, school climate, classroom instructional activities, curriculum alignment, professional community, pedagogical and assessment practices, equitable access to curriculum and instruction, teacher quality, professional development, leadership capacity, resources, etc. To fully understand a school's current performance, it is important to assess a variety of factors and dimensions.

A comprehensive *needs assessment* is a tool for assessing a diversity of factors. The process engages teachers schoolwide in identifying areas they want to learn more about, organizing themselves into teacher-led study teams to research those areas, and bringing that information back to the school community as a whole. This strategy has proven to be a powerful method for discovering change, learning, and improvement.

Before conducting a needs assessment, you may want to spend time identifying the key measures or indicators for your school. Creating a dashboard of these indicators (see Figure 10.1) makes it easier to track progress over time.

The School Dashboard: Keeping an Eye on Improvement Indicators

Before embarking on a comprehensive needs assessment, it is helpful to define the key indicators the school is interested in measuring and monitoring over time. In addition to student achievement, a school will want to keep an eye on other success factors that contribute to successful achievement. A helpful tool is the *dashboard,* first presented to the public by Christopher Meyer (*Harvard Business Review,* May–June 1994, pp. 95–103: "How the Right Measures Help Teams Excel") and adapted here for use in schools. It is portrayed just like a car's dashboard, with the gauges one would periodically review to make sure the school is staying on its continuous improvement course. The first step is to decide which gauges you want to keep an eye on—just as we don't watch every gauge all the time when driving, the *vital few* gauges should be selected for monitoring. Then measures need to be defined and/or developed for those few gauges. These measures should be routinely reviewed, some annually, some more frequently, by the school as a whole. The result of these reviews can be summarized by indicating with the gauges' arrows how well the school is doing.

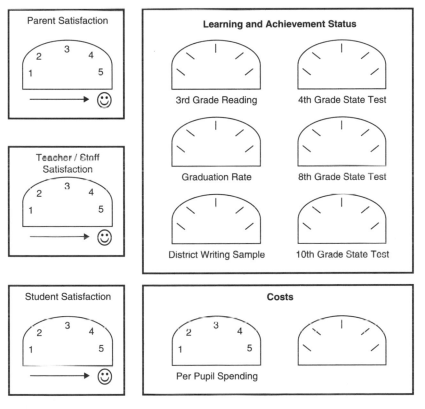

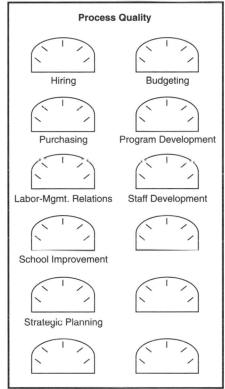

Figure 10.1 The School System Dashboard

There are at least six major areas of study that any school will want to take a look at when conducting a thorough needs assessment:

1. **Community:** the people *inside* the school's walls (students, teachers, paraprofessionals, support staff, and administrators), as well as people *outside* the school's walls (parents, families, community-based organizations, local businesses, labor unions, religious leaders, central office staff, school board members, and others).

2. **Order, discipline, and climate:** the school's internal functioning, specifically policies, procedures, and systems for ensuring safety and a positive learning environment.

3. **Achievement:** students' academic skills, knowledge, and capabilities as measured by standardized tests and classroom/district-based assessments.

4. **Teaching and learning systems:** students' opportunity to learn, processes for identifying and assisting underachieving students, staff development practices, methods of identifying and incorporating best practices into the school, integration of technology as a tool for learning, and the amount of collaborative inquiry that occurs throughout the school.

5. **Curriculum and instruction:** processes for developing and improving curriculum, methods for evaluating outcomes against standards, and the array of teaching and assessment practices used.

6. **Resources:** a catchall category that includes not only the school's use of time and money, but also faculty/staff qualifications and competencies, administrative capabilities, organization of the school, the school's ability to translate goals into actions, communication systems, and the depth and breadth of skillful leadership throughout the school.

The full staff should brainstorm with the following questions: What do we want to know about these areas? and How can we find out? Use a wide range of measures to find the answers.

In addition to gathering information in these six areas, schools will want to get a clear picture of their student demographics—age, gender, race, ethnicity, mobility, socio-economic status, special education status, etc. When students' academic status (as measured by grades, test scores, and other measures) is broken out for different subgroups, often the resulting picture is an eye-opening impetus for improvement.

Friendly Observers

The needs assessment process can be augmented by feedback from a team of friendly observers, experienced educators, and other experts who observe your school at work and provide their own commentary and insights.

More specifically, friendly observers should provide constructive feedback about the school's teaching and learning system, teachers' use of best practices, and the overall climate for leadership and learning.

For the friendly observer process to work well, it is important that the staff—particularly teachers—be fully involved in the process of selection and recruitment, as well as have significant input into what the observers are looking for. A staff that is open to looking in the mirror and really *seeing* what is there has taken a powerful first step toward making improvements.

Process for Using Friendly Observers

1. Have staff brainstorm a list of questions they would like answered about your school.
2. Have staff develop criteria for selecting the friendly observers. Here is a set of criteria developed by one school:
   * Knows our district/school
   * Understands poverty and learning issues
   * Has deep knowledge of reading literacy
   * Has deep knowledge of math literacy
   * Has curriculum, instruction, and assessment experience
   * Holds central office position
   * Holds university position
   * Is a colleague/peer
3. Review the criteria, and then ask staff to brainstorm names of potential friendly observers. The candidates should be people who are highly credible and trusted. As a whole, they should represent a variety of perspectives and areas of knowledge. These brainstormed names become your recruiting list.

4. Create a lead team to work on recruitment and final selection and to organize the logistics (planning their visit, clarifying expectations and needs, designing the process, etc.).

   • Try to recruit 5 to 10 observers.

   • Prepping the observers should include a reminder that their role is to uncover *strengths* as well as opportunities for improvement because the school will need to build on those strengths to achieve its improvement goals.

5. Have the observers visit your school.

   • Schedule the visit over a period of several days, during which they observe classrooms and interview staff, students, parents, and the principal.

   • To create a safe environment for the friendly observer process, allow teachers to opt out when they need uninterrupted teaching time. One option: Simply have teachers post a sign that says "Pass" on the door to their schoolroom. The observers will be instructed to avoid rooms with such signs.

6. Have the observers meet off-site to compare notes and compile a final report highlighting the school's strengths and opportunities for improvement.

7. Share this report among the staff.

Core Questions for SMART Schools

1. Where do we want to be?
2. Where are we now?
→ **3. How will we get there?**
4. What are we learning?
5. Where should we focus next?

Question 3: How Will We Get There?

By this point in your schoolwide improvement process, you will know what your school's mission, values, and vision are (where you *want* to be); you'll also know where you are now. The next question is how you will go from here to there. The planning process begins by translating your mission into concrete *priorities* and *goals* that will help your school decide specific tasks that need to be done.

Priorities

The mission, core values and beliefs, and vision statements discussed earlier in this chapter provide a broad and overarching focus to define what is important to your school community. However, it is your community's *priorities* that help to bring focus in a way that narrows and targets the most important work of the school.

The mission, values, beliefs, and vision help to define what the priority work should be: that which most effectively helps us achieve our vision. Core values and beliefs tell us *how* we must work together to fulfill the mission and achieve the vision; priorities tell us *what* we need to do to achieve our mission and vision. Having priorities means that we are choosing to do the things that help us achieve our vision, that reflect a deep understanding of our school's and our students' needs. Having priorities also means that we are choosing *not* to do things that are nonessential to the vision.

> If you have dozens of priorities you have no priorities.

Selecting Priorities

Select priorities based on what you discover during the "Where are we now?" phase. Priorities should be few in number: If a school has 20 priorities, it has *no* priorities.

The Pareto principle (p. 9) is a useful thinking tool for helping educators select priorities: We need to focus on the *vital few* issues, problems, etc., that will have the biggest impact if addressed. Pareto thinking keeps us from trying to be all things, for all people, in all areas, all the time. It also helps us figure out where to allocate our precious resources of time, energy, and dollars in ways that will have the most likelihood for success.

One way to select priorities is to use brainstorming, affinity, and multivoting to collectively identify *all* the possible priorities and the *vital few* for improvement focus.

1. Review the needs assessment data in depth.
2. Have staff members (and parents and students if possible) brainstorm all the priority needs, using one sticky note per idea.
   - These might appear as high mobility, poor performance in math, too many discipline referrals, lack of curriculum alignment, etc. The point is to write the priorities as *needs* or *gaps*.
3. Group like ideas using the Affinity Process (p. 90). Name the major header categories.
4. Multivote (p. 92) for the top priority needs using sticky-dots, with each member voting on the header cards (not on the details beneath).

5. Count the number of votes for each header card.
6. Create a Pareto diagram (p. 148) showing the largest to smallest category. Include another category for those items receiving no votes.
7. The top vote getters are the priorities to focus on. Some categories may be things the school community can do little about directly (e.g., mobility), but they can focus on ways to make that factor or need less of an issue for student learning.
8. Before making the final decision, be sure to hold another conversation with the whole group to probe whether these are the priorities all are willing to focus on.

Here is another method:

1. Review the needs assessment data from all sources.
2. Review the Pareto principle.
3. Give each faculty member a piece of paper and have them fold the paper in half twice.
4. Have them unfold the paper and in each quadrant write one specific area of need that he or she feels is the highest priority (the vital few) for the school to address.
5. When everyone has finished, have them discard one of their priorities. Go through the discarding process until each person has only one left.
6. Go around the room and collect the top priority from each person and post it on a chart, tallying wherever there are duplications. This becomes the narrow list of priorities that can then be voted on using the multivoting process described on page 92.

Figure 10.2 (p. 243) shows the priorities identified by one school.

Planning Around Your Priorities

Once you've selected your priorities, you need to flesh out what those priorities mean for your school. Here's a simple technique that can help school teams figure out what to do about their priorities. Keep in mind throughout this process that opinions, theories, and suggestions need to be verified with data.

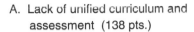

Mendota Elementary School
Survey Results—Summary of Highest Needs

A. Lack of unified curriculum and assessment (138 pts.)

B. Mobile, minority students score lowest (105 pts.)

C. Low reading and writing scores (77 pts.)

D. Little involvement of African American families (71 pts.)

E. Disruptive behaviors (69 pts.)

F. Varying teacher expectations (58 pts.)

G. Safety (50 pts.)

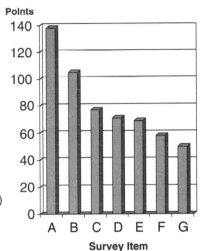

Figure 10.2 Sample of School Priorities

Note. From Mendota Elementary School. Reprinted with permission.

For each priority (remember, you should only have a few),

1. Post three chart papers on the wall, labeled as follows:
   - **Keep doing**—things that we currently do that work well and help us meet our priorities (verify with feedback from friendly observers, see page 239).
   - **Stop doing**—distractions, tangents, and things that may be fun or we are comfortable doing, but don't help us address or meet our priorities.
   - **Start doing**—new needs or areas of neglect where changes, additions, or improvement will significantly and creatively take us to a different place relative to our priorities.

2. Have people post self-stick notes with suggested programs, activities, behaviors, and practices for each of the three areas. Specifically, what content, instructional practices, policies and procedures, behaviors, and professional development activities need to be examined relative to our priorities?

3. Conduct an Affinity Process (p. 90) with the suggestions.

Examples of Priorities

- Improving student achievement for all students
- Assuring a safe, respectful, and welcoming learning environment
- Strengthening community and family partnerships and communication
- Offering a challenging, diverse, and contemporary curriculum and instruction

> **The lack of clear goals may provide the most credible explanation for why we are still only inching along in our effort to improve schooling for U.S. children.**
>
> **—Mike Schmoker**

4. Discuss the potential impact, consequences, and possibilities of the main ideas; verify with data; and analyze the impact using the Relations Diagram (p. 138) and other thinking tools.

5. Create small work teams to follow through on the ideas to which the group agreed.

Goals

Without goals, all of our other focusing efforts remain words on a page. Goals organize our improvement efforts. Collectively and cumulatively, they define the vision in ways that are both actionable and attainable. Good goals are what give specificity and measurability to our priorities. They provide direction, define outcomes, and communicate expectations for improvement in ways that can be measured and monitored over time.

Process and Results Goals

Most goals in education are process goals: They focus on the activities, programs, strategies, and methods that educators want to engage in. Process goals aren't bad; they're just not particularly useful as a way to achieve and measure a particular outcome. Checking a process goal means seeing if the program, strategy, method, or activity was implemented—that is, whether the process was changed. But knowing a process changed doesn't tell you whether the desired outcome or result was achieved.

The problem is not that we use process goals—we need good processes to build capacity. The problem lies in having only process goals, with no goals that measure the effectiveness of the processes we put in place (results goals).

Results goals answer the "so what" question: So what if we did all these things? What actual improvement would we expect or want to see? To be useful tools for measuring performance and progress, goals should be results-oriented rather than process-oriented. They should identify what is desired in terms of performance after, or as a result of, putting new processes in place or improving existing processes.

Table 10.1 offers examples of process- and results-oriented goals.

Table 10.1 Process and Results-Oriented Goals

Process	Results
Means	Ends
Inputs	Outputs
Capacity improvements	Productivity
System interventions	Outcomes
Improvement activities	Improvement targets
Function	Purpose

Examples of Process and Results Goals

Process: Integrate math and science curricula.

—*so that*—

Result: Students are better able to apply math and science concepts to real-life tasks.

Process: Hire star-quality teachers.

—*so that*—

Result: Student achievement improves.

Process: Budget additional time for staff collaboration and professional development.

—*so that*—

Result: Staff are more focused on and skillful in improving student results.

The bottom line is, we need both good processes *and* results.

SMART Schools Set SMART Goals

The Introduction to this book described how SMART goals could become a driving force behind continuous improvement. SMART goals provide us with the means to develop feedback on which of our efforts are making a difference and by how much. This holds true not only for individual teams, but also for a school or district as a whole. Once you're clear about the results you want to achieve as a school, it's time to put even more specificity into your goals.

Examples of SMART Goals

District Level

- All students will be reading at grade level by the end of third grade.
- All students will demonstrate proficiency in all tested areas (reading, language arts, math, science, and social studies) by the time they graduate.
- Our district ranks in the top ten academically in our state.

Classroom Level

- Achieve a 20% increase in the number of students demonstrating advanced proficiency in second grade reading by the end of the semester.
- 80% of first and second graders will be able to auditorially identify musical instruments by the end of the school year using a textbook's pre- and post-tests.
- Increase student attendance by 50% by the end of this school year for students who have been absent seven days or more since the beginning of the school year.

To set SMART goals at the school level, the principals, teachers, staff, parents, and students need to ask broad questions about their particular student population:

- In which areas of the standardized test were our students weakest this year—math, reading, language arts and writing, science, or social studies?
- Has this been a consistently weak area for students over the years or just for a particular cohort of students?
- What patterns do we see in the data? How are girls doing compared to boys? Children of color versus caucasian children? Is mobility a factor? How is our special education population doing?
- Are there other performance measures that verify that this area is weak at our school? Do we have district or classroom assessments to back this up?

Once an academic area has been identified, the school needs to ask these questions: What do we know about the climate at our school? Which aspects of climate are most important to our students, families, and staff? Which are most strongly related to student learning? On which of the most important aspects are we weakest? Also, behavior patterns (attendance, referrals) need to be examined: What impact does attendance have on learning and achievement in our school? Is there a correlation between behavior referrals and low achieving students?

One planning tool that helps people think through multiple indicators, measures, and targets—rather than overly focusing on just standardized test scores—is the Tree Diagram (p. 105). Once you have used it to outline your thinking, you can then write one or two SMART goals that you want to pursue for the year, the semester, or the quarter. Pages 269–272 in the Appendix section show sample tree diagrams for SMART goals at several different grade levels.

Developing SMART goals is not a one-time event. Regular monitoring allows teachers to adjust strategies against intended results. When teachers are using SMART goals to learn, they

- Set specific, measurable, learner-focused goals together
- Plan how to help learners accomplish those goals

- Gather evidence of individual and class progress toward the goal, analyze trends over time, and compare results to exemplar schools as examples of best practices
- Share their results
- Adjust teaching strategies based on what they're learning together
- Develop new plans for meeting their goals, etc.

School improvement plans should include SMART goals that address achievement gaps as well as climate issues, but SMART schools focus on no more than two or three goals at a time. Based on the needs of the school, action plans for achieving goals frequently focus on ways to better serve underachieving students; challenge and enrich all students; increase parent and community communication, involvement, and support; provide continuous professional development for teachers; assist students with transitions; and increase everyone's sense of community and belonging.

Plans for Achieving Priorities and Goals

The use of the PDSA (plan-do-study-act) cycle can help you develop action plans for achieving your SMART goals and priorities. You need to

PLAN for the proposed change; specifically, what actions and tasks should be done by whom? In the first go-round, look at implementing the change on a small scale so that you can learn from the experience.

DO the change according to your plan.

STUDY the results: Did you get the desired results? Did you use the planned methods?

ACT: If the answer to both the Study questions is yes, then use PDSA to implement the change on a bigger scale. If the answer to either or both is no, you need to understand what happened, and either revise the plan or document actual methods before going another round on PDSA to confirm that the methods you're using will achieve the desired results.

Figure 10.3 on page 248 shows the characteristics of effective plans. See page 273 for a sample School Improvement Annual Planning and Reporting Document.

> When an organization has multiple unmeasurable priorities, there's lots of activity, but not much really gets done, and results are slow to come or nonexistent.
>
> —D. Sparks

 A template of a school improvement plan appears on the CD-ROM.

CHARACTERISTICS OF EFFECTIVE PLANS

An effective school improvement plan creates collective understanding of and commitment to the school's future as well as a course of action that will take the school to where it wants to be. When coupled with effective processes, effective school improvement plans lead to better results—and increased school capacity for continuous learning and improvement. Effective school improvement plans are

Essential. Focused on the vital few priorities for the school (usually no more than two to three priority goals). At least one goal should address student learning; another should relate to school climate.

Focused. On results *and* process. Student learning and achievement are always front and center. The processes and methods (such as staff development, instructional programs and structures, school-community building activities, etc.) that support successful learning and achievement are treated as critical success factors.

Fiscally responsible. Implementation strategies and timelines are doable within current constraints and resources. Tap into multiple sources of funding through grants and partnerships to create a bigger "pie" for the improvement work.

Easy to read. The written document is organized into a logical flow. It is concise, complete, and illustrated with graphs and charts that paint an accurate portrait of the school. There is a limited use of jargon, and when it is used, terms are explained.

Collaboratively developed. Document your process for developing and monitoring the plan; show how you will involve multiple stakeholders.

Targeted at specific standards of performance. SMART (specific and strategic, measurable, attainable, results-oriented, and time-bound) goals are focused on outcomes. Data were disaggregated to identify targeted improvements. Standards and specific assessments (classroom and district-based as well as standardized) help establish specific, measurable goals and monitor progress.

Instructionally sound. Strategies address staff development needs as they relate to student learning and achievement needs. Staff development plans are based on a careful review of staff needs and incorporate best practices in staff development implementation. The instructional and programmatic strategies and approaches are based on careful review of educational literature and best practice research.

Vertically and horizontally aligned. Effective plans are linked to the district's strategic plan, priorities, or goals. They connect each grade and school—elementary, middle, and high—creating strong links for students as they transition from grade to grade, level to level. The plans are schoolwide in scope, so that each teacher and staff person understands his or her role and responsibility in helping the school achieve the plan's goals.

Elevating. Plans should include nothing but the highest standards for all students and adults in the school community.

Figure 10.3 Characteristics of Effective Plans
Note. Copyright © 2001 by QLD, LLC. Reprinted with permission.

Question 4: What Are We Learning?

As your school begins to implement its plans, you can use *collaborative inquiry* to make sure you capture lessons learned along the way. Collaborative inquiry is the process of looking at your data, asking penetrating questions of one another, and deciding what is being learned about your students, your instructional strategies and approaches being used, and your professional practice. It is how the data-logic chain introduced in Chapter 3 (p. 63) can be operationalized.

Collaborative inquiry guides people in asking good (logical) questions, letting data provide the answers, and then using the data to lead to the next set of logical questions so that there is a thorough understanding of the current situation *before* solutions are put in place.

A culture of collaborative inquiry requires that certain fundamentals be observed to maintain an environment of dignity, trust, and respect. People will be much more inclined to be open and honest about results when they are assured, through words and deeds, that a continuous *learning* environment exists.

Tips for Conducting Effective Collaborative Inquiry

- Use the advocacy/inquiry method (p. 88) in staff discussions to help uncover people's understanding and interpretation of the outcomes from your plan.
- Gather both perceptual and numerical data to assess performance as your plan is implemented. Measure before and after results as well as ongoing progress.
- Many of the snapshot tools covered in Chapter 6 can help. If you have data that might help you explore cause-and-effect relationships, use a scatterplot (p. 150) to correlate results with an intervention or activity. Scatterplots are a particularly useful tool for assessing the impact of improvements.
- Moving picture tools can be used to monitor ongoing progress and to assess whether the plan is taking effect over time.

Core Questions for SMART Schools

1. Where do we want to be?
2. Where are we now?
3. How will we get there?
→ 4. **What are we learning?**
5. Where should we focus next?

Principles of Collaborative Inquiry

The following principles of collaborative inquiry have been adopted by many schools to assist in creating an environment that supports shared, continuous learning:

- We are in this together to make a difference for children's learning.
- People are basically good and want to do a good job.
- All people deserve to be treated with dignity and respect.
- There is value to be gained by bringing multiple perspectives and skills together.
- All of us are learners . . . all of us are leaders.

Core Questions for SMART Schools

1. Where do we want to be?
2. Where are we now?
3. How will we get there?
4. What are we learning?
→ 5. **Where should we focus next?**

Question 5: Where Should We Focus Next?

As you implement your plans (Question 3) and learn from the results (Question 4), you will generate improvements that begin to shift your priorities. Once a problem or issue is reduced or eliminated, you need to move on to the next priority or goal. To decide when and where to move on, continue to review school trends, compare your school to exemplary schools, and assess your results and processes against your ongoing results and theirs.

Re-establishing goals and strategies based on results involves creating new SMART goals, new staff development plans, and new implementation strategies. Here again, use Pareto thinking to refocus on the new vital few. Use tree diagrams to help in planning new goals; invite friendly observers back to help identify new opportunities for growth and improvement. Throughout this process, you can build confidence and support for schoolwide improvement efforts by inviting stakeholders (parents, community members, and others) from outside the school walls to be part of the ongoing learning process.

To emphasize the need to regularly review and revise your school's or district's goals, you may want to develop a regular calendar for review that occurs in conjunction with annual planning and budgeting processes. This can assure that resources are directed towards true priorities, and that communication occurs throughout the entire school or district. Whitewater School District in Wisconsin has established just such a process (Figure 10.4).

June–August

- Building teams analyze data and plan for improvement.

August–September

- Building teams establish improvement plans based on identified district priorities and building needs.
- Plans specify targets for improvement.

October

- Building teams outline improvement plans for the Board at a public meeting.
- Board provides input regarding plans and targets.

October–May

- Building teams implement improvement plans and gather assessment data.

December

- Budget priorities are set knowing current focus of improvement.

March

- Budget recommendations are presented.

June

- Building teams report results to the Board at a public meeting and provide initial analysis of assessment data.
- Board provides input regarding the results and implemented plan.

June–August

- Repeat the process.

Figure 10.4 Calendar for Improving Student Achievement

Note. From the Whitewater Unified School District. Reprinted with permission.

Engaging All Stakeholders in Leading Improvement

Throughout a schoolwide improvement process, teachers, staff, students, parents, administrators, and community members participate in a variety of ways: providing input, participating on and leading teams, and making decisions collaboratively. Using *community forums* to gather and share information, *team structures* to organize and implement improvement work, and a *skilled facilitator* to help guide the process will all contribute to growing the school's capacity for improving results.

To make sure you reach all the stakeholders, use a variety of forums for discussing your plans and results, including

- Faculty meetings
- Grade level/departmental meetings
- Parent-teacher conferences
- Performance coaching reviews
- Curriculum and assessment meetings
- PTA/PTO meetings
- Community meetings
- E-mail
- Shared Web sites

Final Check: Developing Schoolwide Improvement Plans

 An assessment of the SMART School Improvement Process appears on the CD-ROM.

This chapter has provided instructions for asking the core questions for SMART Schools:

1. Where do we want to be?
2. Where are we now?
3. How will we get there?
4. What are we learning?
5. Where should we focus next?

Obviously, these questions cannot be answered in a single meeting, or even in two or three meetings. Because each school is unique, yours will need to define its own process for obtaining the answers. Here are some tips:

✓ Use a mix of large group meeting and offline work by subteams or individuals.

✓ Use many of the tools and methods described throughout this book. The group process tools described in Chapter 4 will help your meetings be more productive. You may need to gather survey data or perform interviews (Chapter 5); you will likely need to collect and analyze various forms of data (Chapter 6).

✓ Build each question on the answers that came before. Simple, useful documentation will be essential.

✓ Involve a wide range of stakeholders.

Chapter 11
The Role of Professional Development in Learning Communities

"Sheep-dip" in-services are far less effective in building capacity for improved results than we often care to admit.

Dr. W. Edwards Deming often told his seminar participants, "You don't just learn knowledge, you have to create it. You have to re-learn the knowledge, contribute to it, or you don't understand it." This book began with a discussion of learning communities, or, as Dr. Deming would say, SMART schools where everyone is involved in re-learning knowledge and contributing to it.

Effective implementation of the methods, tools, and school improvement plans described in this book relies, to a great extent, on the professional staff development plans that support them. And the *process* used to implement staff development is every bit as important as the plans themselves.

Although workshops and outside consultants certainly have their place, we know that most learning occurs when staff work with their colleagues in ways that help them examine their professional practice more deeply. Dr. Deming's words are a ringing reminder that "sheep-dip" in-services—those that are unconnected to strategic school improvement priorities, scheduled at the end of exhausting teaching days delivered to the faculty as a whole, and presented by outsiders who rarely know the school well—are far less effective in building capacity for improved results than we often care to admit.

When staff development is focused on the school's strategic priority areas for improvement, when staff are involved in determining *how* they want to learn, and then given time to process and make sense of what they're learning in community with others, *then* the goals of a school's improvement plans become reality.

As staff become collectively skilled and share a common knowledge base, they grow in their capacity to move swiftly and decidedly into new arenas of learning and growing.

Principles of Professional Development

High-quality professional development:

- Focuses on teachers as central to student learning, yet includes all other members of the school community.
- Focuses on individual, collegial, and organizational improvement.
- Respects and nurtures the intellectual and leadership capacity of teachers, principals, and others in the school community.
- Reflects the best available research and practice in teaching, learning, and leadership.
- Enables teachers to develop further expertise in subject content, teaching strategies, uses of technologies, and other essential elements in teaching to high standards.
- Promotes continuous inquiry and improvement embedded in the daily life of schools.
- Is planned collaboratively by those who will participate in and facilitate that development.
- Requires substantial time and other resources.
- Is driven by a coherent long-term plan.
- Is evaluated ultimately on the basis of its impact on teacher effectiveness and student learning, and this assessment guides subsequent professional development efforts.

Source: *U.S. Department of Education's Principles for High-quality Professional Development Award Criteria,* 1996.

Putting Staff in the Driver's Seat

When staff are given the opportunity to select the ways they want to learn, they feel more ownership over and commitment to the learning process. Putting them in the driver's seat enables them to control to a certain extent the inevitable vulnerability that arises when we stretch into our discomfort zone. Research is also showing that the most effective staff development is job embedded: Learning happens in the context of professional practice. There are a number of different job-embedded designs for professional staff development to choose from. Some of the most powerful are highlighted here:

- Action research
- Curriculum development
- Examining student work
- Immersion
- Observing model lessons
- Shadowing students
- Shadowing lead or master teachers
- Study groups

Action Research

Action research is a form of disciplined inquiry. It can be conducted by one individual or by a group, but the learning is more far-reaching when a group engages in a question together. An action research process focused on improving student learning often follows these steps:

1. The individual or team raises a question about how to improve an instructional practice. They collect data to verify the problem that generated the question.
2. The team reviews educational literature and conducts research for best practices and/or visits model classrooms or programs.
3. The team selects and implements a strategy or approach. Several strategies or approaches might be chosen, with plans to monitor the results of each.
4. The team collects data to assess the effectiveness of the strategies or approaches.
5. The team shares the results with others in the school and/or district.

Throughout the process, a great deal is learned about subject content, teaching methodologies, problem-solving and research skills, and one's own power to improve one's practice. When coupled with a SMART goal setting, action research can provide a powerful way to target improvement efforts.

Curriculum Development

With growing pressure to teach more while also helping students achieve higher standards, teachers can no longer afford to either "do what I've always done" or simply adopt textbooks wholesale. There is an increasing recognition in the field that teachers should be involved in collaboratively aligning, redesigning, and developing curriculum in more integrated ways. The process of working together to understand the standards, and designing curriculum that works in one's unique school setting, builds capacity to meet and exceed those standards.

Examining Student Work

A close cousin to curriculum development, the practice of bringing teachers together to examine student work is quickly catching on as an important way for teachers to sharpen their practice to improve student learning. Before embarking on this strategy, however, a school should first be sure teachers are already using standards so they have some framework within which to assess student work. Second, teachers need time to do this work together. Third, at least in the beginning, it's helpful to bring in an outside facilitator who has expertise in this process.

Immersion

One of the most critical findings emerging from recent educational research is the fact that a teacher's subject matter expertise has an enormous impact on students' achievement. The competence of a teacher can make as much as a three grade-level difference in student progress. Additionally, new knowledge, particularly in the fields of mathematics and science, is emerging daily. Unfortunately, most teacher certification and recertification programs still do not require teachers to demonstrate up-to-date mastery of the subject areas they teach. As states and districts set tougher standards for students and teachers, teachers need to actively seek out immersion opportunities —such as subject-related jobs, internships, and specialized training— to gain first-hand experience in their subject areas.

Action Research Steps

Step 1. Define the research project.
- Identify improvement area.
- Develop SMART goal.
- Gather support from others for working on the project.

Step 2. Analyze the situation.
- Establish baseline data.
- Identify unique student characteristics.

Step 3. Generate hypotheses.
- Develop hypotheses about causes of performance and potential solutions.

Step 4. Try solutions and check results.
- Brainstorm potential solutions.
- Select one set based on criteria.
- Try solution strategy for several months.
- Assess results against baseline.
- Adjust until goal is achieved (or revise original project).

Step 5. Capture lessons learned.
- Document results in graphs and narrative.
- Share what was learned about making improvements in this system.
- Share what was learned about student learning.
- Develop ways to maintain the gain.
- Identify possibilities for next research focus.
- Celebrate!

 The Collaborative Action Research Steps and a template for the Collaborative Action Research Guide appear on the CD-ROM.

Standards in Practice

This method was developed by The Education Trust as a way to analyze and improve instructional quality. Small teams of teachers, guidance counselors, and even parents get together bimonthly to examine teachers' assignments, student work, and the relevant standard or set of standards.

TIME: 90–120 minutes

DIRECTIONS:

1. A volunteer teacher brings in student work along with the assignment.
2. Team members do the assignment themselves in order to experience the task given to the students.
3. Team members identify the state, local, or national standards that align with the assignment.
4. Without looking at the student work, the team constructs a scoring guide (rubric) for this specific assignment. Scores go from 4 (highest proficiency) down to 1 (minimal proficiency). The rubric includes detailed descriptions of what successful work looks like.
5. The team uses the scoring guide to score the student work.
6. The team summarizes insights gained during the session and creates a plan of action.

Source: "Examining student work," by Ruth Michell, *Journal of Staff Development,* Summer 1999 (Vol. 20, No. 3). For more information see Education Trust's Web site: www.edtrust.org. To learn about more options for examining student work, visit the *Learning About Student Work* Web site maintained by the Annenberg Institute for School Reform (www.lasw.org)

Observing Model Lessons

In Japan, teachers collaboratively develop model lessons with their colleagues, which they then demonstrate live with their students while other teachers (from their own school, from neighboring schools, from other districts) observe. After the lesson, the teachers gather to share notes, dialogue about what they saw, and discuss applications to their own practice. Although very time-intensive, planning, conducting, and evaluating instruction promises rich learning for teachers. The observers become aware of new approaches to teaching and learning, and assess these against what might work with their own students. The model teachers sharpen their own instructional practice as they carefully think through the logic and value of their lessons. This process, with adaptations, is beginning to catch on in the United States.

Shadowing Students

Although time-intensive, the process of following a student and systematically recording that student's instructional experiences provides a rich base of understanding about the link between pedagogical practices in the classroom and student performance. This approach requires a deep sense of trust between the observer and his or her colleagues and between the observer and the student. The purpose is not to play "gotcha," but to use the experience as an opportunity for further dialogue, reflection, and school improvement.

Shadowing Lead or Master Teachers

Another professional development approach is to allow teachers to shadow each other throughout the day. This is common practice with student teachers, but not so common with licensed teachers. When someone is identified as having a wealth of skills, knowledge, and expertise, there is tremendous value in teaming him or her with another teacher for a day or more, with time for collaborative reflection and dialogue. The observing teacher need not be new to the profession; the process of watching and reflecting with those who exhibit masterful skills can be a powerful learning practice for anyone interested in continuous improvement of their professional practice.

Study Groups

Study groups are among the most commonly used approaches to job-embedded staff development. Groups of teachers and/or administrators come together to learn more about a particular topic such as discipline, brain-based learning, balanced literacy, accelerated curriculum, etc. The groups usually meet at least every other week to review the literature, visit model programs, and discuss the potential of the practices or program for their school or classrooms.

Tips for Continuous Learning

As teachers well know, learning can happen anywhere at anytime. It doesn't have to happen in the context of professional development. There are many ways for your team to build learning opportunities into your everyday work. Here are just a few tips:

- Invite people from outside your team to come in and make a brief presentation on a topic of interest to the group.
- Visit other schools and school districts or other noneducational organizations to learn how they approach the same problem or issue.
- Build learning time into every meeting agenda:
  - At the beginning of a meeting, ask people to tell one thing they learned between meetings that would be helpful to their work.
  - Have one person be responsible for summarizing an article of his or her choice that relates to a topic the team has to address.
  - Build 15 minutes into each agenda to have a team member share a teaching strategy or new resource he or she has used this year.
  - At the end of every meeting, ask people to tell one thing they learned during the course of the meeting. This could be something about the content, the process, or the people.
- Build learning opportunities into everyday work:
  - Work with a teaching colleague to plan lessons.
  - Consult an expert.
  - Ask an expert or peer to coach you in skills you'd like to improve.
  - Coach a colleague.
  - Ask experts, colleagues, or others to observe you and give you feedback.
  - Lead a schoolwide committee or project.
  - Participate in school improvement planning.
  - Do a self-assessment.
  - Keep a journal.

A Special Word About Teacher Portfolios Linked to School Improvement Plans

Schools are beginning to make the link between schoolwide improvement plans and the classroom by helping teachers develop their own classroom portfolios that demonstrate the results of their SMART goals work and strategies for improvement (pp. 269–272). In the high school portfolio example provided in the Appendix (p. 272), a high school faculty focused on a SMART goal for writing. They then researched best practices around writing and developed plans for incorporating these practices into their classrooms. The teachers agreed to use the same classroom and district-based assessment tools so they would be able to compare results across the whole school. The portfolio example shows the progress made by students in one history teacher's classroom.

> **Commitment is the daily triumph of integrity over skepticism.**
>
> —Dr. Joseph M. Juran

- Create your own additional learning opportunities:
    - Enroll in a university course.
    - View educational videos.
    - Listen to video/audio recordings.
    - Research on the Internet.
    - Join a professional network.
    - Write an article about your work.
    - Read journals, educational magazines, books.

Final Check: Professional Development Evaluation Criteria

How do you know whether your professional development plan will be effective? Assess your plan against the following checklist. Our plan

✓ Is linked to the district's overall strategic plan and priorities

✓ Is linked to the school's strategic plan and priorities

✓ Addresses verifiable staff learning needs

✓ Incorporates a variety of methods

✓ Is job-embedded—reflects real work and can be addressed in concert with real work

✓ Has well-defined goals with achievable outcomes

✓ Supports a variety of individual learning styles and needs

✓ Addresses various levels of need—awareness, implementation, proficiency, mastery

✓ Has a basis in learning and teaching best practice research

✓ Was developed through collaboration of teachers

Appendix
Tools for SMART Schools

The 30+ Minute Meeting Series

These meetings can be done by the whole staff, by grade level teams, or by departments.

Meeting #1: Identify and isolate the opportunity or "gap" between what is wanted and the current situation.

5 min.	The presenting question: What are the student *learning* issues we are struggling with the most?
10 min.	Brainstorm responses.
5 min.	Identify top three priorities by multi-voting.
10 min.	What more do we need to know? How can we find out?

Between meetings, gather student data and information on priority areas.

Meeting #2: Identify SMART Goals for priority area(s).

10 min.	Present graphs of student performance in area of concern. (Focus on skill areas or proficiency/performance levels.)
10 min.	Brainstorm results-oriented goal(s) for priority area(s).
5 min.	Select 1 results-oriented goal for each priority area.
10 min.	Make the results-oriented goal SMART: Individuals write indicators, measures, and targets for 1 goal.
	(Consider indicators by skill/competence/performance expectations aligned to standards; consider both standardized and classroom-based measures; consider student data when writing targets.)
5 min.	Share SMART goals round robin one at a time.
15 min.	Group selects "best of" indicators, measures, and targets to write group SMART goal.
10 min.	What do we need to know to affect student learning for this SMART goal?

Between meetings do literature, research, or best practice review.

Meeting #3: Correlate best practices to current practices.

10 min. Share information gathered between meetings.

10 min. Matrix: What are we already doing that supports best practice in this area? What else would we like to learn about?

10 min. Identify instructional strategies we want to do more of, start doing, and stop doing.

Between meetings, research ways to develop professional knowledge to learn best practices.

Meeting #4: Identify staff development methods we want to use.

10 min. Share information about various staff development methods.

10 min. Matrix: Individuals select preferred strategy for learning about best practices, identifying areas about which they are willing to coach/teach others.

15 min. Discuss implementation. How will we implement staff development for best practices? What support do we need? How will we measure progress on the SMART goal?

Between meetings, implement staff development and integration of best practices, and then gather data to measure against baseline.

Meeting #5: Analyze results and refocus.

10 min. Present graphs of new data.

15 min. Discuss what worked, what didn't, and why.

15 min. If the instructional strategy worked well, discuss how to "hold the gains." If the strategy did not work well, decide next steps: START doing the strategy differently, STOP doing the strategy altogether, START a new strategy.

Start the cycle over again.

Sample Size Chart—95% confidence level

Size of Population N / ERROR	Sample Size for Reliability of				
	+−1%	+−2%	+−3%	+−4%	+−5%
100	—	—	—	—	79
200	—	—	—	—	132
300	—	—	—	—	168
400	—	—	—	—	196
500	—	—	—	—	217
600	—	—	—	—	234
700	—	—	—	—	248
800	—	—	—	—	260
900	—	—	—	—	269
1,000	M*	M*	M*	375	278
2,000	M*	M*	696	462	322
3,000	M*	1,334	787	500	341
4,000	M*	1,500	842	522	350
5,000	M*	1,622	879	536	357
10,000	4,899	1,936	964	566	370
20,000	6,489	2,144	1,013	583	377
50,000	8,057	2,291	1,045	593	381
100,000	8,763	2,345	1,056	597	383
500,000 and more	9,423	2,390	1,065	600	384

M* = more than 50% of the population is required in the sample
Source: University of Wisconsin—Madison Office of Quality Improvement. Reprinted with permission.

Random Number Table

	1	2	3	4	5	6	7	8
1	0.7676	0.3167	0.8677	0.2342	0.9632	0.5291	0.5781	0.1489
2	0.7576	0.193	0.4166	0.7144	0.0719	0.8109	0.6874	0.5396
3	0.7635	0.9429	0.7015	0.7051	0.0164	0.1228	0.3966	0.4541
4	0.5705	0.8117	0.6033	0.2638	0.1578	0.5438	0.6836	0.5774
5	0.8637	0.7397	0.6554	0.8405	0.9351	0.0394	0.9147	0.5302
6	0.1985	0.5586	0.9588	0.8467	0.6	0.4007	0.8252	0.7829
7	0.2833	0.5231	0.1909	0.9423	0.2408	0.6079	0.7498	0.8159
8	0.5994	0.5298	0.13	0.183	0.2456	0.7644	0.8986	0.6278
9	0.9683	0.334	0.1977	0.3994	0.0891	0.9699	0.4013	0.1678
10	0.5599	0.5284	0.0624	0.3389	0.8004	0.9871	0.3657	0.3169
11	0.9567	0.1537	0.8563	0.3627	0.0158	0.7101	0.9796	0.1562
12	0.4396	0.2521	0.347	0.4246	0.7202	0.17	0.9671	0.3592
13	0.6546	0.2547	0.8725	0.4444	0.8648	0.793	0.0735	0.4079
14	0.5019	0.7787	0.3192	0.8516	0.5052	0.4754	0.6017	0.7394
15	0.1437	0.8561	0.3068	0.7349	0.0269	0.585	0.4837	0.4863
16	0.0118	0.6226	0.1932	0.3416	0.0957	0.6994	0.3828	0.8618
17	0.0086	0.209	0.3931	0.7363	0.2027	0.106	0.8662	0.9639
18	0.4973	0.7744	0.8074	0.0329	0.8665	0.6009	0.8186	0.0413
19	0.0401	0.6316	0.5995	0.5628	0.1518	0.0423	0.6101	0.7079
20	0.174	0.0698	0.0293	0.6006	0.9853	0.3564	0.6712	0.7989
21	0.7165	0.0924	0.0814	0.8343	0.9135	0.2701	0.4702	0.1825
22	0.377	0.3578	0.2	0.8596	0.2007	0.7491	0.5916	0.0735
23	0.1243	0.2708	0.758	0.3208	0.6268	0.9726	0.9281	0.75
24	0.1483	0.6169	0.2639	0.6042	0.3687	0.1393	0.1018	0.4156
25	0.4745	0.9524	0.0583	0.2908	0.1338	0.5646	0.4359	0.6868
26	0.3884	0.7946	0.9486	0.9847	0.2294	0.7557	0.7186	0.6235
27	0.9892	0.1696	0.9944	0.1819	0.0374	0.6021	0.3918	0.1692
28	0.1135	0.2734	0.7844	0.0304	0.4494	0.5873	0.2608	0.8112

Gap Analysis Survey

IMPORTANCE **How important is this?** 5 = Extremely important 4 = Very important 3 = Somewhat important 2 = Not very important 1 = Not important NA = Not Applicable DK = Don't Know	*Section I. School Climate* *Rate the IMPORTANCE and your AGREEMENT with the following items.*	CURRENT SITUATION **What's your perception?** 5 – Strongly Agree 4 = Agree 3 = Neutral 2 = Disagree 1 = Strongly Disagree NA = Not Applicable DK – Don't Know
5 4 3 2 1 NA DK	1. Expectations for student behavior are clear.	5 4 3 2 1 NA DK
5 4 3 2 1 NA DK	2. There are logical consequences for misbehavior.	5 4 3 2 1 NA DK
5 4 3 2 1 NA DK	3. Students treat each other with respect.	5 4 3 2 1 NA DK

High School Climate Survey

Grade: (circle one)   9   10   11   12

Gender: (circle one)   Male   Female

Directions: Please complete the following survey items **honestly**—your viewpoints are important and very helpful. This survey is entirely anonymous. THANK YOU!

1 = never
2 = sometimes
3 = frequently
4 = always
5 = I don't know

Leadership:

	1	2	3	4	5
1. I see my principal as the leader of my high school.	❑	❑	❑	❑	❑
2. My principal is visible (outside of the office, in classrooms, halls, at activities, etc.).	❑	❑	❑	❑	❑
3. I receive prompt and efficient service in the high school office.	❑	❑	❑	❑	❑
4. My principal works to make our school a better school.	❑	❑	❑	❑	❑

Runs Table

Number of Data Points Not on Median	Lower Limit for Number of Runs	Upper Limit for Number of Runs		Number of Data Points Not on Median	Lower Limit for Number of Runs	Upper Limit for Number of Runs
10	3	8		34	12	23
11	3	9		35	13	23
12	3	10		36	13	24
13	4	10		37	13	25
14	4	11		38	14	25
15	4	12		39	14	26
16	5	12		40	15	26
17	5	13		41	16	26
18	6	13		42	16	27
19	6	14		43	17	27
20	6	14		44	17	28
21	7	15		45	17	29
22	7	16		46	17	30
23	8	16		47	18	30
24	8	17		48	18	31
25	9	17		49	19	31
26	9	18		50	19	32
27	9	19		60	24	37
28	10	19		70	28	43
29	10	20		80	33	48
30	11	20		90	37	54
31	11	21		100	42	59
32	11	22		110	46	65
33	11	22		120	51	70

Source: *Oriel Incorporated*
Reprinted with Permission.

Airplane Rubric

Paper Airplanes, Controlled Tests, and Newton's Laws of Physics

	Ultra Light Pilot	Airplane Pilot	Super Sonic Jet Pilot
Following Written Directions	Followed some directions, may have needed help. Accurately folded 1-2 different planes.	Generally followed directions, may have received help. Accurately folded 3-4 different airplanes.	Followed written directions carefully, may offer to help others. Accurately folded 5-6 different airplanes.
Collaborative & Independent Work	Generally focused, on task. Cooperative with groups.	Uses time wisely, focused, on task. Cooperative with groups, contributes to good balance of work load.	Uses time wisely, always on task. Cooperative, helpful to others, shows leadership and balance of tasks and workload.
Design/Execute Controlled Test	Much review or assistance needed in test design or identification of variables. Procedure may be incomplete. Supplies used appropriately. Some monitoring of controls. Measurements may require help.	Minimal review of assistance in design. Test is reasonable. Supplies used appropriately and safely. Measurements are accurate. Showed care in control of variables. Ran recorded/multiple trials.	Questions, hypothesis, controlled and manipulated variables, procedure is clear. Test is procedure, no review of assistance needed. Supplies used appropriately and safely. Measurements accurate, transposes between units. Carefully controlled variables. Ran multiple trials, dealt accurately with outlyers.
Collect, Organize, and Graph Data	Assistance needed to collect data, record data, design data table or graph.	Collected, recorded data. May have had minimal assistance to design table, graph.	Collected, recorded data in neat organized way. Designed and used effective table and graph.
Draw Conclusions	Attempted conclusion, or based on only one component.	Drew conclusion on only one part of the test.	Drew conclusion in response to questions based on data.
Application Four Forces of Flight	Identifies 2 forces of flight, positions of potential and kinetic energy.	Identifies effects of 4 forces of flight on own tests, positions of potential and kinetic energy.	Recognizes the application of Newton's Laws in flight.
Airplane Re-Design	Prepares a folded design, may be similar to patterns given. Writes sample directions for fold.	Prepares a folded design with qualities based on results of flight tests. Writes directions that another can reproduce.	Prepares an improved folded design with qualities and rationale based on results of flight tests. Writes complete directions that most could reproduce.

Source: Judy Singletary, Sun Prairie Area School District. Reprinted with permission.

Tree Diagram for SMART Climate Goal (generic)

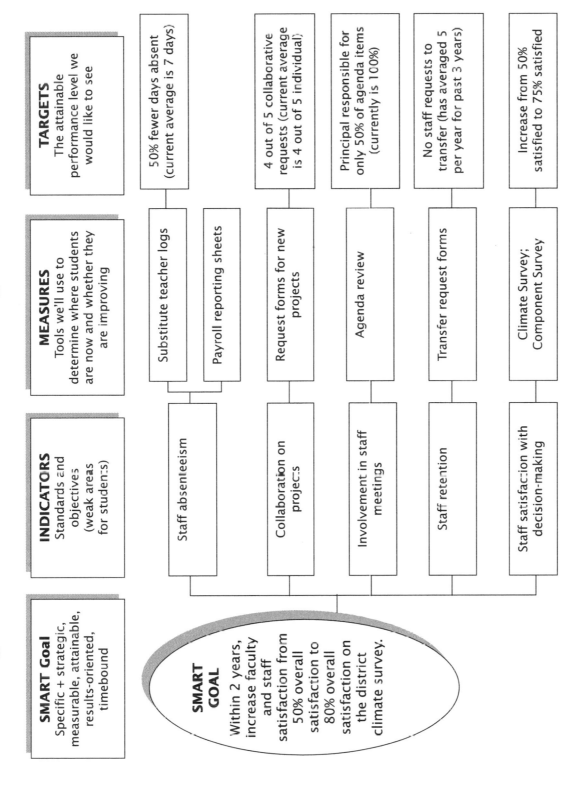

SMART Goal
Specific + strategic, measurable, attainable, results-oriented, timebound

INDICATORS
Standards and objectives (weak areas for students)

MEASURES
Tools we'll use to determine where students are now and whether they are improving

TARGETS
The attainable performance level we would like to see

SMART GOAL
Within 2 years, increase faculty and staff satisfaction from 50% overall satisfaction to 80% overall satisfaction on the district climate survey.

Staff absenteeism — Substitute teacher logs; Payroll reporting sheets — 50% fewer days absent (current average is 7 days)

Collaboration on projects — Request forms for new projects — 4 out of 5 collaborative requests (current average is 4 out of 5 individual)

Involvement in staff meetings — Agenda review — Principal responsible for only 50% of agenda items (currently is 100%)

Staff retention — Transfer request forms — No staff requests to transfer (has averaged 5 per year for past 3 years)

Staff satisfaction with decision-making — Climate Survey; Component Survey — Increase from 50% satisfied to 75% satisfied

Tree Diagram for SMART Reading Goal (elementary)

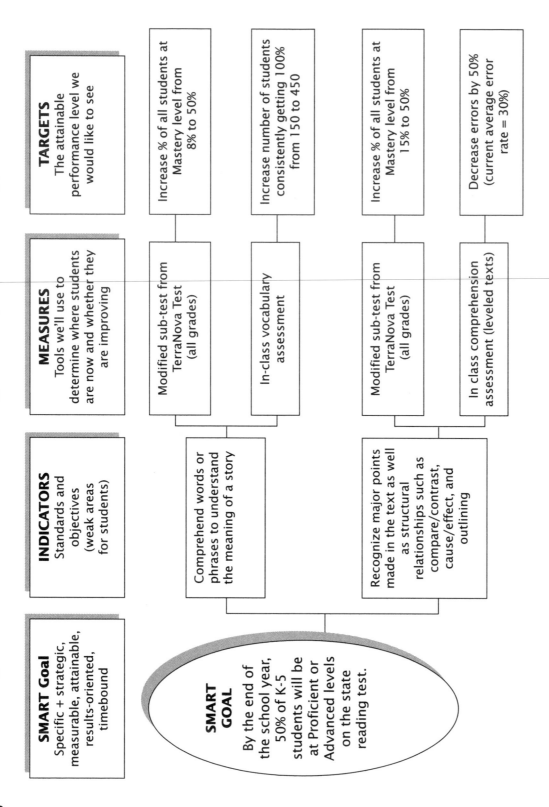

SMART Goal
Specific + strategic, measurable, attainable, results-oriented, timebound

INDICATORS
Standards and objectives (weak areas for students)

MEASURES
Tools we'll use to determine where students are now and whether they are improving

TARGETS
The attainable performance level we would like to see

SMART GOAL
By the end of the school year, 50% of K-5 students will be at Proficient or Advanced levels on the state reading test.

Comprehend words or phrases to understand the meaning of a story

Modified sub-test from TerraNova Test (all grades)

Increase % of all students at Mastery level from 8% to 50%

In-class vocabulary assessment

Increase number of students consistently getting 100% from 150 to 450

Recognize major points made in the text as well as structural relationships such as compare/contrast, cause/effect, and outlining

Modified sub-test from TerraNova Test (all grades)

Increase % of all students at Mastery level from 15% to 50%

In class comprehension assessment (leveled texts)

Decrease errors by 50% (current average error rate = 30%)

Note. Copyright © 2001 by QLD, LLC. Reprinted with permission.

Tree Diagram for SMART Analytical Thinking Goal (middle school)

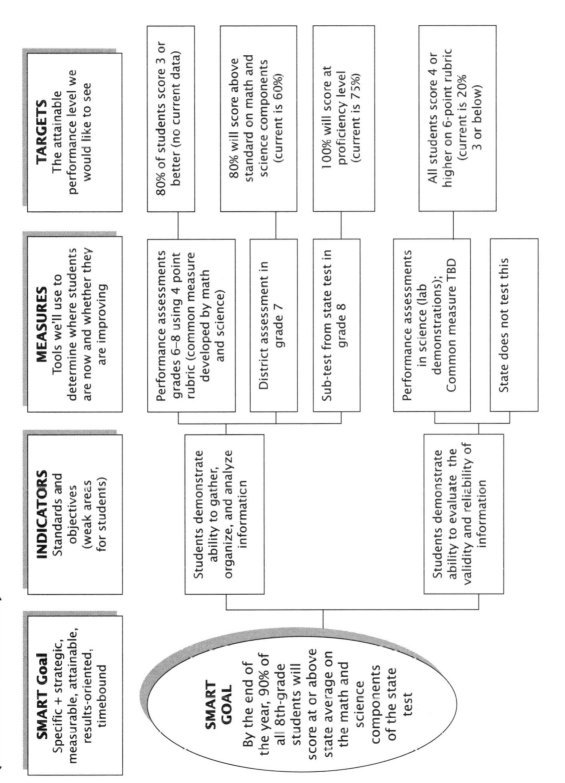

SMART Goal
Specific + strategic, measurable, attainable, results-oriented, timebound

SMART GOAL
By the end of the year, 90% of all 8th-grade students will score at or above state average on the math and science components of the state test

INDICATORS
Standards and objectives (weak areas for students)

Students demonstrate ability to gather, organize, and analyze information

Students demonstrate ability to evaluate the validity and reliability of information

MEASURES
Tools we'll use to determine where students are now and whether they are improving

Performance assessments grades 6–8 using 4 point rubric (common measure developed by math and science)

District assessment in grade 7

Sub-test from state test in grade 8

Performance assessments in science (lab demonstrations); Common measure TBD

State does not test this

TARGETS
The attainable performance level we would like to see

80% of students score 3 or better (no current data)

80% will score above standard on math and science components (current is 60%)

100% will score at proficiency level (current is 75%)

All students score 4 or higher on 6-point rubric (current is 20% 3 or below)

Tools for SMART Schools

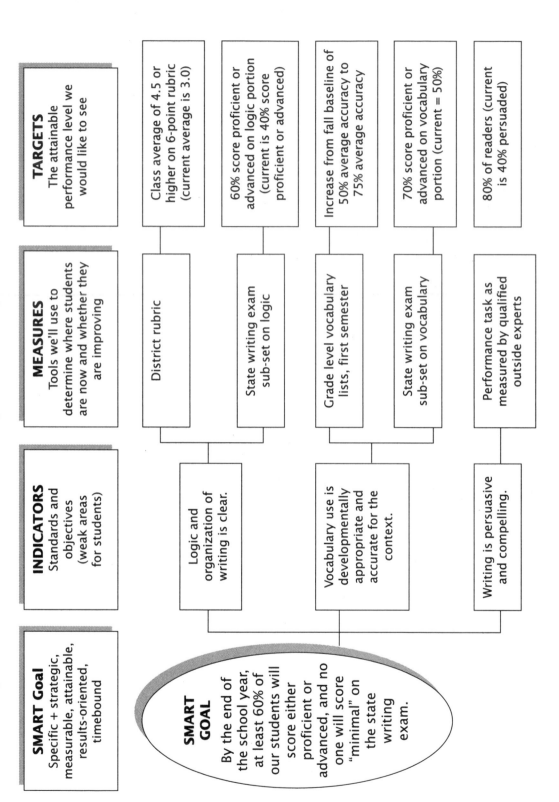

Tree Diagram for SMART Writing Goal (high school)

SMART Goal
Specific + strategic, measurable, attainable, results-oriented, timebound

INDICATORS
Standards and objectives (weak areas for students)

MEASURES
Tools we'll use to determine where students are now and whether they are improving

TARGETS
The attainable performance level we would like to see

SMART GOAL
By the end of the school year, at least 60% of our students will score either proficient or advanced, and no one will score "minimal" on the state writing exam.

Logic and organization of writing is clear.
— District rubric — Class average of 4.5 or higher on 6-point rubric (current average is 3.0)
— State writing exam sub-set on logic — 60% score proficient or advanced on logic portion (current is 40% score proficient or advanced)

Vocabulary use is developmentally appropriate and accurate for the context.
— Grade level vocabulary lists, first semester — Increase from fall baseline of 50% average accuracy to 75% average accuracy
— State writing exam sub-set on vocabulary — 70% score proficient or advanced on vocabulary portion (current = 50%)

Writing is persuasive and compelling.
— Performance task as measured by qualified outside experts — 80% of readers (current is 40% persuaded)

School Improvement Annual Planning and Reporting Document

–SAMPLE–

School Name: Eagle Ridge Elementary School

School Year: 2001-2002

Date of Plan: August, 2001

I. District Strategic Priorities Addressed by this Plan:

Three of the five district priorities are addressed in this plan. They are

1. Improving student achievement
2. Offering challenging, diverse, and contemporary curriculum and instruction
3. Assuring a safe, respectful, and welcoming learning environment

II. School-based Achievement Gaps to be addressed by this Plan (provide evidential data and rationale):

Our school data show achievement gaps in reading and writing. Only 13% of our students scored in the "high" category of the school writing sample while 24% scored in the "low" category over the past 2 years. 22% of our third graders and 32% of our fourth graders fell below the proficient category on the state reading tests with specific weaknesses in comprehension.

School behavioral referrals have risen by 25% over the last 2 years.

III. Building-Level SMART Goals

1. Each year for the next 3 years, we will increase the proportion of students in each grade who score in the "high" category, and decrease the proportion who score in the "low" category on the school writing sample.

2. Increase by 5% each year the number of third graders and fourth graders who move into the proficient range on the statewide reading assessments.

3. Reduce by 25% per year, over the course of the next 3 years, the number of behavioral referrals received for disciplinary action.

(continued on page 274)

IV. Implementation Plan—Use

SMART Goal #1

- Each year for the next 3 years, we will increase the proportion of students in each grade who score in the "high" category, and decrease the proportion who score in the "low" category on the school writing sample.

Best Practices/Strategies Associated with this Goal:

- Plenty of opportunities for students to express themselves in writing
- Frequent and varied feedback to students on their writing
- Vocabulary lists of key words at each grade leve—monitor use of vocabulary words in all writing tasks

#	Action Steps (List each step on a separate line. Add lines as needed.)	Timeline (month and year to start this step)	Person(s) Responsible	Action Step Completed (month and year)
1	All teachers attend the writer's workshop to learn effective instructional strategies for writing.	1/3 of staff to complete each year	Individual teachers and principal	
2	Grade-level teams meet to create key word vocabulary lists.	Sept. 2001	Grade-level teams	
3	Create a checklist to monitor number of writing opportunities students are getting and number and types of feedback strategies being used.	Sept. 2001	Grade-level teams	
4	Implement new instructional strategies and monitor results.	Third week of Sept. 2001; Monitor every 6 weeks.	Grade-level teams	
5	Share vocabulary lists with other staff members. Align, reinforce, and reduce duplication.	Third week of Sept. 2001	All teachers and principal	
6	Share results and chart schoolwide data on number of writing opportunities, number, and types of feedback.	Sixth week of school	All teachers and principal	

CD-ROM Contents

Improving Processes and Systems

Becoming a SMART School

The Role of Professional Development in Learning Communities

SMART Schools Self-Assessment

INSTRUCTIONS: Complete the following survey with several other people from your school if possible. Circle the number that best indicates where you believe your school currently functions.

FOCUS

1. There is a shared vision for continuous school improvement that is focused on student learning.

1	2	3	4	5	6	7	8	9	10
We don't have a shared vision.				There is a formal vision statement, but it is seldom referenced.					The school's vision for student success regularly guides our staff discussions and decision-making.

2. School goals focus on improved student achievement.

1	2	3	4	5	6	7	8	9	10
We don't have written goals.				Our goals focus on process and program enhancement.					Our goals address student learning needs with regard to standards and expectations.

3. School goals are SMART.

1	2	3	4	5	6	7	8	9	10
Our goals are hard to measure.				Our goals are measurable and specific.					Our goals focus on student results and target needs based on a careful analysis of data on student performance.

REFLECTION

4. Staff, faculty, and administration reflect and dialogue together about professional matters that impact student learning.

1	2	3	4	5	6	7	8	9	10
We never meet to discuss substantive issues related to student learning.				We occasionally discuss student-centered issues focused on learning.					Our discussions focus on the quality of teaching and learning in our school.

1

5. Staff members know how effectively current practices work and continuously seek to find new methods to improve student performance.

1	2	3	4	5	6	7	8	9	10

Staff members do not talk about instruction, results, or improvement.

Staff members occasionally look at how they are doing and make adjustments/improvements.

Staff members regularly reflect on and assess the impact of their instruction and make revisions based on the results.

COLLABORATION
6. There is a high degree of trust among individuals.

1	2	3	4	5	6	7	8	9	10

Low trust and conflict characterize our school's working relationships

We generally trust each other but are not always as open as we could be.

Trust and openness characterize the way we work.

7. The structure of the day and year provide flexibility and time for people to work together.

1	2	3	4	5	6	7	8	9	10

There are no specific arrangements made to create time for school improvement teams' interaction.

Time is arranged, but it is either inadequate or inconsistent.

The school day and year have been restructured so as to make collaborative decision-making and team learning the way we do business.

LEADERSHIP
8. There is full participation in leadership. Staff, faculty, administrators, community members, parents, and students all have important and defined leadership roles.

1	2	3	4	5	6	7	8	9	10

There is one leader in the school.

Leadership is an assignment based on a specific task, committee appointment, or position.

All members of the school community take leadership action for improving school results.

9. Individuals have well developed leadership skills and consistently use them in collaborative ways.

1	2	3	4	5	6	7	8	9	10

The development of leadership skills is limited to a few "positional" leaders.

Broad-based, skillful leadership is valued but not systemically developed.

Leadership skills are developed, valued, and consistently applied across a wide variety of stakeholders.

2

3.

TOTALS
Add all numbers circled and put the total below.

[ ] TOTAL (out of 90 possible)

Strength areas to celebrate (the way it is comes close to the way you want it to be):

Priority areas (biggest gaps between the way it is and the way you want it to be):

One step you can take that will address the priority area this year (preferably something you have direct control or influence over):

Team Charter

Team Members (List all members.):

Mission (A brief statement of purpose that includes specific end results or outcomes.):

Tasks to Complete (A sequential list of activities that the team will use to achieve the end results/outcomes provided in the mission.):

Timeline (Either phases or a specific timeline that the group will follow to achieve its mission. Ad hoc groups will most likely have a stated date for completion; ongoing groups will have a timeline that targets incremental progress within specified time ranges.):

Meeting Agenda Template

Facilitator:

Timekeeper:

Recorder:

Other:

Meeting Purpose:

Estimated Time	Topic	Lead Person	Method	Outcome
5 min.	Check-In	All	Round Robin	We're all present!
5 min.	Agenda Review	Facilitator	Discussion	Agenda adjusted as needed
5 min.	Next Agenda	All	Brainstorm	Input for next meeting agenda
5 min.	Meeting Evaluation		+/- on flipchart	Meeting process improvements for next time

Meeting Evaluation Form

Date: **Time of Day:**

	Yes	No	Comments
1. Did the meeting start on time?	☐	☐	
2. Were meeting objectives met?	☐	☐	
3. Was the agenda followed?	☐	☐	
4. Did the discussion remain focused?	☐	☐	
5. Were participants adequately prepared?	☐	☐	
6. Was the location appropriate?	☐	☐	
7. Did the meeting end on time?	☐	☐	
8. Has a follow-up report been sent?	☐	☐	
9. Were ground rules adhered to?	☐	☐	
10. Was everyone involved?	☐	☐	

The strengths of this meeting were:

This meeting could have been improved by:

I could have assisted in making this meeting more effective by:

Meeting Record

Team Name:

Date: **Time:**   **Location:**

Members Present:

Y	N	Name	Facilitator	Timekeeper	Recorder	Other

Next Meeting(s):

Date: Time: Location:

Date: Time: Location:

Facilitator: Recorder:

Timekeeper: Other:

Agenda for Next Meeting:
Check-In:

Check-Out:

1

Topic	Discussion Points	Decisions

Issues/Ideas for Future Meetings:

Assignments:

What	Who	When

2

Meeting Skills Self-Assessment

Instructions: Each statement below represents a valuable meeting skill. Learning to identify, practice, and improve these skills is part of being a team member. Check the appropriate column for each statement indicating how often you practice that behavior. Your team may want to compare answers to find areas that the team as a whole should be working on.

Meeting Skill	I frequently do this.	I need to do more of this.
Goal Setting I help the group stay focused on the results we're working toward. I suggest interim benchmarks along the way.		
Resource Assessing I see the big picture of what will be required to get tasks done, and I share my thoughts with the group.		
Initiating I suggest methods, procedures, and plans as needed. I offer to take the lead on getting tasks done.		
Information Giving I offer facts, research, and background as needed.		
Opinion Sharing I contribute to the group's work by offering my thoughts, feelings, perceptions, and beliefs.		
Clarifying I help clear up confusion about the task by defining terms and offering additional information.		
Harmonizing I try to help group members find agreement in conflicting points of view; I help reduce tension by getting people to explore difficulties.		
Encouraging I am friendly, warm, and responsive; I celebrate successes; I validate others' points of view; I use non-destructive humor.		
Compromising I modify my thinking or position as appropriate by exploring other members' ideas rather than debating or defending each idea that comes up.		
Gatekeeping I create opportunities for others to participate in the discussion.		
Regulating I point out when ground rules are being broken; I ask whether the group is satisfied with its progress.		
Summarizing I synthesize what's been said, and then check the accuracy of my summary with the group; when I hear the group repeat itself, I help us close discussion and reach a decision.		

Decision Matrix

Alternatives / Criteria						Vote Totals

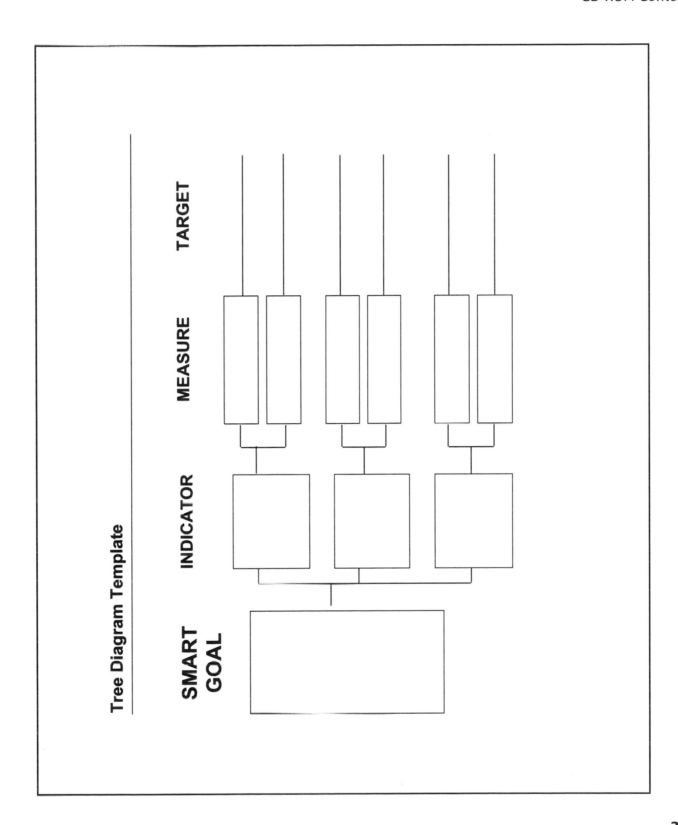

Tree Diagram Template

Responsibility Matrix

Name of Core Process	Decision Maker	Process Manager	Back-up	Involved Stakeholders
1.				
2.				
3.				
4.				
5.				
6.				

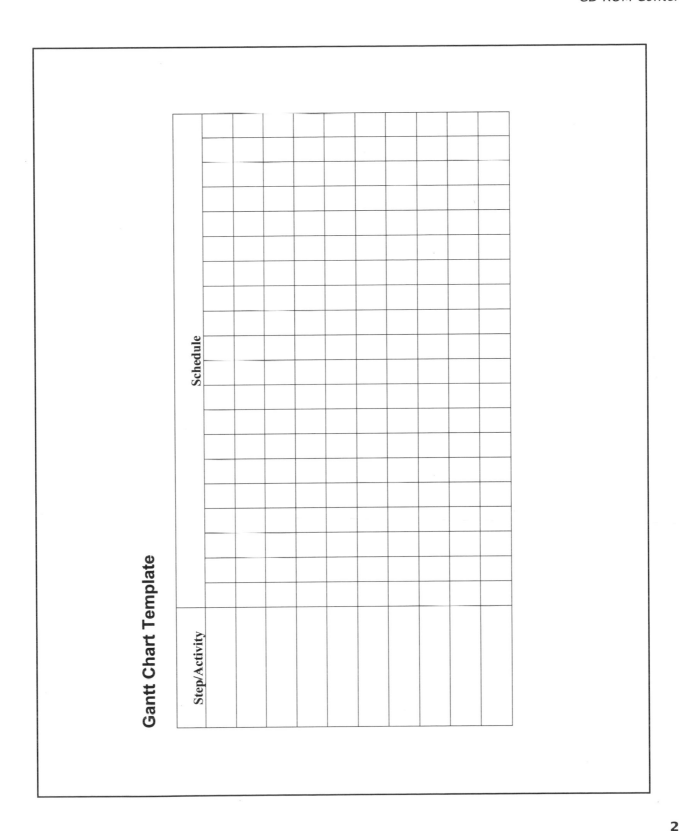

Gantt Chart Template

Data Needs Chart

Use this matrix to organize the data you have on students. Note where you have gaps (missing information) for cohorts of students. Consider standards-based standardized test data, curriculum-embedded assessment data, as well as climate (satisfaction/behavior/attendance) data. Note where the data are available in disaggregated form.

- Cohort group by year
- Name/title of assessment/measure
- Disaggregation available (D)

Cohort Group	Type of Data		
	Standards-based Assessments	Curriculum-embedded Assessments	Climate/ Behavior Data

Data Analysis Worksheet

School/Grade Level/Department:

Source of Data	Years Available	Form/Type of Data

Can the data be disaggregated by: Yes   No
- Free and Reduced Lunch   ☐   ☐
- Special Education/Non-special Ed   ☐   ☐
- Gender   ☐   ☐
- Race/Ethnic Group/ESL   ☐   ☐
- Classroom   ☐   ☐

Use highlighters to note areas of strength and weakness.

GREEN   Super! Exceeds expectations!
BLUE   Good. Meets expectations.
ORANGE   Caution. Doesn't quite meet expectations.
RED   Top priority! Needs immediate attention!

1

Whether you are using state test data, district data, or school/classroom data, look for differences across subgroups in all academic areas:

- ◆ Percent at different proficiency levels
- ◆ Percent in different quartiles
- ◆ Percent exceeding, meeting, almost meeting, or not meeting expectations

How are subgroups of students doing relative to:
- Previous years?

- Other subject areas?

- Other schools in the district?

- The district at large?

- Other schools of similar size in the area?

What patterns do you see?

What reasons can you think of for these patterns?

What other forms or sources of data would be helpful to you in understanding your students' performance? (Consider correlating with attendance, truancy, mobility, GPA, satisfaction, etc.)

What questions do you have about your students' performance?

2

Worksheet for Computing Control Limits

Date/Time	Data Points in Time Order	Range

Sums		
Divided by	# of Data Points	# of Ranges
$\overline{X}$ or $\overline{R}$	Average of Data Points	Average of Ranges

Average of Scores **Average of Ranges**

UCL = _____ + (2.66 X _____) = _____

LCL = _____ - (2.66 X _____) = _____

AIP Pre-Work Meeting Agenda Template

Date: Time:

Location:

Attendees:

Purpose: Define project mission and measures of success.

Time Needed: 4–8 hours

Meeting Outcomes:
- Completed Project Definition Template
- Completed Project Timeline Template
- Completed Current and Ideal Process Flowcharts
- Data/Information Gathering Assignments

Time   **Agenda**
- Welcome, Introductions, & Meeting Guidelines
- Overview of Accelerated Improvement Process (AIP)
- Define the Project

- BREAK

- Flowchart Current Process
- Flowchart Ideal Process

- BREAK

- Decide Data Gathering Assignments
- Complete Project Timeline
- Adjourn

Note: From the Office of Quality Improvement, University of Wisconsin—
Madison. Adapted with permission.

AIP Team Meeting #1 Agenda Template

Date: Time:
Location:
Attendees:

Time Needed: 4–8 hours

Meeting Outcomes:
- Confirm ideal process
- Develop solutions and ideas to close the gap between current and ideal process
- Select and prioritize solutions
- Assign team members to analyze solutions

Materials needed:
- Project Definition and Timeline
- Current process flowchart
- Ideal process flowchart
- Data/process information

Time	**Agenda**
	- Introductions
	- Overview of the project and key AIP concepts (if different participants than pre-work meeting)
	- BREAK
	- Confirm current process (with data)
	- Confirm ideal process (with input from others involved in the process)
	- Brainstorm solutions to close gap between current and ideal process
	- BREAK
	- Select and prioritize solutions
	- Assign team members to analyze solutions
	- Schedule next meeting

Note: From the Office of Quality Improvement, University of Wisconsin—Madison. Adapted with permission.

AIP Team Meeting #2 Agenda Template

Date: Time:
Location:
Attendees:

Time Needed: 4–8 hours

Meeting Outcomes:
- Agree upon solutions to close gap between current and ideal process
- Develop new flowchart for proposed process
- Develop Implementation Plan (including timeline)
- Review recommendations with sponsor for approval

Materials to send ahead to members:
- Analysis of recommendations

Time	**Agenda**
	• Summary of where we are
	• Finalize recommendations
	• Agree upon final solutions/recommendations
	• Integrate recommendations into a new flowchart
	• BREAK
	• Develop Implementation Plan (including timeline)
	• Prepare for sponsor presentation
	• Present to sponsor for approval
	• Decide next steps for implementation

Note: From the Office of Quality Improvement, University of Wisconsin—Madison. Adapted with permission.

AIP Project Definition Template

Project Name: _____

Project Sponsor: _____

Pre-Work Team Members: _____
_____

Project Mission: _____
_____

Process To Be Improved: _____
_____

AIP Team Members: _____
_____

AIP Team Leader: _____

AIP Facilitator: _____

Project Recorder: _____

Project Measures of Success:

Note: From the Office of Quality Improvement, University of Wisconsin—Madison. Adapted with permission.

AIP Project Report Template

This template is a suggested outline for communicating the work of an AIP team. It is best if a team begins using this report at the start of the project to organize information as it goes. That way, the team's report will already be completed at the conclusion of the project.

I. Project Description
- Completed Project Definition
- Completed Project Timeline showing planned and actual

II. Understanding the Process
- Flowchart of the process at the beginning
- Flowchart of the ideal process
- Data/information gathered/learned about the process

III. Identifying Solutions
- Include the list of possible solutions considered
- Include criteria used to select solution(s)
- Include solution(s) selected

IV. Improvement Plan—New Process
- New flowchart showing new process
- Include measures
- Include rationale

V. Implementation
- Implementation action plan
- Implementation timeline and costs

VI. Results
- Include data gathered over time on identified measures (e.g., time saved, quality improved, resources reallocated)

Note: From the Office of Quality Improvement, University of Wisconsin—Madison. Adapted with permission.

AIP Project Timeline Template

Month																
Week	1	2	3	4	1	2	3	4	1	2	3	4	1	2	3	4
Define Project																
• Pre-work meeting																
• Team selection																
• Project scope																
Design Improvements																
• AIP meeting #1																
• Gather data/verify process																
• AIP meeting																
• Approve recommendations																
Implement Improvements																
• Train staff in new process																
• Gather data																
Follow-up																
• Evaluate results																
• Decide next steps																

Note: From the Office of Quality Improvement, University of Wisconsin—Madison. Adapted with permission.

Assessment of the SMART School Improvement Process

The purpose of this assessment is to gather the perceptions of school principals and district administrators regarding the effectiveness of the *SMART School Improvement Process (SSIP)*. The information from the assessment will be used to identify areas and ways for improving the process.

Instructions: Listed below are several statements about various aspects and features of the SSIP. For each of these statements you are asked to make two (2) responses:

1. **Importance.** How *important* is this aspect or feature to the SSIP, or how important should it be?
2. **Current Status.** To what extend does this aspect or feature *currently exist* in the SSIP?

For each statement below, circle the response that best describes your perception of the *importance* of the statement, and circle the response that best describes your perception of the *current status* of the statement.

IMPORTANCE How important is this? 5 = Extremely Important 4 = Very Important 3 = Somewhat Important 2 = Not very Important 1 = Not Important NA = Not Applicable DK = Don't Know	Section I. Purpose	CURRENT STATUS What's your perception? 5 = Strongly Agree 4 = Agree 3 = Neutral 2 = Disagree 1 = Strongly Disagree NA = Not Applicable DK = Don't Know
5 4 3 2 1 NA DK	1. The primary purpose of the SSIP is to improve student achievement.	5 4 3 2 1 NA DK
5 4 3 2 1 NA DK	2. The SSIP serves as an accountability mechanism to the public.	5 4 3 2 1 NA DK
5 4 3 2 1 NA DK	3. The SSIP formalizes instructional decision-making in the school.	5 4 3 2 1 NA DK
5 4 3 2 1 NA DK	4. A systematic planning process is needed for schools to improve their students' achievement.	5 4 3 2 1 NA DK

1

IMPORTANCE How important is this? 5 = Extremely Important 4 = Very Important 3 = Somewhat Important 2 = Not very Important 1 = Not Important NA = Not Applicable DK = Don't Know	Section II. Data Analysis	CURRENT STATUS What's your perception? 5 = Strongly Agree 4 = Agree 3 = Neutral 2 = Disagree 1 = Strongly Disagree NA = Not Applicable DK = Don't Know
5 4 3 2 1 NA DK	5. Data from both the district and the school are systematically analyzed and summarized for use in the SSIP.	5 4 3 2 1 NA DK
5 4 3 2 1 NA DK	6. A school data summary is presented in a user-friendly format for use in the SSIP.	5 4 3 2 1 NA DK
5 4 3 2 1 NA DK	7. The school's data are used to identify discrepancies between actual student/school performance and desired performance based on the school's vision/mission.	5 4 3 2 1 NA DK
5 4 3 2 1 NA DK	8. The school's data are used to identify discrepancies between actual student/school performance and desired performance oward district standards.	5 4 3 2 1 NA DK
5 4 3 2 1 NA DK	9. The school's data are used to measure progress on existing SSIP goals.	5 4 3 2 1 NA DK
5 4 3 2 1 NA DK	10. The school's data are used to identify additional data needed.	5 4 3 2 1 NA DK
5 4 3 2 1 NA DK	11. The school's data are used to modify existing goals and/or identify additional goals.	5 4 3 2 1 NA DK
5 4 3 2 1 NA DK	12. The school's data are used to construct a rationale for identified goals.	5 4 3 2 1 NA DK
5 4 3 2 1 NA DK	13. The school's data are used to suggest improvement and implementation strategies.	5 4 3 2 1 NA DK
5 4 3 2 1 NA DK	14. The school's data are used to monitor and demonstrate progress.	5 4 3 2 1 NA DK

2

IMPORTANCE
How important is this?
5 = Extremely Important
4 = Very Important
3 = Somewhat Important
2 = Not very Important
1 = Not Important
NA = Not Applicable
DK = Don't Know

CURRENT STATUS
What's your perception?
5 = Strongly Agree
4 = Agree
3 = Neutral
2 = Disagree
1 = Strongly Disagree
NA = Not Applicable
DK = Don't Know

Section III. Improvement Goals

Importance	Item	Current Status
5 4 3 2 1 NA DK	15. Each SSIP goal clearly describes a specific improvement result (not an activity).	5 4 3 2 1 NA DK
5 4 3 2 1 NA DK	16. Each SSIP goal provides a specific and complete description of *who* will improve and *what* they will be able to do.	5 4 3 2 1 NA DK
5 4 3 2 1 NA DK	17. Each SSIP goal specifies a *measurement strategy* and a *standard* (or baseline) that will be used to measure progress.	5 4 3 2 1 NA DK
5 4 3 2 1 NA DK	18. Each SSIP goal specifies the *timeframe* in which the improvement will be accomplished.	5 4 3 2 1 NA DK
5 4 3 2 1 NA DK	19. Each SSIP goal is justified with a clear, strong *rationale*, which references a thorough school-based data analysis.	5 4 3 2 1 NA DK
5 4 3 2 1 NA DK	20. All of the SSIP goals together in a school's Continuous Improvement Plan comprise a *comprehensive improvement plan* for the school.	5 4 3 2 1 NA DK

Section IV. Improvement Activities

Importance	Item	Current Status
5 4 3 2 1 NA DK	21. The SSIP activities are directly related to the SSIP goals in ways that will result in significant improvement.	5 4 3 2 1 NA DK
5 4 3 2 1 NA DK	22. The SSIP activities include only those efforts that go beyond the school's current practices.	5 4 3 2 1 NA DK
5 4 3 2 1 NA DK	23. The SSIP activities include the necessary staff and organization development strategies to prepare staff members to use new practices.	5 4 3 2 1 NA DK
5 4 3 2 1 NA DK	24. The SSIP activities reflect what is known about effective classroom and/or school practices.	5 4 3 2 1 NA DK

3

IMPORTANCE
How important is this?
5 = Extremely Important
4 = Very Important
3 = Somewhat Important
2 = Not very Important
1 = Not Important
NA = Not Applicable
DK = Don't Know

CURRENT STATUS
What's your perception?
5 = Strongly Agree
4 = Agree
3 = Neutral
2 = Disagree
1 = Strongly Disagree
NA = Not Applicable
DK = Don't Know

Section IV. Improvement Activities
(continued)

Importance	Item	Current Status
5 4 3 2 1 NA DK	25. The SSIP practices are powerful enough to result in the desired improvement.	5 4 3 2 1 NA DK
5 4 3 2 1 NA DK	26. The SSIP activities are realistic in terms of timelines, expectations, and resources.	5 4 3 2 1 NA DK
5 4 3 2 1 NA DK	27. All of the SSIP activities together comprise an interrelated effort that is comprehensive and significant enough to result in improved classroom practices and student learning.	5 4 3 2 1 NA DK

Section V. Implementation

Importance	Item	Current Status
5 4 3 2 1 NA DK	28. Most or all of the school staff members are involved in implementing some aspect of the SSIP.	5 4 3 2 1 NA DK
5 4 3 2 1 NA DK	29. Students, parents, and other community members are involved in SSIP implementation activities.	5 4 3 2 1 NA DK
5 4 3 2 1 NA DK	30. Appropriate groups/individuals are assigned responsibility for leading/directing SSIP implementation activities.	5 4 3 2 1 NA DK
5 4 3 2 1 NA DK	31. Each SSIP implementation group (team, committee, etc.) has a clear understanding of its charge.	5 4 3 2 1 NA DK
5 4 3 2 1 NA DK	32. Each SSIP implementation group systematically implements and monitors the improvement activities for which it is responsible.	5 4 3 2 1 NA DK
5 4 3 2 1 NA DK	33. The activities of each SSIP implementation group are coordinated with each other, they are monitored, evaluated, and revised as needed; and the results are shared with all stakeholders.	5 4 3 2 1 NA DK

4

IMPORTANCE — How important is this? 5 = Extremely Important 4 = Very Important 3 = Somewhat Important 2 = Not very Important 1 = Not Important NA = Not Applicable DK = Don't Know	Section VI. Involvement and Communication	CURRENT STATUS — What's your perception? 5 = Strongly Agree 4 = Agree 3 = Neutral 2 = Disagree 1 = Strongly Disagree NA = Not Applicable DK = Don't Know
5 4 3 2 1 NA DK	34. The ultimate responsibility for the development, implementation, and evaluation of the CAIP resides with the school principal.	5 4 3 2 1 NA DK
5 4 3 2 1 NA DK	35. A planning team representative of staff, students, parents, and community members oversees the SSIP for its school.	5 4 3 2 1 NA DK
5 4 3 2 1 NA DK	36. The district's central office staff provides the necessary support (direction, resources, technical assistance) to enable the school's principal and SSIP planning team to effectively do their improvement work.	5 4 3 2 1 NA DK
5 4 3 2 1 NA DK	37. The SSIP planning team seeks input from staff, students, parents, and community members.	5 4 3 2 1 NA DK
5 4 3 2 1 NA DK	38. Written copies of the Continuous Improvement Plan are shared with all school staff members and with interested students, parents, and community members.	5 4 3 2 1 NA DK
5 4 3 2 1 NA DK	39. The SSIP planning team and implementation groups use consensus decision-making methods.	5 4 3 2 1 NA DK
5 4 3 2 1 NA DK	40. The SSIP planning team and implementation groups work to ensure that all members feel valued and included and that they participate fully in the group's work and decision-making.	5 4 3 2 1 NA DK
5 4 3 2 1 NA DK	41. The SSIP planning team and implementation groups inform the full school community of their activities and results.	5 4 3 2 1 NA DK
5 4 3 2 1 NA DK	42. Regular SSIP progress reports are published in the school newsletter and discussed at staff and parent meetings.	5 4 3 2 1 NA DK

5

School Improvement Plan Template

This information should be the narrative introduction to the templates that spell out the goals and action steps for the school's 1- to 3-year plan.

School Name: _____ **School Year:** _____

Mission: _____

_____

Vision: _____

_____

Core Values: _____

_____

A. Site Leadership Team
   1. Membership
   2. Roles (Chair/Co-Chairs, etc.)
   3. Meeting schedule
   4. Purpose statement for leadership team

B. Assessment of Student Learning Progress
   1. Assessments used and curricular areas covered
   2. Climate information gathered (internal and external surveys, student behavioral data, etc.)
   3. Student follow-up data collected/used
   4. New assessments to be developed

C. Staff Development
   1. Areas of development to be provided and for whom
   2. Various types or strategies of staff development to be employed
   3. Link of staff development to strategic and site plans

D. Budget Considerations
   1. New budget initiatives needed to address this plan
   2. Attach school budget items linked to school improvement plan

E. System Issues
   1. System concerns or issues that need to be addressed
   2. Technology tools and training needed
   3. District-wide curriculum issues that need to be addressed

Collaborative Action Research Steps

STEP 1: **Define the research project**
- Identify improvement area
- Develop SMART goal
- Gather support from others for working on this project

STEP 2: **Analyze the situation**
- Establish baseline data
- Profile the students

STEP 3: **Generate hypotheses**
- Develop hypotheses about causes of performance and potential solutions

STEP 4: **Try solutions and check results**
- Brainstorm potential solutions to try
- Select one solution or a set of solutions based on criteria
- Try the solution strategy for several months
- Assess results against baseline
- Adjust as needed until goal is achieved (or revise original project)

STEP 5: **Capture lessons learned**
- Document results in graphs and narrative
- Share what was learned about making improvements in this system
- Share what was learned about student learning
- Develop ways to "maintain the gain"
- Identify possibilities for next research focus
- Celebrate!

Collaborative Action Research Guide

Step 1: Define the Research Project
The purpose of this step is to focus improvement efforts on a particular area. The outcome of this step is the development of one SMART goal.

What improvement opportunity will you work on? There are a number of ways to identify a specific area. If at all possible, try to select an area where you already have some baseline data.[1] Examples:

- Analyze standardized test results to identify weak areas for students, or areas where all students are not achieving at the expected level.
- Analyze customized district-wide assessment data.
- Use information from your classroom assessments.
- Consider national research that indicates areas of weakness or opportunity.
- Use your intuition to narrow and prioritize where to focus improvement efforts.

Improvement area:

Analyze **items** on the assessments that your students are weakest in to further narrow, prioritize, and focus. For example, persuasive or expressive writing, math problem-solving or computation, capitals or punctuation, etc. State the improvement opportunity as a gap to close, using SMART goal language:

SMART goal: Improve _____ by _____
                                   specific, measurable item   attainable (how much)

by _____ .
         time-bound (by when)

Example: "Increase by 10% the number of students achieving at 'meets standards' level in persuasive writing by end of February."

---
[1] To identify the "gap" between what is and what should be, compare your students' results to standards, benchmarks, averages, and rubrics.

Plan for Collaborating With Others

Who will you use as a reality check to make sure you get feedback and advice on the direction and impact of your project? Who else will really care about this project? What will they care about? Who do you need help from in order to do this project? Develop a plan for involving them and communicating about this project.

Who I Plan to Involve	How I Will Involve Them	When I Will Involve Them

2

Step 2: Analyze the Situation

The purpose of this step is to further clarify and understand performance levels. The outcome of this step is a clear picture of what is happening with the students' performance.

What data exists today to describe the gap? Is the gap related only to this group of students or have students been demonstrating this gap over the years?

- To answer the first question, look at assessment results for this year's students going back as many years as possible.
- To answer the second question, compare this year's students to assessment results for all students over the years.

Use run charts, control charts, and scatterplots to look at data over time. Use histograms and bar charts when comparing student results.

Profile the students. Generate questions about the students and their programming. Examples:

- What instructional strategies have been tried?
- What curriculum have students been exposed to?
- What is the pattern of attendance?
- What are the students' learning styles?
- What are the students' study and work habits?

Questions:

Collect data to answer your questions by talking with previous teachers, examining school records, and looking at other information available. When possible, graph the data to get a picture of what is going on.

3

Step 3: Generate Hypotheses

The purpose of this step is to generate hypotheses to further investigate before you move to solution strategies. This step, if thoroughly done, ensures that solution strategies are not built around symptoms.

Once you have gathered answers to your questions, you can begin generating hypotheses about what might make an improvement. Here are some examples of hypotheses, based on data:

Data	Hypothesis
1. Students missed needed curriculum.	1. Exposing students to _____ curriculum component will improve their performance.
2. Students were taught using "whole group" instruction.	2. Teaching students one-on-one and in small groups will improve their performance.
3. Students' attendance was poor; they were not present for needed instruction.	3. Improving students' attendance will improve performance.

Data	Hypothesis

4

Before jumping to solutions, however, probe your thinking a little further. Use a cause-and-effect analysis tool such as a Fishbone Diagram, a Tree Diagram, or a Relationship Diagram to ask "why" five times. Examples:

- Why are these students having attendance problems? *(and why and why and why...)*
- Why didn't whole group instruction work for these students? *(and why and why and why...)*
- Why didn't phonics help them? *(and why and why and why...)*

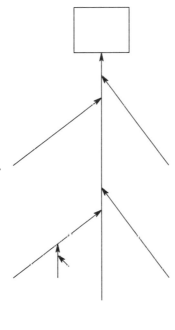

Also, check research and other sources of best practice to verify that your hypotheses about what might work are based on solid data. Take another look at your hypotheses after you've completed a causal analysis and checked with other sources. Are these hypotheses still on track?

5

Step 4: Try Solutions and Check Results

The purpose of this step is to test solutions in action and measure results against the baseline to see if they worked. The outcome is a "before-after" graph showing results of this improvement effort.

Keeping your hypotheses in mind, what do you think should happen? Strategies...programs...policies...training...new instructional methods...process improvements...? Develop an implementation plan. Consider criteria as you select an improvement plan. Examples:

- Improvement can be tested within a 3–6 month time period.
- Improvement is targeted (clearly linked to the performance gap).
- Improvement is cost-effective.
- Teachers are supportive.
- Parents are supportive.
- Students are supportive.

Implementation Step	Lead Person	By When	Product/Output

Try the improvement plan for a period of no more than 6 months (3 months is ideal). Assess results using the same assessment(s) that were used to generate the baseline performance. Compare before/after results. Adjust as needed until the desired performance level is attained.

6

Step 5: Capture Lessons Learned

The purpose of this step is to help the system as a whole learn from this improvement effort. The outcome is a summary of what has been learned—both in terms of process and in terms of results—and recommendations about next steps.

Document results of your improvement research using graphs and narrative. Share what you learned with others in your system.

- What did you learn about your hypotheses?
- What improvement plan really worked?
- What were the final results?
- What did you learn about how students learn in your system?
- What tools were useful along the way?
- What questions were useful along the way?
- Where did you lose your way and how did you get back on track?
- What barriers did you have to contend with?
- What new collaborations resulted from this work?
- What did you learn about building a safe environment for talking about data and results?
- What impact did your work have on others in your system?
- How might those barriers be addressed in the future?
- What was the most rewarding part of this effort?

Ensure that the gains are maintained through development of policies, training, instructional materials, curriculum, practices, etc.

7

8

Based on what you learned, where should the next research effort focus?

CELEBRATE your progress toward closing the gap!

NOTES (Things to remember next time I'm involved in an improvement project):

References & Resources

Educational Reform

Conzemius, A., & O Neill, J. (2001). *Building Shared Responsibility for Student Learning.* Alexandria,VA: Association for Supervision and Curriculum Development (ASCD).

Conzemius, A., & O Neill, J. (May, 1999). Improving results: Putting energy where it counts. *Wisconsin School News.* Madison, WI: Wisconsin School Board Association (WASB).

Dolan, P. (1994). *Restructuring our schools: A primer on systemic change.* Kansas City, KS: Systems and Organizations.

DuFour, R., & Eaker, R. (1998). *Professional learning communities at work: Best practices for enhancing student achievement.* Bloomington, IN: Solution Tree (formerly National Educational Service).

Eaker, R., DuFour, R., & Burnette, R. (2002). *Getting started: Reculturing schools to become professional learning communities.* Bloomington, IN: Solution Tree (formerly National Educational Service).

Langford, D., & Cleary, B. (1995). *Orchestrating learning with quality.* ASQC Quality Press. 1-800-248-1946.

Markova, D., & Powell, A. (1992). *How your child is smart: A life-changing approach to learning.* Emeryville, CA: Conari Press.

Markova, D.(1996). *The open mind: Exploring the 6 patterns of natural intelligence.* Berkley, CA: Conari Press.

Marzano, R. J., & Kendall, J. S. (1996). *A comprehensive guide to designing standards-based districts, schools and classrooms.* Alexandria, VA: Association for Supervision and Curriculum Development (ASCD).

Newmann, F., & Associates. (1996). *Authentic achievement: Restructuring schools for intellectual quality.* San Francisco, CA: Jossey-Bass.

Newmann, F., & Wehlage, G. (1995). *Successful school restructuring.* Madison, WI: Center for Organization and Restructuring of Schools. 608-263-7575.

Newmann, F., Secada, W., & Wehlage, G. (1995). *A guide to authentic instruction and assessment: Vision, standards and scoring.* Madison, WI: Wisconsin Center for Education Research.

Palmer, P. (1998). *The courage to teach.* San Francisco, CA: Jossey-Bass.

Sparks, D. (1999). "Using lesson study to improve teaching." *Results.* National Staff Development Council (NSDC).

Stiggins, R. J. (1997, 2nd edition). *Student-centered classroom assessment.* Upper Saddle River, NJ: Prentice-Hall, Inc.

Wiggins, G. P., & McTighe, J. (1998). *Understanding by design.* Alexandria,VA: Association for Supervision and Curriculum Development (ASCD).

School Improvement

Bernhardt, V. L. (1999, 2nd edition). *The school portfolio: A comprehensive framework for school improvement.* Gardiner, NY: Eye on Education.

Bernhardt, V. L. (2002). *The school portfolio toolkit.* Larchmont, NY: Eye on Education.

Conzemius, A. (Winter, 2000). "Framework." Journal for Staff Development, 21(1).

O'Neill, J., & Conzemius, A. (1998). Facilitator's guide for school improvement. *Creating meaning through measurement: How our school got SMART about accountability.* Madison, WI: Quality Leadership by Design, LLC. (QLD). 1-888-700-9535.

O'Neill, J. (February, 2000). SMART goals, SMART schools. *Educational Leadership,* 57(5).

Sagor, R. (2000). *Guiding school improvement with action research.* Alexandria, VA: Association for Supervision and Curriculum Development (ASCD).

Saphier, J., & D'Auria, J. (1993). *How to bring vision to school improvement.* Carlisle, MA: Research for Better Teaching.

Schmoker, M. (1999, 2nd Edition). *Results: The key to continuous school improvement.* Alexandria, VA: Association for Supervision and Curriculum Development (ASCD).

Schmoker, M. (2001). *The results fieldbook.* Alexandria, VA: Association for Supervision and Curriculum Development (ASCD).

Teams and Teamwork

Francis, D., & Young, D. (1992). *Improving work groups: A practical guide for team building.* San Diego, CA: Pfeiffer & Co.

Garmstom, R., & Wellman, B. (1999). *The adaptive school: A sourcebook for developing collaborative groups.* Norwood, MA: Christopher-Gorden.

Harington-Mackin, D. (1994). *The team building tool kit.* New York: American Management Association.

Harper, R., & Harper, A. (1992). *Skill building for self-directed team members: A complete course.* New York: MW Corporation.

Hirsch, S., Delehant, A., & Sparks, D. (1994). *Keys to successful meetings.* Oxford, OH: National Staff Development Council (NSDC).

Peck, M. S. (1988). *The different drum: Community making and peace.* New York: Simon & Schuster.

Phillips, S. (1989) *The team building source book.* San Diego: University Associates.

Robinson, R. (1995). *An introduction to dynamics of group leadership and organizational change.* West Bend, WI: Omnibook Co.

Scholtes, P. (1993). *The team handbook.* Madison, WI: Oriel, Inc. 608-238-8134.

Using Data

Bernhardt, V. L. (1998). *Data analysis for comprehensive schoolwide improvement.* Larchmont, NY: Eye on Education.

Holcombe, E. L. (1999). *Getting excited about data: How to combine people, passion, and proof.* Thousand Oaks, CA: Corwin Press, Inc.

Tufte, E. R. (1983). *The visual display of quantitative information.* Chesire, CT: Graphics Press.

Professional Development and Action Research

Caro-Bruce, C. (2000). *Action research facilitator's handbook.* Oxford, OH: National Staff Development Council (NSDC).

Hassel, E. (1999). *Professional development: Learning from the best. A toolkit for schools and districts based on the national awards program for model professional development.* Oak Brook, IL: North Central Regional Educational Laboratory (NCREL).

Sagor, R. (2000). *Guiding school improvement with action research.* Alexandria, VA: Association for Supervision and Curriculum Development (ASCD).

Leadership

Conzemius, A. (Fall, 1999). Ally in the office. *Journal for Staff Development, 20*(4).

Cotter, M., & Seymour, D. (1993). *Kidgets.* ASQC Quality Press. 1-800-248-1946.

Covey, S. (1989). *The 7 habits of highly effective people.* New York: Fireside Books.

Deal, T. E., & Peterson, K. D. (1999). *Shaping school culture.* San Francisco: Jossey-Bass.

Deal, T. E., & Peterson, K. D. (1990). *The principals' role in shaping school culture.* Washington DC: U.S. Department of Education Office of Educational Research and Improvement.

Lambert, L. (1998). *Building leadership capacity in schools.* Alexandria, VA: Association for Supervision and Curriculum Development (ASCD).

Organizational Dynamics and Systems Change

Deming, W. E. (1982). *Out of the crisis.* Cambridge, MA: Massachusetts Institute of Technology.

Fullan, M. G. (1991) *The new meaning of educational change.* New York: Teachers College Press.

O'Neill, J. (April, 2000). "Capturing an organization's oral history." *Educational Leadership, 57*(7).

Schein, E. (1997, 2nd edition). *Organizational culture and leadership.* San Francisco: Jossey-Bass.

Senge, P. (1990). *The fifth discipline: The art and practice of the learning organization.* New York: Doubleday.

Senge, P., Kleiner, A., Roberts, C., Ross, R., & Smith, B. (1994). *The fifth discipline fieldbook: Strategies and tools for building a learning organization.* New York: Doubleday.

Senge, P., Cambron-McCabe, N., Lucas, T., Smith, B., Dutton, J., & Smith, B. (2000). *Schools that learn.* New York: Doubleday Dell.

Weisbord, M. (1987). *Productive workplaces: organizing and managing for dignity, meaning and community.* San Francisco: Jossey-Bass.

Index

End-User License Agreement

You should carefully read these terms and conditions before using the CD-ROM included with this book. This is a license agreement between you and Solution Tree (formerly National Educational Service). By opening the accompanying CD-ROM packet, you acknowledge that you have read and accept the following terms and conditions. If you do not agree and do not want to be bound by such terms and conditions, promptly return the book to the place from which you obtained it for a full refund.

License Grant

Solution Tree grants to you (either an individual or entity) a nonexclusive license to use the files solely for your own personal or business purposes on a single computer (whether a standard computer or a workstation component of a multi-user network). The files are in use on a computer when it is loaded into temporary memory (RAM) or installed into permanent memory (hard disk, CD-ROM, or other storage device). Solution Tree reserves all rights not expressly granted herein.

Ownership

Solution Tree is the owner of all rights, title, and interests, including copyright, in and to the compilation of the files recorded on the CD-ROM. Copyright to the individual files and programs recorded on the software media is owned by the author or other authorized copyright owner of each file or program. Ownership of the software and all proprietary rights relating thereto remain with Solution Tree and its licensers.

Restrictions On Use and Transfer

(a) You may only (i) make one copy of the software for backup or archival purposes, or (ii) transfer the software to a single hard disk, provided that you keep the original for backup or archival purposes. You may not (i) rent or lease the software, (ii) copy or reproduce the software through a LAN or other network system or through any computer subscriber system or bulletin-board system, or (iii) adapt or create derivative works based on the software.

(b) You may not reverse engineer, decompile, or disassemble the software. You may transfer the software and user documentation on a permanent basis, provided that the transferee agrees to accept the terms and conditions of the agreement and you retain no copies. If the software is an update or has been updated, any transfer must include the most recent update and all prior versions.

General

This agreement constitutes the entire understanding of the parties and revokes and supersedes all prior agreements, oral or written, between them and may not be modified or amended except in writing signed by both parties hereto that specifically refers to this agreement. This agreement shall take precedence over any other documents that may be in conflict herewith. If any one or more provisions contained in this agreement are held by any court or tribunal to be invalid, illegal, or otherwise unenforceable, each and every other provision shall remain in full force and effect.

Make the Most of Your Professional Development Investment

Let Solution Tree (formerly National Educational Service) schedule time for you and your staff with leading practitioners in the areas of:

- **Professional Learning Communities** with Richard DuFour, Robert Eaker, Rebecca DuFour, and associates
- **Effective Schools** with associates of Larry Lezotte
- **Assessment *for* Learning** with Rick Stiggins and associates
- **Crisis Management and Response** with Cheri Lovre
- **Discipline With Dignity** with Richard Curwin and Allen Mendler
- **SMART School Teams** with Jan O'Neill and Anne Conzemius
- **PASSport to Success** (parental involvement) with Vickie Burt
- **Peacemakers** (violence prevention) with Jeremy Shapiro

Additional presentations are available in the following areas:

- At-Risk Youth Issues
- Bullying Prevention/Teasing and Harassment
- Team Building and Collaborative Teams
- Data Collection and Analysis
- Embracing Diversity
- Literacy Development
- Motivating Techniques for Staff and Students

Solution Tree

(formerly National Educational Service)
304 W. Kirkwood Avenue
Bloomington, IN 47404-5132
(812) 336-7700 • (800) 733-6786 (toll-free number)
FAX (812) 336-7790
e-mail: info@solution-tree.com
www.solution-tree.com

NEED MORE COPIES OR ADDITIONAL RESOURCES ON THIS TOPIC?

Need more copies of this book? Want your own copy? Need additional resources on this topic? If so, you can order additional materials by using this form or by calling us toll free at (800) 733-6786 or (812) 336-7700. Or you can order by FAX at (812) 336-7790, or visit our web site at www.solution-tree.com.

Title	Price*	Quantity	Total
The Handbook for SMART School Teams	$ 54.95		
Getting Started: Reculturing Schools to Become Professional Learning Communities	19.95		
Professional Learning Communities at Work (video set)	495.00		
Professional Learning Communities at Work (book)	24.95		
Creating the New American School	21.95		
EdMarketing: How Smart Schools Get and Keep Community Support	24.95		
How to Create Alternative, Magnet, and Charter Schools	24.95		
Leading Schools to Quality (video and leader's guide)	250.00		
		SUBTOTAL	
		SHIPPING	
Continental U.S.: Please add 6% of order total. Outside continental U.S.: Please add 8% of order total.			
		HANDLING	
Continental U.S.: Please add $4. Outside continental U.S.: Please add $6.			
		TOTAL (U.S. funds)	

*Price subject to change without notice.

❏ Check enclosed ❏ Purchase order enclosed
❏ Money order ❏ VISA, MasterCard, Discover, or American Express (circle one)

Credit Card No._____ Exp. Date_____
Cardholder Signature _____

SHIP TO:
First Name_____ Last Name _____
Position _____
Institution Name _____
Address _____
City_____ State_____ ZIP _____
Phone_____ FAX _____
E-mail _____

Solution Tree
(formerly National Educational Service)
304 W. Kirkwood Avenue
Bloomington, IN 47404-5132
(812) 336-7700 • (800) 733-6786 (toll-free number)
FAX (812) 336-7790
e-mail: orders@solution-tree.com • www.solution-tree.com